Music as Alchemy

Tom Service writes about music for the *Guardian*, where he was Chief Classical Music Critic, and broadcasts for BBC Radio 3. He has presented Radio 3's flagship magazine programme, *Music Matters*, since 2003. He was the inaugural recipient of the ICMP/CIEM Classical Music Critic of the Year Award, and was Guest Artistic Director of the Huddersfield Contemporary Music Festival. After years practising in the mirror, he once conducted Bruckner's Ninth Symphony. *Music as Alchemy* was shortlisted for the Royal Philharmonic Society Music Awards.

Further praise for *Music as Alchemy*:

'Service eavesdrops on the rehearsals of a handful of greats and discovers a striking variety of approaches to cultural leadership.' Helen Wallace, *Financial Times*

'What sets Mr Service's book apart, in addition to its breezy tone and infectious, easily worn enthusiasm, is his focus on the relationship between the conductor and his or her orchestral musicians. Many hours have been spent not just in concerts given by the six conductor-orchestra pairs taken as his subject, but in observing them in the rehearsals beforehand and quizzing members of the orchestra about their side of the experience . . . The book's strength is in its mix of stories and perspectives, which ably convey the murky process by which orchestras and conductors build a bond of mutual trust . . . As the book's title suggests, it may indeed be most appropriate to think of this listening process as a kind of magic. But if so, it is a magic that comes through dedication, not sorcery.' *Economist*

'Dictator, teacher, magician: in *Music as Alchemy*, Tom Service sneaks into rehearsals to fathom the role of the conductor, interviewing the likes of Claudio Abbado and Simon Rattle' Liz Thomson, *Independent*

Music as Alchemy

TOM SERVICE

FABER & FABER

First published in 2012
by Faber and Faber Ltd
Bloomsbury House
74–77 Great Russell Street
London WC1B 3DA

This paperback edition first published in 2014

Typeset by RefineCatch Limited, Bungay, Suffolk
Printed and bound in the UK by CPI Group (UK) Ltd, Croydon, CR0 4YY

A CIP record for this book
is available from the British Library

ISBN 978-0-571-24048-7

FSC
www.fsc.org
MIX
Paper from
responsible sources
FSC® C013604

2 4 6 8 10 9 7 5 3

To my parents,
Jo and MacIain

Contents

Introduction

It seemed like magic then, and it still does. The first orchestral concert I ever saw was in the lino-clad glory of Glasgow's City Hall when I was seven, in 1983. I had expressed no desire to see an orchestra play: I had just started to make my first faltering fingerings through beginners' piano books, and only went along because a friend of the family was ill and there was a spare ticket. But what happened after the Scottish Chamber Orchestra assembled on stage, about six feet above my seat near the front of the stalls, would change my life. I craned my neck and saw a very young-looking Richard Hickox step on to the concert platform, after the musicians had made some weird, tuneless scratchings and scrapings. There was some applause for Hickox, though he didn't seem to have an instrument anywhere underneath his tails, so why everyone thought he was so special was beyond me. He stood in front of the players, he made a couple of arcane signs in the air with what looked like a magician's wand, and the music started. And something opened up in me, some place of resonance and meaning, which I've been exploring ever since.

The music was the main thing. I found out that it was by Mozart, his Symphony No. 29 in A major, K201 (all part of the trainspottery information I quickly started to imbibe as a new and zealous convert), and I was unstoppable in my quest to hear more, discover more. It was Mozart's symphonies, concertos, sonatas, and operas I threw myself into first, my early Walkman devouring tapes on long car journeys until they wore out (and the Walkmen too, over the years): Herbert von Karajan conducting the Berlin Philharmonic Orchestra, Daniel Barenboim with the English Chamber Orchestra, Karl Böhm with the Berlin Philharmonic again (that orchestra seemed to be everywhere, especially on a record label that styled itself with big yellow stickers, and the Berliners quickly became one of my favourites). Then there was Neville Marriner with the glamorously named Academy of St Martin in the Fields, Leonard Bernstein with the Vienna Philharmonic (a close second to the Berlin Phil in my affections), Otto Klemperer with the New Philharmonia (there was obviously an 'Old Philharmonia' I had never heard of), the extravagantly mustachioed Arturo Toscanini with the NBC Orchestra, John Eliot Gardiner and the English Baroque Soloists, and the charismatic Nikolaus Harnoncourt with his wild staring eyes and the Chamber Orchestra of Europe. I gorged myself on all of them and more playing Mozart, Bruckner, Beethoven, Mahler, Brahms, Schoenberg, Stravinsky, Bach, Elgar, Scriabin, Ligeti, James MacMillan, Joonas Kokkonen: anything I could get my hands on, and everything I heard and liked on BBC Radio 3.

But there was something else, too. I didn't hear this canon of orchestral music as monuments of sound, great things that one really ought to know about, to be worshipped and adored from a safe distance. To me, all the pieces of music I loved were visceral experiences that did things to my insides, to my brain and body, things I still can't fully explain, because of the way they moved through and manipulated time.

And when I started going to more concerts, the person who seemed to be at the centre of this flow of time, both moving with it and apparently shaping it, was the person – usually a man – who stood where Richard Hickox had taken his place: in the centre of the podium at the front of the City Hall, almost always using nothing more than a white stick, and making no sound at all, bar the odd expressive grunt. The conductor wasn't the composer but he seemed to be the closest person to the source of the music, wherever that was, since without conductors, most orchestral performances would never get started. The conductors I saw most often in concert, like Walter Weller, Bryden Thomson, and Neeme Järvi, with the Scottish National Orchestra (now Royal Scottish National Orchestra), were the ones responsible for the music happening, for creating and shaping the time-flow of the music.

That was what I wanted to do. At home, my impressions of Toscanini and Karajan in their pomp were legendary. At least, they were to me and my mute audience of tapes, CDs, and music dictionaries. That was before I had even seen film of either of them conducting: but leading the Berlin Philharmonic or the NBC Symphony in my window (which, I admit, acted like a mirror after dark), I felt the music flow through me as I thought it must flow through them.

And I still do it, after teenage years of conducting courses and forcing myself on unsuspecting orchestras, choirs, and contemporary music ensembles at university and afterwards. Even knowing a bit about the technique of conducting hasn't dimmed my appalling habit of sitting in concert halls listening to the world's great orchestras and conductors and giving an involuntary downbeat at the start of a Beethoven scherzo, or showing the oboist how to shape that melody in the slow movement of Brahms's Violin Concerto.

But my ideal was: be Simon Rattle or bust. I quickly discovered the shocking truth that there is, in fact, more to conducting than moving your arms in time with the music, or emoting along to your favourite Bruckner or Mahler symphonies. My skills as a performer were never good enough to equip me for the traditional routes into conducting – becoming a pianist at an opera house and being given the chance to pick up a baton, or playing in an orchestra and learning how others do it before moving to the podium – and so my dreams of conducting the Berlin Philharmonic remain unrealised.

Yet my fascination with conducting has never dimmed, and that's what this book is about. In part, it's an attempt to answer the simplest question of all: what is it that conductors do up there? How can a person who makes no sound occupy the attention of more than a hundred musicians – who really do make a sound – and of the audience, too? But the book also deals with a bigger question, exploring what that hackneyed old phrase, 'the art of the conductor', might actually mean. If conducting is about anything, it's about communication. It's significant real-time interaction between one person and a larger group of musicians. Far from being mystical, conducting is about things that happen and which can be described. Something is passed from the conductor to the orchestra, and vice versa, and it's the quality and intensity of that communication that is responsible for what happens in orchestral performance.

It's been a centuries-long cultural development to get to this point. The roots of conducting in the sense we understand it today – a person with a stick controlling the musical impulse of serried ranks of musicians playing instruments – go back to the seventeenth century, but the basic idea of someone commanding a large group of singers or players goes back much further. There's a report from Greece in 709 BC of a group of eight hundred musicians being led by on 'Pherekydes of Patrae, giver of Rhythm', who waved a golden staff so that the 'men began in one and the same time . . . [beating] his stave up and down in equal movements so that all might keep together'. The Greeks also gave us the idea of 'cheironomy', a system of moving the hands to indicate pitch level and melodic contour to singers, something employed in India, China, Egypt, and Israel; and in the first millennium AD there were traditions of Jewish Torah-singing which used the right hand to signal different melodic formulae. In modern times, the first evidence of a baton being used comes with the nuns of St Vita in 1594: 'Finally the Maestra of the concert sits down at one end of the table and with a long, slender and well-polished wand . . . gives them without noise several signs to begin, and then continues by beating the measure of the time which they must obey in singing and playing.' The sort of silent baton used by the Maestra of St Vita was not generally adopted straight away, as the story of Lully shows. Jean-Baptiste Lully was the most famous composer-conductor of the seventeenth century, and he's also the most celebrated casualty of a conducting accident. Lully was so important a part of Louis XIV's court that he was de facto the head of all music-making throughout France. Instead of a baton, this early musical dictator used a long staff to beat time on the floor, and while directing a Te Deum for the Sun King in 1687, he stabbed his toe. The injury developed into an abscess, became gangrenous, and killed him two months later. Many have suffered for the art of conducting, but only a few, like Lully, have died from an injury sustained in the act.

Once conductors had taken up the baton again (after experimenting with rolls of paper, sticks of ivory, wands of ebony, and the like) it was the early nineteenth century that saw the conductor start to flourish as an essential component of musical performance. It was not simply an extension of the roles of leader of the first violins or keyboard player in the eighteenth-century orchestra: the bigger demands composers made from their musicians in the nineteenth century made conductors essential instead of optional. The heroes of the podium in this era were all composers: Beethoven, Mendelssohn, Spohr, Weber, Spontini, Berlioz, Liszt, von Bülow, and above all, Wagner. *On Conducting*, Wagner's treatise, is a manifesto for realising what he calls 'the very life of music' through a careful understanding of the tempo fluctuations and modifications demanded by the music of Beethoven, Weber, and a certain Richard Wagner. As with so much of his writing, Wagner is making a polemical claim to territory that was previously the preserve of brilliant Jewish musicians, above all Meyerbeer and Mendelssohn. According to Wagner, Mendelssohn's method is capable of realising only the most 'superficial' aspects of music like Beethoven's symphonies, as opposed to the revelations (naturally) of his own performance practice.

After another generation of brilliant composer-conductors, like Gustav Mahler and Richard Strauss, a new phenomenon emerged: career conductors such as Hans Richter and Arthur Nikisch who, for the first time in musical history, could make a living simply by working with orchestras. The stage was set for the titans of the podium of the twentieth century and the recording era: the 'classical' Arturo Toscanini and his 'romantic' anti-pode, Wilhelm Furtwängler (also a minor composer), the prodigious Herbert von Karajan and the enigmatic genius Carlos Kleiber, the charismatic Leonard Bernstein (also a great composer) and the guru-like Sergiu Celibidache – and so on.

But such a list of names, from Pherekydes to Furtwängler, gives rather less than half the story of conducting. All of these maestros are nothing without their musicians. The story of how conducting has changed over the millennia, from the Greeks' cheironomy to the choreography of today's maes-tros, is not so much a drama of treatises, diktats, and titanic figures standing in front of their orchestras, but rather a story of ever-developing communication and interaction. It's about how different generations of musicians have reacted to different kinds of leaders. In other words, con-ducting is about collaboration, politics, and society. In the recent past, that has often meant a top-down model of communication that many have compared to dictatorship – fascist, communist, or otherwise. It hardly needs the forensic equipment of a cultural historian to unpick the symbol-ism of a man with a stick telling a hierarchically arranged phalanx of well-dressed men (orchestras were mostly all male up to the 1930s and 1940s) what to do, and shouting at them for not doing it well enough. As Elias Canetti puts it in a famous passage in *Crowds and Power*, 'There is no more obvious expression of power than the performance of a conductor ... He is the living embodiment of law, both positive and negative. His hands decree and prohibit. His ears search out profanation.' More recently, artist Christian

Marclay has revealed the hollowness of the cult of the conductor in his *Dictators*, stitching together twenty-five LP sleeves of maestros in variously vainglorious poses, creating a wall-size mosaic of images of unwitting impotence. The conductors are shown eyes closed, fists clenched, batons aloft, hair gelled, all of them male, all of them well lit, and all of them fetish objects of pure, menacing power – power without responsibility, since none of the photos shows any of the musicians at the end of their sticks. It's as if the conductors have ascended to an ethereal realm where they no longer need their humble orchestras in order to make music. Many conductors have themselves indulged the fetish of their supposed superiority, celebrating the ontological slippage that my young mind identified, which is that in the absence of the real-live composers – everyone from Bach to Stockhausen being now a dead composer – the conductor can all too easily assume ultimate musical authority. That's why on Karajan's later record sleeves, his name is bigger than Beethoven's or Wagner's. But even in the most otiose caricature of the conductor as despot, they still need their musicians. Without their players, they are all armchair conductors. They're no better than me, in other words.

However, in most books about living conductors, which are often collections of interviews, it's possible to come away with the illusion that all conductors do is arrive at a rehearsal with an idea about a piece of music, and that orchestras simply enact their instructions and respect their authority. As with any other discipline, if you talk only to conductors themselves, the danger is that you might believe what they say. My approach is different. Every orchestral concert is the tip of an iceberg of human and musical relationships. To find out what conductors really do, it's

8

essential to find out what their orchestras do as well. Each chapter of the book puts the particular concert or concerts I saw being prepared and performed (taking place over a three-year period in cities throughout Europe) in the context of the orchestra's life: its place in the musical culture of the city, its relationship to audiences past and present, its political situation. Most crucially, there's the story of the relationship between the conductors and their musicians, and the myriad relationships within the orchestras themselves, from one player to another, one section to another. That thickness of description, and that multitude of voices, informs the essential discussion of each chapter, which is the relationship between rehearsal and performance, and how conductor and orchestra transmute these infinite stories and histories into the music they play, from Mahler to Debussy, Dvořák to Rachmaninov.

So who are the conductors and orchestras you will meet in the six main chapters of the book? The choice was driven by a desire to find a wide range of different approaches to situations that look superficially similar. All six conductor-and-orchestra pairings were preparing symphonic, and occasionally choral, concerts of music of the core romantic and early modernist repertoire. All the conductors in this book are musicians I deeply respect and admire, and all have given performances among those I treasure the most in a lifetime of concert-going.

The players in all the orchestras you will encounter are as central to the musical journeys as the conductors. Talking to orchestra members provided the key insights into the creative process of music-making that I witnessed in each city. It's one thing to have an inkling of what's going on when you're following a score of a symphony in a rehearsal, and another to talk to the conductor about what they thought was happening, but it's another to actually ask the oboist, the timpanist, or the bassoonist what was really happening in that place, to find out what mix of psychology, man-management, technical know-how and musical shenanigans was really afoot.

There are obvious things the conductors in this book are not: most obviously of all, they are not women. The gender imbalance of the conducting profession may be scarcely different from the higher echelons of politics or business, including major arts organisations, but it's a grotesque difference when you consider the constitution of most major orchestras, which are steadily reaching a point of equality (especially in Britain, but around the world too). Judging from the composition of the world's youth orchestras, there soon will be – or should be – more women than men in professional orchestras all over the world. That's less true of conducting courses worldwide, but it's another truism that there are many more women student conductors, proportionally, than there are in professional jobs. However, this is now as much a generational phenomenon as a question of cultural or sexual politics. In China, for example, there are whole dynasties of female conductors. The most celebrated female conductor to have made a career in the West, Xian Zhang, was taught by a woman, who herself was taught by a woman conductor. And in Portugal, major musical jobs are held by women, notably the English conductor Julia Jones, who is principal conductor of the Teatro Nacional de São Carlos in Lisbon, and guest conducts at the Vienna State Opera and the Royal Opera House, Covent Garden. Slowly, the balance will change. But we aren't there yet, and the simple fact remains: the top conducting jobs at the world's great orchestras in London, Berlin, and Amsterdam are in the hands of men, despite the early influence of the Maestra of St Vita. However, at least Susanna Mälkki, Marin Alsop, and Joana Carneiro are no longer referred to as 'women conductors', but 'conductors', pure and simple.

There are other obvious things the conductors and orchestras are not: in order to highlight the huge differences between the apparently similar phenomena of orchestral concerts from London to Lucerne, there are no new-music ensembles, nor are there early-music ensembles or conductors who specialise in this field, nor is there any opera. It was a deliberate choice, too, that Daniel Barenboim, Pierre Boulez, and Nikolaus Harnoncourt would not appear as major focuses of the book, given how much all of them have published on conducting and their philosophies of music-making. To have done justice to all the world's finest conductors and orchestras in the way I wanted would have overstretched even the fattest dust jacket, although the ghosts and axioms of other conductors, from Herbert von Karajan to Carlos Kleiber, nonetheless stalk the book's pages.

So in the symphonic patchwork of the chapters that follow, there is a variety of locations and types of orchestra, from those with an impregnable and sometimes daunting history, like the Concertgebouw or Berlin Philharmonic, to the relatively new and ad hoc, such as the Festival Orchestras of Budapest and Lucerne. All of them want to do the same thing: to play orchestral music to the highest standard possible, and to change audiences' lives through the power of music, just as their own lives are indebted to the artform. But they go about it in completely different ways.

As Kolja Blacher, the leader of the Lucerne Festival

Orchestra, a soloist and ex-leader of the Berlin Philhar-monic, puts it, 'There is a sociological difficulty nowadays, where personal liberty is so important to everybody. So why stick with this very un-free job of being an orchestral musi-cian?' Nearly all conductors nowadays – although not all of them, as you'll find out – style themselves democrats. They espouse models of authority that are much less hierarchical than earlier decades, especially the era of the shouty tyrants like Toscanini and the less noisy but equally despotic Fritz Reiner. But it's easier to say you're a democrat than to be one in practice on the podium. How do you lead an ensem-ble of a hundred-odd rampant individualists – as nearly all orchestral players instinctively are – without simply tell-ing them what to do? How can you be a democrat when there's not much rehearsal time, the concert's the next day, and the piece still isn't taking off as you would wish? And here's the thing: while the musicians might tell you they all want to have their say as individuals, that's only part of the complicated psychology of orchestral playing. Conversely, as a collective, they want and need to feel they're going in the same direction, that they're being led.

One of the differences between conducting today and conducting half a century ago is that the gaps between what conductors say is happening and what's really going on are more obvious, and orchestras are less willing to believe the hype of the maestro. As audiences are too. And yet that figurehead for orchestral performance is still a nec-essary lightning rod, even for those who think there should no more be conductors in the world than there should be omnipotent political leaders. Whether we like it or not, we read orchestral performances through the conductor's gestures as well as through the sounds and movements the musicians make, and whether we like it or not, it's easier to have a single person to refer to when we talk about a performance than a hundred (so we talk, paradoxically, of 'Jurowski's Mahler' or 'Furtwängler's Beethoven', as if the conductors possessed the composers, and as if they were solely responsible for the sounds the orchestra made).

Each conductor you will meet – and every conductor working today – wants you to think that they are serving the music rather than their own ego through their performances. And that can't always be true. Not least because 'serving the music' sometimes means going as far into the depths of your own ego as any psychoanalysis to get to the truth about a Mahler symphony, a Bruckner slow movement, or a Rachmaninov piano concerto. But what if they were right? Colin Davis has had a career of more than six decades, leading orchestras in America, Germany, and Britain, where he was principal conductor of the London Symphony Orchestra from 1995 to 2006. Reflecting on his life in music, he told me with disarming honesty, 'You don't matter at all as a conductor. And if you think you do, you're on a hiding to nothing. You have to get rid of your ego.' Behind Davis's self-deprecation is a deadly serious truth about conducting. There is something that happens between the music, the conductor, and the musicians that is, in performance, greater than the sum of its parts. At those moments, conductors really do think that the music is simply flowing through them.

It happened to me once, when thanks to a concatenation of happy circumstance, I came to be conducting an orchestra – an actual orchestra of real people, not one in my imagination or my mirror – in my favourite symphony, Bruckner's Ninth. The final section of the first movement is one of the most thrilling ratchetings-up of tension, dissonance, and volume in the whole repertoire. It's music I've imagined countless times: how I would shape it, control it, make it happen if I were ever lucky enough to do so. And then, in the moment, actually doing it and being there on the podium, something strange happened. I wasn't aware of doing anything at all, instead simply letting this symphonic cosmos achieve its natural momentum and power. It felt like the music was flowing through me, that I was hardly there in any meaningful physical sense. It could have been that I simply stopped conducting and started listening. But I don't think that's what was going on. It was as if I was feeling the energy-filled stillness at the centre of a storm.

It wasn't a great performance, thanks to my manifold conductorly incompetencies, but it was an insight into what professional conductors and orchestras experience, day after day, night after night. I believe in the life-changing, mind-bending, and ear-enhancing power of those experiences, demonstrated in the rehearsals and concerts I describe in this book. It's a journey that starts in London, with Britain's most highly regarded orchestra and its talismanic, dangerously inspirational principal conductor.

Valery Gergiev

London Symphony Orchestra and World Orchestra for Peace

It's one of the great riddles of conducting: the relationship between the physical movements a conductor makes and the sound that results from the orchestra. If you read any of the dozens of handbooks that claim to teach you a basic technique of conducting, you'll discover that what every conductor should be aiming for is a clarity and transparency of beating pattern, so that the orchestra can instantly understand the rhythmic impetus of the music, and at the same time interpret the conductor's expressive intentions. The vast majority of these books turn conducting into a kind of musical semaphore, in which if you swish the baton in the correct shapes through the air, you should be guaranteed a reasonable musical result. These tomes are full of diagrams that show you how your right hand and your baton should move, whether you're conducting music with two beats in the bar, a waltzing three-time, the most common four-beat pattern, a compound six-time, or the more exotic combinations of five, seven, eleven, or thirteen beats. The diagrams resemble the Laban notation that ballet dancers use as a mnemonic for choreography. They suggest that all you have to do to become a virtuoso conductor is to execute these moves fluently.

Supposedly, this spatial geometry in the mime of the conductor's hands can be transformed into an instant musical result. Lazare Saminsky, in his *Essentials of*

Conducting, propounds a typical theory. 'The rhythm being marked by the right wrist, its movement must be confined to a triangle or a rhombus with the sharp angle pointed to the focus, where the initial down-beat originates. The right hand alone is the legitimate organ of rhythm; the left must be considered chiefly as the means whereby shading is defined.' That's an idea shared by many of the technicians of the art of conducting: use the right hand and its attendant spatial rhomboid to mark out the rhythm and to keep the players together, and use the left hand to communicate the expressive and emotional dimensions of the music. It ought to be easy – and it ought to mean not only that it's possible to teach conducting, but also that there should be a gold standard of technical excellence that is as quantifiable and assessable as any other musical discipline. Getting your triangles and rhombuses right is the conductor's equivalent of playing your scales and arpeggios as an instrumentalist.

Some pedagogues of conducting turn that ethos into practice. Each summer at a public school in Dorset, conductor George Hurst leads one of the most celebrated conducting summer camps in the world. The tuition begins every day with an extraordinary colloquy of conductors, one of the most astonishing anthropological sights in musical culture. On the lawn at Sherborne School – at the summer course that took place for many decades at the nearby Canford School – the students on the other music programmes look out over their breakfasts with bemusement as eighty or so conductors assemble on the grass, batons deployed. With right arms stretched, these fledgling maestros practise the beating patterns that have become known to generations of student conductors as the 'Canford method', a silent mimetic ballet that proceeds according to the instructions of a teacher who calls out mysterious commands such as '12/8 with an accent on the sixth quaver!', '4/4 with a fortissimo entry on the upbeat!', '7/4, split into two, two, and three!', 'a slow 5/4, three and two!', 'fast 3/4, moving into one beat in the bar!' There is no better illustration of the fundamental impotence of the conductor as an individual musician than this bizarre musical drill. There are no musicians watching these maestros, there are no sounds produced other than a self-satisfied chuckle when you carve out a perfect 12/8 with your baton, or an ironic guffaw at the sheer ridiculousness of belonging to a field of conductors who have suddenly transformed into an assemblage of synchronised swimmers, of trainee Harry Potter-like wizards. And I know, because I was one of them for two years, making these 'Canford Christmas trees' in the air (you can often tell a Canford graduate, thanks to the smooth shapes of Yuletide arboreality they describe with their batons). I dutifully practised in front of mirrors, I had videoed lessons with one of the tutors, who assessed my potential without any musicians being present, and I felt thoroughly confused by the whole thing. Was conducting a journey of musical exploration, or just, after all, a technical acrobatic exercise? At Canford the feeling was that if you made a technical mistake – an extra flick of the wrist that upset the pre-ordained patterns of your ethereal carving – you were committing a musical crime, as if the gesture *was* the music.

George Hurst himself is a brilliant and visionary conductor, but the attempt to deduce a one-size-fits-all technique from his personal physical language is a hopeless cause. And any attempt to find a single gestural methodology of conducting from a historical model is doomed to failure. John Barbirolli's maxim that 'a conductor is born and not made' is only half true – conductors are formed by circumstance and experience, and they can only learn the necessary musicianship through hours of study and sheer hard work – but in terms of physical technique, he was absolutely right. Anyone can learn a beating pattern, but that won't make you a conductor, as any number of experiments over the years have proved. And not just at Canford or any other conducting school, either: one of the latest attempts to make conducting technique legible to a wider audience was BBC Television's *Maestro*, a series in which celebrities with varying degrees of musical ability attempted to learn the rudiments of conducting, with mostly dire results. The two musicians of real talent, comedian Sue Perkins and electronica artist Goldie, were the finalists, both of whom had an innate musicality and a convincing personal body language instead of a perfect, Canford-style technique.

Gunther Schuller, in his *The Compleat Conductor*, a magisterial, painstaking diatribe against what he sees as the paucity of musical intelligence of conductors throughout recorded history and their often abject failure to respect the authority of the composer's score, is nobody's fool. He knows that there's no single true way for conductors to move their hands through the air:

The most important thing, from a technical point of view, is what a conductor does *between* the beats. Beating time is something that almost anybody can do – and unfortunately too many conductors are merely 'time-beaters' – but the real art of conducting resides in how you shape the music, give it its appropriate character and mood and essence by *how* you move from beat to beat, what you do *between* the beats.

But Schuller is no conductorial relativist, and censures the worst excesses of podium antics. 'A simple definition of the art of conducting could be that it involves eliciting from the orchestra with the most appropriate minimum of conductorial (if you will, choreographic) gestures a maximum of accurate acoustical results,' to which he adds a footnote: 'Fritz Reiner ... put it similarly in an interview ... One wishes that Leonard Bernstein, Reiner's pupil, but later one of the world's most histrionic and exhibitionist conductors, would have taken his teacher's advice to heart.' Schuller describes Bernstein as one of a handful of 'perfect conducting machines' (the others are Seiji Ozawa, Carlos Kleiber, and Reiner), but misses no opportunity to criticise him for his immodest interpretative indulgences. Saminsky, writing in 1958, would probably agree with Schuller's assessment of Bernstein: 'The abuse of large and expressive gesticulation, which certain conductors bring to the verge of hysterics, quickly exhausts both the psychic strength and the enthusiasm of the players. They are likely to be found non-responsive, emotionally paralysed just when a special effort – a powerful sonority, an emotion of high potency – is demanded of them.'

Schuller's ideal conductorial physicality amounts to a transcendence of any individual's bodily attributes and limitations: 'Almost all of us are to one extent or another variously inept in one area or another.' These physiological obstacles need to be surmounted so that the conductor 'may accurately reflect and transmit to the orchestra (and thence to the audience) that which the music requires us to express'. Saminsky has a more precise piece of advice, regarding the necessity, as he sees it, of using a baton to conduct (unlike Pierre Boulez, Kurt Masur, and

Leopold Stokowski, to name but three famously batonless conductors):

The baton has a special value, and it is scarcely wise to abolish the use of it. The gesture of a batonless hand grows less concise. It loses the neatness of rhythmic punctuation which the movement from the wrist transmits to the baton-point with such clarity. The ensemble feels the absence of the baton at once, particularly when sharply rhythmic music is played. [Not using a baton makes] an additional demand on the orchestra's attention, [and is] wasteful and consequently harmful.

So what Saminsky and Schuller would make of Russian conductor Valery Gergiev is anyone's guess. Gergiev's hand and arm movements – almost always without a baton, although he did use a stick in his earlier career, and has occasionally made use in concerts of a strange object the size of a toothpick between the thumb and index finger of his right hand – are among the most fascinating phenomena of contemporary conducting. For anybody seeing Gergiev for the first time, it's difficult to decode what you're witnessing. Gergiev doesn't bring music into being with upbeats or downbeats, but with tremors and vibrations of his fingers, with explosive propulsions of his elbows, with violent convulsions of his shoulders, and even with bestial laryngeal grunts. There is no perfectly observed rhombus or triangle anywhere in his technical or physical apparatus. Instead, there is a tremulating mass of nervous energy that infects the air around his hands and which somehow communicates something to his players. At first sight, you wonder how any musician in any of the orchestras he regularly conducts – the orchestra of the Mariinsky Theatre in St Petersburg, the institution he has masterminded from penury to international fame over the last twenty years, the London Symphony Orchestra, where he has been principal conductor since 2007, the Metropolitan Opera in New York, the Vienna Philharmonic, and the occasionally convened international super-band of the World Orchestra for Peace – manages to follow him at all. Any textbook conceptions of the division of labour between the left and right hands, any two-dimensional diagrams of what conventional beating patterns should look like, any conception of proper conductorial decorum – all of these go out of the window when you are confronted, either as a player or a listener, with Gergiev's unique physicality on the podium. A drawing of Gergiev's path through even the most mundane of 4/4 bars would resemble a spider's web more than a neat diagrammatic representation; you would produce a labyrinth of lines and judders and doodles from the independent movements of all ten of his fingers, and the unpredictable oscillations of his forearms and wrists. The Gergiev technique is unique and unteachable: the Canford lawn would look like a shoal of jellyfish rather than a collection of militarily disciplined Christmas trees if they tried to turn Gergiev's movements into a model for aspiring conductors to follow.

But Gergiev's movements are not, apparently, incomprehensible. He works with the world's most accomplished and experienced orchestral musicians, day-in, day-out. Sometimes on the same day, in fact: no other conductor, apart perhaps from Daniel Barenboim, clocks up the air miles like Gergiev does. If his physical gestures really were as gnomic and cryptic as they sometimes appear, his career in music could never have happened. If Schuller is right, and every conductor's gestural language is the result of compensating for physical deficiencies of one kind or another, it's tempting to ponder what Gergiev's might be. What defects could the trembling spasms of his hands be disguising? The easiest answer might be an inability to keep still, a continual or even clinical need for constant movement. Yet off the podium, Gergiev is poised and serene. A compensation for that most common of conductorly traits, a lack of physical stature? Not really: Gergiev is above average height, and heftily built. A deliberate attempt to give his players something unclear to decode, to make them work harder, because of an inherent lack of weight or intensity in his other physical gestures? Impossible: because of his manic self-imposed work schedule (which more often than not requires the use of private planes to supplement commercial flights around the world), Gergiev works more intensively and in a more concentrated fashion than most other conductors. No. The answer has to be the other part of Schuller's formulation: that Gergiev's physical language is the most direct route he has found to communicate his vision of what the music 'requires him to express'.

That vision is a singular one, and amounts to a philosophy of performance, of rehearsal, of music-making, that sets Gergiev apart from all of the other conductors in this book. It's a vision that is symbiotically related to his gestures, that flows from the filigree dances of his fingertips – surprisingly slender and delicate, when you shake his hand, compared to the strength and bulk of the rest of his body – to the core of his musical being.

And to explore it properly, you need to have seen Gergiev throughout the process of moulding his performances. In London, in autumn 2008, fifty-five-year-old Gergiev rehearsed the three concerts that would open the London Symphony Orchestra's season: a Rachmaninov festival, with his three symphonies and the Third and Fourth Piano Concertos. On paper, this was a schedule that would have tested all but the most resilient conductors and most tolerant orchestras. They had just two and a half days of rehearsals before the first concert, scant time to prepare four and a half hours of uniquely demanding music. Together, they would play just about as many notes as it is humanly possible to perform in so short a space of time.

Yet such a punishing workload is nothing unusual for the LSO players or for Gergiev. Unlike most of the other orchestras in this book, but in common with every other professional symphony orchestra in London (apart from the BBC ensembles), the LSO engages even its most seasoned principal players as freelancers. This is an orchestra whose players are proudly in charge of their own destiny, as they have been since their founding in 1904, but they have to work extraordinarily hard for their survival. Proportionally, their salaries are much lower than those of, say, the Concertgebouw or the Berlin Philharmonic, and each musician is expected to put in far more hours, sessions, and concerts, than their counterparts in continental orchestras. When I explained the mechanics of the LSO's season to players in orchestras in Berlin and Munich, they looked appalled.

When the LSO musicians convene on the afternoon of Thursday 18 September, the atmosphere is hardly red-hot with excitement at the prospect of the dawning of a new season. Unlike professional footballers, who enjoy a close season of pampering and resting ahead of the autumn calendar, the London Symphony Orchestra musicians have had no chance to relax. They have just returned on a delayed flight the night before from a ten-day tour to Italy, in which time they played all seven symphonies of Prokofiev with Gergiev – rehearsed in just three days – and concerts with their previous chief conductor, Colin Davis. This was their twenty-second tour of the season, in addition to fulfilling their regular season-long residency at the Barbican Centre in London, just down the road from their rehearsal space, the converted church of LSO St Luke's. 'We're just back from the lovely seaside town of Rimini,' jokes Andrew Marriner, this week's principal clarinet. 'Actually, it was like off-season Blackpool.' Their tours have taken them everywhere from Florida to Japan, and the sheer pressure of having to maintain their hugely high standards as individuals and as an orchestra, as well as learn and play the massive volume of music they get through, takes its toll. Joost Bosdijk, the orchestra's second bassoon, says, 'I have hardly been home all summer'; Andrew Marriner tells a colleague, 'I can hardly stand up.'

This superhuman level of stamina, sustained by necessities financial as well as artistic, will be tested over the next few days by their immersion in Rachmaninov. And by Gergiev. But at the start of the first rehearsal, despite the fatigue, the late night, and the sense of the mountain of music ahead of them, there's optimism in the ranks. 'Valery is mesmerising,' Marriner says. 'We played two performances of Prokofiev's Fourth Symphony, and I was amazed at how different they were. And this is how he likes to work – under pressure, like this.'

Gergiev puts the same pressure on himself as he does on his musicians. The way he has turned around the fortunes of the Mariinsky Theatre embodies everything about his personality and his approach to music-making. Not content with securing the artistic future of the orchestra, the theatre, and the ballet, Gergiev built a new concert hall in St Petersburg in a couple of years – the same time it would take a planning application to get approval in a major Western European or American city. He knows how to operate within the labyrinth of Russian politics, and he knows that the Mariinsky brand has become the most famous exporter of Russian musical culture around the world: they opened Beijing's new concert hall with a residency in 2008, they have played complete cycles of Shostakovich's fifteen symphonies all over the world, given Prokofiev's operas their most compelling contemporary advocacy, defined a twenty-first-century performance practice of Tchaikovsky's and Rimsky-Korsakov's music, and revealed the essential Russianness of Stravinsky in their performances of his ballets. In short, the Mariinsky orchestra has become synonymous with the nineteenth- and twentieth-century repertoires of Russian music.

But the Mariinsky company without Gergiev is almost unthinkable. When he was just about to take over the LSO job, he told me that the Mariinsky was still the centre of his musical life, and that it always would be. He was proud of the repertoire that he and his orchestra instantly had at their disposal: 'Who else in the world can do this? We can do a Shostakovich cycle if needed, Prokofiev cycle if needed, Brahms and Beethoven cycle if needed, Wagner *Ring* cycle if needed – who else?' To which the obvious response is: who would want to? If the simple volume of music is the measure of an orchestra's achievement, rather than the potential quality of those performances, is having all this repertoire at his febrile fingertips really such a good thing? Gergiev's visionary musical dreams have sometimes been hoisted by the petard of his ambition. One nadir was a staging of Wagner's *Ring* that he toured in Cardiff, New York, and London, whose production values and quality of singing were damagingly impoverished, and which he performed in four consecutive days (usually, the cycle takes six, with two rest days, allowing the musicians – especially the string players – time to recover). Only Gergiev's orchestra would agree to this inhuman schedule; and probably, they had no choice.

For Gergiev, pressure is a necessary part of the game, adding to the adrenalin-fuelled alchemy essential for his performances. And things can happen in a Gergiev performance with an orchestra that are impossible with any other conductor. 'I really like this Gergiev way of working,' says Lennox Mackenzie, one of the LSO's most experienced first violinists. That's because the risk-taking of the Gergiev approach matches the LSO's sense of adventure – and the time pressure under which both conductor and orchestra continually put themselves. For other orchestras and other conductors, this kind of pressure-cooker would be anathema – the Concertgebouw, for example, would never tolerate so intense a workload – but in London, the schedule works. Not least, because it has to.

'I don't know this piece, I've only heard a few bars of it,' Joost says. That's not surprising. Rachmaninov's First Symphony, with which Gergiev begins his rehearsal, is a rare symphonic bird on concert programmes; a pity, since the work's big-boned romanticism allows any orchestra the chance to indulge the full gamut of colours and expression.

Their performance gives the players the opportunity to save the reputation of an unjustly neglected minor masterpiece. The premiere of Rachmaninov's symphony, in St Petersburg in 1897, was one of the great catastrophes of the composer's life. Teacher and composer Alexander Glazunov conducted the performance, possibly under the influence of alcohol, with a hopelessly under-prepared orchestra; Glazunov also made nonsensical cuts in the symphony, a piece he couldn't fathom: 'There is a lot of feeling ... but no sense whatever,' he said. As if the lamentable quality of the performance weren't enough – Rachmaninov left before the farrago had even finished – he suffered the indignity of some especially vitriolic criticism, from fellow composer César Cui:

If there were a conservatory in Hell, and if one of its talented students were to compose a programme symphony based on the story of the Ten Plagues of Egypt, and if he were to compose a symphony like Mr Rachmaninov's, then he would have fulfilled his task brilliantly and would delight Hell's inhabitants. To us this music leaves an evil impression with its broken rhythms, obscurity and vagueness of form, meaningless repetition of the same short tricks, the nasal sound of the orchestra, the strained crash of the brass, and above all its sickly perverse harmonisation and quasi-melodic outlines, the complete absence of simplicity and naturalness, the complete absence of themes.

The creative collapse that Rachmaninov suffered in the wake of this experience left him unable to compose for three years (the Second Piano Concerto, completed in 1901, was the next work he composed), and the First Symphony was not performed again until 1945, two years after Rachmaninov's death. So Gergiev's responsibilities with the LSO are awesome and multi-dimensional: to teach the vast majority of his players how the symphony goes, to try and inject its essence into their musical bloodstream before the performance in seventy-two hours' time, and even more significantly, to make a case for this symphony in the wider context of music history, to convince an audience that the First deserves a place in the repertoire alongside Rachmaninov's most famous symphony, the Second.

It all starts somewhat inauspiciously. Gergiev is on his mobile phone when he appears in the rehearsal room, wearing a baseball cap that he won't remove for the duration of the rehearsal. His bearing is not that of an overpowering maestro but a shambling, overworked, and pretty knackered-looking human being. There's some confusion about which symphony he wants to rehearse initially, but together, he and the orchestra agree on the First. Gergiev's strategy is inscrutable. In its simplicity, it's closest to Thomas Beecham's disarmingly simple description of how he rehearsed: that he played the whole piece through, played it again and then picked out some places that weren't working. Gergiev is sitting on a high chair, his eyes only occasionally coming up from the score, and he plays through the first movement, only stopping once to correct a tiny rhythmic error; the second movement, a wild scherzo, receives the same treatment. It's hard to know what Gergiev is doing in this rehearsal, beyond simply allowing the players to become acquainted with Rachmaninov's least performed symphony. But in the last two movements, he makes some general requests of the LSO musicians, going into more detail in the third movement, a slow Largo – 'to help the orchestra to understand the rhythm, we play the horns solo' – so that the rest of the musicians know where to play against the repeated syncopated rhythms in the horn parts: 'you heroically resisted the temptation to go with the wrong stress, thank you.' In the finale, there are some infelicitous moments of tuning and ensemble in the woodwind and strings, but Gergiev does not stop to correct these mistakes.

The atmosphere is a strange mix of the pressurised – Gergiev looks at his watch every few minutes during the rehearsal, and reminds the orchestra that 'we do not have much time to prepare this music' – and the relaxed, given the fact that this is basically a sight-reading session through the piece. Gergiev's gestures are shimmering shadows of the shakes and tremors that he uses in his performances, his hands making smaller shapes and convulsions than he uses in concert. And yet, even if his eyes are usually affixed on the black and white symbology of the notes in front of him, he is not disconnected from the players. It's as if those slender fingers, with all their weird tremblings, are connected through a web of gossamer filaments to each of the players. There's a moment in the coda of the last movement, as Rachmaninov builds his gigantic D major peroration, a hard-won victory against the fatalistic gloom of much of the rest of the symphony, when Gergiev and the London Symphony Orchestra players suddenly come alive. He jumps up from his seat, and is able with a single look at the trombones to perfectly balance the orchestral texture – and for just a moment, the rehearsal is transformed into a performance. The energy in the room lifts as the players give themselves to Rachmaninov's musical climax, and Gergiev gives a glimpse of the excitement and finesse he wants to generate in the concert.

For all that, this is a baffling rehearsal. It's obvious from those final few minutes that Gergiev and the orchestra are capable of working with intensity and commitment, but the rest of the session seems neither to have familiarised the players with music that the vast majority of them don't know at all, nor to have gone into any meaningful detail on what it is that Gergiev wants to say or do with it. All that would not be a problem, were it not for the tightness of the schedule, and the sheer volume of music they still have to get through: another two symphonies, and two piano concertos.

Nonetheless, none of the players seems worried by the way things are going. They know enough about Gergiev's working methods to understand that this relaxed rehearsal is a way of preserving energy for the concert, and trust themselves and their conductor enough to know what has to be done in the next forty-eight hours to turn the base metal of this rehearsal into the gold of a proper LSO performance. 'The more I work with him,' Joost says, 'the more I think he knows exactly what he's doing. The problem sometimes, having played a lot with him in Holland, is that he trusts his musicians so much. Which sometimes I don't like, because in rehearsal it means if things go wrong, he doesn't correct them, and just trusts and knows that it will work in the performance. You're thinking, we should really do that again, but it doesn't happen!' Andrew Marriner tells me that 'he's so clear in what he wants, what he shows with his hands. He can balance an orchestra as it's playing' – as the conclusion of the First Symphony showed.

Another day dawns, in which the LSO have two gigantic symphonies on their plates, Rachmaninov's Second and Third, as well as the mythical virtuosity of the 'Rach Three' – his Third Piano Concerto, played by the young

Russian pianist and Gergiev protégé, Alexei Volodin. It's a relief for the musicians to turn to the Second Symphony, a piece that's part of their repertoire, which they recorded famously with André Previn, and which they don't have to learn from scratch. And it's in this piece that Gergiev's musical philosophy emerges; the essence of what he wants to do in these Rachmaninov concerts. The Second Symphony is the longest orchestral work Rachmaninov ever composed, especially in the complete, uncut version of the piece that Gergiev plays, as most conductors do today. The first movement is a massive outpouring of lyricism and melody, but the music's voluptuous charms can sound cloyingly sentimental if every one of Rachmaninov's big tunes – and there are a lot of them in this twenty-minute movement – is indulged with overwrought emotion. It's a temptation to which it's all too easy to succumb. But it's something from which Gergiev wants to rescue Rachmaninov, at all costs. 'We have to follow the accents melodically, not rhythmically,' he tells the players, 'and each bar should never be the same. We have to save Rachmaninov from sounding repetitive; we should use such a range of sonority that it is always different.' Later on, as the orchestra swells to an over-enthusiastic climax: 'it's beautiful – but it's dangerous'; and specifically to the horns: 'you play wonderfully, corni, beautifully, but it's too smooth. Does it work in this context? It is not sure.' And again: 'I will do my best with the strings to make each bar different. The feeling with every new bar should be like when a new guest comes into a room, and everyone looks round.' Gergiev leans into his string section, imploring them to re-imagine each bar of Rachmaninov's music.

It's not just his gestures that transform the sound: his words do, too. 'Strings, the sound is always there, but we need to keep it speaking, singing; we are always against the brass, so we need to sing.' Repeated again, the problematic passage is sorted out. There is a moment of humour when Gergiev asks the orchestra to play 'from figure 69' – the players give a round of applause at the single entendre, the sort of schoolboy and -girl humour that never leaves a British orchestra's psyche, whatever their collective brilliance and individual maturity – and at the end of the movement, there is a cursory 'good' from the podium. The orchestra pauses for a well-earned coffee and fag break, while Gergiev attends to messages accrued over the last hour and a half on at least two of his mobile phones.

Throughout the symphony, Gergiev's concern is to make Rachmaninov's melodic and harmonic lines speak, so that the music has 'presence'. His continued request is that every section and every player articulates their part in the context of what's happening around them. This rehearsal is a lesson to the players to develop a three-dimensional awareness of the entirety of Rachmaninov's orchestration. In Rachmaninov's quicksilver scherzo: 'It sounds good, strings, but we need to make it more present, we need a better connection between all the parts. It's easier for me to read because I have the whole score – but you need to know too.' The third movement, Rachmaninov's sumptuously emotional slow movement: 'This music is an endless line, all the time, line . . . the line continues, so please play all legato, not just your part, but create the whole line with the rest of the orchestra.' He gives the violins a technical solution to creating this enormously long horizontality, a span of musical time infinitely longer than the length of the string players' bows: 'Please, you have to have the fingers vibrating before the bow comes down on the string – I can hear the difference.' A tune in the huge finale 'should not be sentimental, but it needs to be a proud melody'. And there is more of Gergiev's insistence on making individual lines felt within the texture, making them speak. 'Celli and contrabassi, may I encourage you to play with more presence . . . horns, your change of harmony should be very present.'

This idea of 'presence' is not just a musical request to clarify a passage of harmony. It's one of Gergiev's calls to arms for his players: that every note they perform should be played with intensity and understanding. What looks on the page like a routine bit of passage-work – repeated quavers in the viola parts, sustaining tones in the brass or woodwind – Gergiev wants to be performed with a complete comprehension of the character of the music at that point. What he is aiming for is that each player should be conscious of the whole musical organism of the piece they're playing, not just focused on getting their own part played accurately. Character, line, presence: these are Gergiev's watchwords in the Second Symphony.

Later, it's the same in the Third Symphony, which he rehearses in detail, especially the opening page of the piece, when the cameras from CNN arrive in the rehearsal room for a documentary about Gergiev. After they're gone, he reverts to a more generalised rehearsal technique, similar to his work on the First Symphony. The Third is another rare visitor to the stage of the Barbican Hall, and Gergiev needs his musicians to have a feel for the architecture of the whole piece. That's not easy in what is Rachmaninov's most complex symphonic structure, with its second movement

that fuses together elements of scherzo and slow movement, its moments of surprising, garish orchestration, and
some of the most daring harmonies he ever wrote. Gergiev's
watchwords are identical to those in the Second Symphony.
'Horns, these triplets are not leggiero, they're very full, very
present – very what you call "in your face".' At another
passage, later in the scherzo section of the symphony, he
tells them that 'my philosophy is not equality of parts, but
speaking, making the music, the line speak', as he picks out
the piquant dissonances Rachmaninov composes for the
celesta above a viola ostinato, making the soft-focused bells
of this sugar-plum instrument sound creepy, uncanny, and
chromatic.

The time for the rehearsal is up. Working longer than
the allotted time is almost always a social and professional
no-no – as well as contravening Musicians' Union regulations – but Gergiev asks 'for five more minutes on the finale
of this symphony, then it will be right', and he gets them
without a murmur from the orchestra. It's a moment that
crystallises the two irrefutable facts of the LSO's schedule
in these few days: they are working too hard, more intensively than any of them would choose to, and yet they have
no choice but to plough on through this stamina-testing
mass of Rachmaninov, or risk giving a performance that is
not up to their high standards. For the opening concerts of
the season, in the glare of large audiences and a full com-
plement of critics, no one wants to take any chances.

There is no let-up for the musicians when the weekend of
concerts comes. On the day of their first concert – the Third
Piano Concerto and the first of two performances of the
Second Symphony during the weekend – the players have

another rehearsal in the Barbican Hall, their first experience for a couple of months of their home turf (they are the sole resident orchestra there), after a long summer of tours. Before the concert, Joost Bosdijk and the tuba player, Patrick Harrild, field questions from the audience on their relationship with Gergiev. Harrild, one of the LSO's most experienced players, describes how the myths of Gergiev not rehearsing properly, or not having time to prepare, are completely untrue, and says that he can be obsessed with twenty bars of a piece, 'to go to the core of the sound-world', after which he can push through the rest of the piece relatively quickly. Joost defines Gergiev's approach as 'creating melody through a continuum of harmony. That's how he sustains slow tempos, because it's as if there's a great big river of harmony underpinning the whole orchestra.' A river that requires each of the players to be fully alert and awake, to stay afloat. 'He is challenging to play for, because he demands that you really listen, that you really join in with creating the performance. You can never just follow him. If at times his gestures are not clear, he is doing that deliberately, to create atmosphere.' Patrick describes how 'every performance is different, you never know what's going to happen'.

And the LSO has to be ready to react instantaneously when the concert starts. In performance, Volodin lifts the Third Piano Concerto from the mundane prestidigitation of the rehearsal room into something special. This isn't just a run-through of Rachmaninov's massively demanding music, but an edge-of-the-seat event. In the first movement, Gergiev throws a look along with an exploding tangle of fingers at the cellos, and their accompaniment is suddenly alive with an intensity and immediacy that changes the character – the 'presence' – of the music in an instant, from languid accompaniment to searing expressive line. As Joost has told me, 'he does so much with his eyes,' and even if in the audience we can't see those big, dark eyes boring into the players, you can hear the results of Gergiev's visual engagement with his musicians throughout the concert. Rachmaninov's music flickers with luminous colours and murky half-lights. If Volodin's brand of pianism is brasher than the orchestra's playing, the performance still reveals unexplored dimensions to this concerto. Gergiev finds expressive ambiguities in the light and shade of Rachmaninov's orchestration; instead of a flashy, self-indulgent heroism, the music becomes questioning and introverted, without losing its shape or its line. Gergiev never loses his grip on the performance, and Volodin has to obey the conductor's speeds, his phrasing, and his architecture. Having invited his soloist to make these debut appearances with the LSO, there's no doubt that Gergiev expects Volodin to do his musical bidding, rather than the other way round.

The Second Symphony receives a superficially exciting performance, but whether it's because another account of the piece looms as the climax of this Rachmaninov festival at the end of tomorrow's concerts, not every element of the symphony sings with the line that Gergiev wants to find. There are moments of episodic brilliance, like Andrew Marriner's clarinet solo in the slow movement, but somehow the symphony isn't connected from beginning to end with the same intensity as the concerto.

Marriner offers another interpretation of Gergiev's musical goals. 'Everything – every performance – for him is a work in progress. He's not looking for *the* definitive performance. If something happens during a concert that he's not expecting, if someone plays with a new phrasing or articulation or intensity, he's able to incorporate that into his performance, to make it part of the whole.' And that gives a clue to the physical conundrum of Gergiev's tremulous hands. Those shakes and vibrations are invitations to his musicians to conceive music and sound as he does. His movements seem to have no beginning or end, since every beat, every phrase, and every paragraph of his performances is connected by the same field of energy. For Gergiev, sound is a plasma that surrounds him and his players during a concert. It is his job to guide and shape that aura of energy, which has no definite start or end point. The players' fingers need to vibrate before the bow comes into contact with the strings, the woodwind players need to be imagining the next note they play before it sounds on their instruments; the whole orchestra needs to have a perception of the piece of music as a continuous structure that is bigger than the individual notes they play. Those shaking fingers and arms of Gergiev's are nothing less than quantum conducting, manipulations of musical space-time. The difference between Gergiev and a conductor who is a perfect time-beater or metronome, for whom music is about making the right noises in the right places, is the difference between a Newtonian physicist and a professor of string theory. For Gergiev, sound, music, and performance are all relative.

It is the morning after the night before, and the London Symphony Orchestra has two concerts still to play, in the afternoon and the evening. And they also have another rehearsal in the morning. It's a stupefying workload, and it's no surprise that the end of that final rehearsal is a little chaotic. In the finale of Rachmaninov's Fourth Piano Concerto (as seldom played as the Third Symphony, and even more unjustifiably: the piece is a masterpiece that fuses romanticism and modernism with a unique virtuosity), orchestra and soloist come unstuck. The problem is that it's Gergiev who sets the tempo, after which the pianist (Alexei Volodin again) has no choice but to get on with it. In the rehearsal, the speed Gergiev has set is just too fast, so poor Volodin is sent crashing around the keyboard without a hope of getting the notes right. And it's not his fault – and neither is it the orchestra's, who are almost equally stretched by Gergiev's speed. 'Don't worry,' Gergiev says to Volodin and his trumpeters, who fared especially badly, 'in performance, we agree that the tempo will be a little slower.' There is a collective sigh of relief.

About an hour before the players are due to reconvene for the first of the day's concerts, Gergiev manages to outline his philosophy of rehearsal and performance to me, as we walk through backstage corridors, into a chauffeur-driven car, through a hotel lobby, and back to the Barbican foyer. 'You must have wanted the schedule to be like this,' I ask him, 'to have crammed all of this music, all of these rehearsals and performances into such a short space of time?'

VALERY GERGIEV: Sometimes that's the way it has to be. And yes, so far, I do like it. I think it was a good concert last night. And we are sweating here, we are really working in these sessions. Whatever I want the musicians to give in the concert, we have to prepare. It is a question of how you inspire the orchestra, how you find the right sonority for Rachmaninov. Sometimes it is even a technical question of asking musicians to change their technique, to ask them to play their instruments differently, and working in a lot of detail on one small section to have a big result. It was a very big work to achieve in these days, I must say.

TOM SERVICE: *It is as if you work so hard on one particular section, to teach the orchestra what principles you want them to apply to the whole piece, the whole symphony or concerto. Is that your strategy?*

VG: Yes, correct. You have to realise that the modern orchestra can play in many different ways. Some people believe that sound should be very articulated, that musicians should play always with clear attacks and heavy articulation. And others think that the sonority should be very flexible and transparent and light. And I just happened to become a conductor who believes that all these elements are important – and all of them are necessary in Rachmaninov. So you have to achieve very different things at the same time, which includes lightness and transparency at the same time as utmost power. So I have to work in detail to arrive at these results.

But the rehearsal process – my rehearsal process – is also about something which is very rarely done: making sure that there is a strong sense of presence in the concerts. This is very, very important. I want the flow of the music to feel so natural in the concert, that there is always a sense of direction and even what you call 'drive'. That energy should always be present in the concert.

TS: *So how do you achieve that? Is it a question of deliberately holding back in rehearsal, deliberately leaving room for the live improvisation of the concert?*

VG: You know you can talk a lot in rehearsal, tell the orchestra what you want to do and how to do it – but finally, you have to do something in the concert, not in the rehearsal room! This is the most difficult thing, making sure that the performance never loses shape and energy. The challenge is making a sixty-minute-long symphony, like Rachmaninov Second, not seem like a long, boring speech, which you want to interrupt, or if possible just leave the room.

To get to that point, you have to prepare a lot. And of course I choose the things that I decide will be most important in our performance. So when we play through the second movement of the symphony, say, I am looking for those small but important details. The musicians then quickly understand that they need to take this point and put it in the context of the rest of the symphony, and feel how that principle will be projected across the whole performance. And I can be completely open and honest with these musicians. I just go straight to the most important thing – what is the colour, what is the character of this music, what is the principal voice? And that means we are working immediately on what I call light and shade, the relationship between all the parts, which is a huge coordination between all of us. And especially for me: what I do with the bass line, the harmony, the texture.

The point of understanding all these things is the performance – the ability to change things in performance, all the time. And that is what I can do; that is why I am in these shoes, and why I have been in them for the past thirty years in my career as a conductor. And that ability is probably the reason people and orchestras around the world keep me busy, and ask me to do certain things. I never want to lose the direction of a performance. I want to lead that direction and demonstrate it in the performance.

We have reached his hotel in the car; there is a hiatus in our conversation as Gergiev's manager, a shadowy American suit, tells him he has half an hour before he needs to get back to the concert hall. He goes up to his room to make some calls, and comes down the lobby a few minutes later.

VG: I couldn't even get any lunch.

TS: *I'm sorry. Now, the thing about last night's concert was that it was both a more expressive performance of the Second Symphony than I'm used to hearing, and a more structurally coherent one, too: it showed how great Rachmaninov was as a symphonist, not just that he could write a good tune.*

VG: That's because the performance had that direction, that energy I was looking for. And that's what conducting is really about. Real conducting is the furthest possible thing from giving entrances to musicians, making sure they play in the right place. It's about doing whatever you can to help the composer, and having the strength of will and gesture to get the sound you want. There are very different ways to do that: Fritz Reiner hardly moved his hands, whereas Toscanini was very expressive and passionate, and Lenny Bernstein was unbelievably extrovert – he jumped even more than I do on the podium. But inside, they all knew the sound they wanted to hear and communicated it powerfully to the players. There was no way orchestras could resist doing what they wanted! These were strong-willed artists. The best conductors work in such a way that the orchestra doesn't understand why it plays how it does – they just have no room to think about what they are doing. The process is almost a little bit mystical: you just – you are emotionally involved, and you know, it just happens.

TS: *But there's a paradox here, because you aren't the same conductor in rehearsal as you are in performance – you're less emotionally involved in rehearsals, because you have to be more objective and analytical.*

VG: Of course rehearsal and performance are absolutely different things. There are times when you give the energy a little bit like you would in a concert, but for me, the time has long gone when each rehearsal is like a concert. I'm completely aware now of the empty hall. And I don't want to tire the orchestra out before the performance.

Talking of which, we arrive back at the Barbican in

Gergiev's car. There are just ten minutes to go before he is due on stage to conduct the First and Third Symphonies. He hasn't changed into his concert gear yet, and as soon as he steps out of the Mercedes, a group of French friends of his collar him. I rush to take my seat in the hall, as Gergiev engages in what sounds like relaxed conversation. Stories of Gergiev's lackadaisical approach to time-keeping are legion in the classical music world: interviews given in intervals, attempting to rehearse an orchestra for one concert in the morning in Russia before flying to the UK to give a concert that evening with another ensemble. But the impression he gives is the opposite of chaos: he emanates a sense of relaxed calm. After all, it only takes three minutes to walk from the foyer to the backstage of the Barbican, and probably ninety seconds to change. So what's the rush?

Some of the players, however, are less sanguine about the day's schedule. Second oboist John Lawley, shortly to retire, says, 'We've never done a day like today, with a full working rehearsal in the morning, a concert in the after-noon, and another in the evening.' And the truth is that for all that Gergiev doesn't want to tire out his players, the fact that they are human beings rather than musical machines means that some of them are mentally and physi-cally worn out. Yet the adrenalin of performance – and the special atmosphere created by a Gergiev concert – brings its own ineluctable energy, because the players launch themselves into a performance of the First Symphony that's driven with a dark intensity that leaves me and the rest of the audience breathlessly wondering why the piece isn't performed more.

After the interval, the Third Symphony is more contro-versial. Gunther Schuller, the patron saint of conductorly rectitude, would not be pleased with Gergiev's approach: he flagrantly ignores Rachmaninov's metronome marking for the main body of the first movement, an Allegro moderato that the composer means to flow, albeit melancholically, at a speed of crotchet = 100, the pace of a fast heartbeat or a steady walk. But Gergiev takes the movement at a lugubrious tread of around crotchet = 80, making Rachmaninov's already baggy symphonic structure almost come apart at the seams. What's more, he repeats the long first section in this opening movement, further robbing the piece of forward momentum – the 'drive' he has just been telling me about. And if the finale comes off more energetically, the performance isn't helped by a sense of anticlimax in the Barbican Hall. This afternoon concert is far from sold out, and on the opening weekend of the orchestra's season, too; and it is in the back of the players' minds that they will have to do it all over again in just a couple of hours, performing the Fourth Piano Concerto and the gigantic Second Symphony again.

The Fourth Piano Concerto is full of pitfalls for the players and the soloist. It's not just the speed of the last movement: throughout the final rehearsal, the number of passages of shaky ensemble pointed to a lack of familiarity on all sides with this music. At one point in the first movement, Gergiev himself asks the players 'What should I do?', as the strings and bassoons could not coordinate either with each other or with the soloist. There are places where Gergiev's habit of not correcting mistakes goes too far in the direction of trusting that it will be all right on the night. There are raised eyebrows from the horns as another solo goes awry and fails to gel with the pianist, while the percussion and brass complain that they have never had the chance to get another place in the final movement properly together. What's more, Gergiev is unconcerned by details of dynamics. Rachmaninov's carefully notated gradations of pianissimo and piano, forte and fortissimo, are sacrificed on the altar of just getting through the piece.

There is an intriguing atmosphere backstage before the performance at seven o'clock that evening, as if no-one is quite sure what's going to happen in the concert, whether Gergiev and the orchestra's collective throw of the musical dice will make them winners or losers. Gergiev's solution in the performance is to make the most of what he has worked on in rehearsal: whatever subtleties of dynamic shading may be missed, the first movement is propelled by an irresistible single-mindedness, and the second by a piquant, nostalgic poetry. But the finale is another story. Gergiev's promise that the tempo would be slower must have been in the pianist's mind as he waited to make his first entry. But Gergiev has sold him and the orchestra a pup. The speed is faster, if anything, than in the rehearsal. I imagine Volodin's internal curse to the musical gods, and to Gergiev in particular, at that moment. 'Thanks a lot, Valery,' would be putting it mildly. The conductor must have known what he was doing; it can only have been a deliberate sense of surprise and danger that he wanted to create in his musicians and in the performance. That's one way to generate 'drive and direction', but it's pretty crude. And it doesn't work. The whole finale is a helter-skelter ride that's sometimes as uncomfortable to listen to as it must be to play. Gergiev's gamble – or his calculated decision to add another level of excitement to the performance – does not pay off.

And yet: the Second Symphony after the interval is a performance in a different class from anything else in the weekend of concerts. Somehow, from the crucible of the huge stresses and strains of the last few days – some of them inflicted by the pressures of their schedule, the rehearsal-as-endurance-sport they have had to put up with, and the extra unknowns and excitements of what Gergiev has got up his sleeve during the performances – the London Symphony Orchestra players pull off one of the most intense and moving interpretations of a late-romantic symphony you could ever hope to hear. It's a vindication of at least three musical fundamentals: the orchestra's ability as a group of players and professionals to give themselves to the moment of performance, whatever their physical and mental state, to Rachmaninov's genius as a symphonist, and to Gergiev's ideology of performance. The risk with his approach is that it might not work, that Gergiev's commitment to creating excitement, drive, and direction in his concerts at all costs means that quality and accuracy are compromised. But in this performance of the Second Symphony, the alchemy works, however tortuous the process of achieving it has been for the players. The LSO musicians, never prone to over-exaggeration, are capable of objectively criticising the performance even in the afterglow of the music, back-stage at the Barbican. 'I actually thought the scherzo was too fast,' Andrew Marriner says. Joost Bosdijk tells me, 'I think he knows this particular piece very well, and with a symphony like that, he's always looking for something new to say.'

My own assessment is that Rachmaninov could not have been better served than by this performance of the Second Symphony. But it has come at a cost – one that Gergiev himself thinks was too high. In his room after the concert, as he swaps his sweat-drenched clothes, he tells a group of musicians and administrators from the orchestra that 'three sessions in one day is too much. Two concerts is possible, but that final rehearsal was the killer. Maybe just one hour would have been possible, but not a whole session. I am tired. I lose two or three kilos in each concert, you know. So the afternoon concert was a bit, maybe, compromised. But tonight's concert was good, the concerto as well.' I disagree with Gergiev on that point, and Rachel Gough, the orchestra's principal bassoonist, refers to 'that concerto we didn't know', and says to Gergiev, 'I've never seen you tired before!' Gergiev looks physically drained, 'like in that photo they used of me to advertise the Mahler cycle with the orchestra' – a black-and-white image that shows Gergiev as a sweatily feral maestro, committed more to the music than to mundanities of personal hygiene or vanity. Whether the orchestra or the conductor would plan a Rachmaninov festival like this again, the audience have ultimately been the winners, joining Gergiev and the players on a Russian music thrill-ride for a weekend.

If Gergiev wanted to use the Rachmaninov experience as a catalyst to slow down, to know his own physical limits and those of his players, his subsequent months of performances with the Mariinsky, operas at the Met, and more concerts with the London Symphony Orchestra, show no sign of it. I immerse myself in his musical maelstrom again a year later in Kraków. Gergiev is also music director of the World Orchestra for Peace, an international ensemble which before September 2009 had played precisely twelve times since 1995, when Georg Solti had the idea of convening an orchestra made up from players all over the world to show politicians that music can unite the globe. If players from Russia, America, Austria, Poland, Georgia, and dozens of other nations can transcend their cultural differences for a higher goal of harmony, why can't the world's political leaders? Solti only lived long enough to conduct the World Orchestra for Peace once before his death in 1997. Scheduled to open the Festspielhaus in Baden-Baden in Germany the year after, Charles Kaye, the orchestra's manager, needed to find a replacement, and Gergiev has conducted this elite ensemble ever since.

The format might have been designed for Gergiev, since the whole project puts an extraordinary pressure on the musicians. In 2009, they prepared their thirteenth concert together in Kraków, a performance on 1 September in the Church of St Peter and St Paul that marked the seventieth anniversary of the start of World War II. Gergiev and his 120 players had just two days to put together Mahler's Fifth Symphony and the world premiere of a new piece by Krzysztof Penderecki for brass and percussion. This ensemble is the ultimate test of a conductor's communicative skills: to try and mould a huge gathering of the world's most experienced orchestral players into a cohesive unit in just three rehearsals in forty-eight hours, and then make them give a performance that is not just a pedestrian run-through, but a fully-fledged interpretation.

It seems an impossible task, but Gergiev has some things in his favour in Kraków, which even the LSO can't give him: each player is there because they have decided to get on a plane from Australia, from America, from Russia, to play for no fee, and to be part of the ensemble. There are none of the sometimes divisive politics of a conventional orchestra to deal with, and none of the working conditions, either. Gergiev can rehearse as long as he wants, and he can be safe in the knowledge that the musicians themselves do not have time to question his judgement or build up close enough relationships either to fall in love or fall out. Ed Vanderspar is the principal viola of the LSO, and leads the section in the World Orchestra for Peace. 'We're here because we want to be, for the music, for the project – and for Valery.'

From the first rehearsal, this is music-making in the raw. Players from the Vienna Philharmonic and Irish Chamber Orchestra, from the Hong Kong Symphony and Pittsburgh Symphony, sit next to one another, but there's hardly time for them to introduce themselves to each other in whatever common language they can find before Gergiev starts the rehearsal. The acoustic of the church is ruinous for the detail and subtlety of Mahler's symphony: its gigantic ecclesiastical space swallows up the orchestral sound, and gives it back to the musicians about five seconds later after it has reverberated around the gigantic rococo dome. Even the leader of the first violins, the Vienna Philharmonic's Rainer Küchl, looks bemused. But Gergiev does not complain – and there is no point in any case: the concert, televised live on Polish TV and broadcast on the internet, will happen in two days' time, whether the players and the conductor like the venue or not. The only choice is to make Mahler work in this appalling acoustic, and for the players to transcend their differences as fast as they can.

And the magic that makes the World Orchestra for Peace work at all is Gergiev's rehearsal technique, his conception of performance, and the power of his gestural language. There is no choice but to leave any number of interpretative decisions to the performance. There is no possibility of over-preparing, and no time for it, either. Instead, Gergiev is virtually assured an excitement, drive, and energy in the performance, since the players are unsure how their musical neighbours are going to react in the concert, and are in the dark as to precisely what Gergiev will do. His basic approach is the same as with the London Symphony Orchestra: after running through each of the five movements, he teases out a particular passage to work on – the climax of the Adagietto, a contrapuntal tempest in the finale, a moment of difficult rhythmic coordination in the scherzo – but there is far more that he has to leave to chance, which he has to trust his virtuosic musicians simply to correct themselves. There are no complaints from the players, just words of encouragement from those who have already been through the Gergiev whirlwind to those who are playing for him for the first time, and guidance from musicians like Ed, who have been fixtures in the World Orchestra for Peace virtually since the start.

Above all, the orchestra has to go with Gergiev wherever his musical instincts take them. The musicians simply have no choice. He has them in the same situation that Toscanini and Reiner had their musicians, gripped by sheer musical will and force of personality. Monica Curro is sitting on the first desk of the second violins, a long way from her day job with the Melbourne Symphony Orchestra, beside Tibor Kovác, the leader of the same section in the Vienna Philharmonic. It is her first time playing for Gergiev. She marvels at Gergiev's turn of phrase, how he refers to a handful of chords separated by pauses in the Fifth Symphony as being like 'diamonds, each one needs to be joined to the other like diamonds on a necklace: they are separate, but they need to connect with one another' – a description that automatically transforms the way the players think of the resonance of one chord to the next, each joined by a shimmer of musical luminescence. But she has another word for what Gergiev's physicality achieves. 'It's psychokinesis,' she says. 'He's a creature – he's just got this ability to think something, and it happens.'

Investing conductors with paranormal powers, the mystical, indeed mythical ability to move objects, or to change a musical situation, simply by thought, is dangerous territory. But Monica has experienced the phenomenon with Gergiev. 'I'm playing exactly the way he wants me to – and he doesn't even have to say what it is, I just know that he wants this phrase to go this way, to have that particular colour.' Joost Bosdijk at the LSO talked about Gergiev's eyes, and Gunther Schuller confirms the power that a maestro's eyes can have, even greater than their hands, their baton, their physical movements. But Monica is talking about something else, a telepathic connection of brainwaves that is more fundamental than any of Gergiev's physical apparatus: really, it's the essence of his musical being. I have never seen Gergiev lift a chair with his brainwaves alone, but I have heard him and the World Orchestra for Peace play Mahler's Fifth Symphony with a rawness and power that completely transcended what seemed like an unworkable acoustic and impossible conditions and which was fuelled by a drive and energy that seemed to come from another dimension.

Psychokinesis? Possibly. But there's a good explanation for what I saw and what Monica experienced in the shadow of Gergiev's tremulating hands and the glare of his gaze. The schedule of the World Orchestra for Peace's rehearsals and concert in Kraków guarantees an unusual concentration on the part of the players, who cannot take anything for granted as they can in their day jobs, whether that's with the Vienna or Berlin Philharmonics or the Melbourne Symphony. Whatever the peaceful, harmonious, symbolic and political function of the orchestra, there is national and personal pride at stake in how each of the individual players performs, how they compare to their desk partner in the strings, whether they feel they are on the same technical and musical level as their colleagues in the more soloistic woodwind and brass sections. Combine that with the pressure of TV broadcasts, the sense of how important the occasion of 1 September 2009 was to Poland and the viewing millions, and the inherent specialness of the World Orchestra for Peace as an ensemble that convenes only rarely, and there are all the conditions in place to generate a unique atmosphere between the musicians and the conductor.

Psychokinesis, in conducting terms at least, is a two-way process. Gergiev can only move what wants to be moved, he can only bore into his musicians' hearts (Monica told me that she felt Gergiev 'was looking into my soul') if they are open to being penetrated in that way. His gestures focus the players' attention still further, given the deliberate lack of clarity of the vibrations of his arms and hands, their creation of that immersive musical plasma rather than a clock of clicks and points. In Kraków, Gergiev's hands and eyes were aerials of connection that reached out to his players' powers of musical and mental concentration. His philosophy of spontaneity and excitement may have no more complete fulfilment. As the ultimate pick-up band, the World Orchestra for Peace is the realisation of Gergiev's ideal musical situation. The features of his personality and his way of working that both inspire and frustrate the London Symphony Orchestra had no impediment in Poland: there was only improvisation, excitement, and the thrill of the unexpected in that shocking, extreme, unforgettable – psychokinetic? – performance of Mahler's Fifth Symphony.

2

Mariss Jansons
Royal Concertgebouw Orchestra

The Concertgebouw – 'Concert Building' – Amsterdam, 6 February 2009. It's late on a wet, cold Friday night, but the players of the 'World's Greatest Orchestra' – as voted for by a panel of experts in *Gramophone* magazine just a couple of months before – are on a high. The musicians of the Concertgebouw Orchestra (the Koninklijk Concertgebouworkest, to give them their full Dutch title) have just played an astonishing performance of Dvořák's Requiem with their chief conductor Mariss Jansons, to a sold-out audience – no surprise, since tickets for the orchestra's concerts have been the hottest classical music commodity in Amsterdam ever since the orchestra inaugurated its hall in 1888. It's a piece that the orchestra were playing for the first time this week, and that most of the audience would never have heard in concert. 'The Dvořák Requiem? I didn't even know he'd written one': this was the orchestra's English principal flautist, Emily Beynon, when she saw the piece on their programme.

It was all so different just twenty-four hours before. The Requiem's first performance, on the Thursday, was technically polished and at times shimmeringly moving – as it should have been, with the combination of the Concertgebouw, the choir of the Vienna Singverein, and a team of soloists that included arguably Germany's greatest singer, bass-baritone Thomas Quasthoff. And yet the piece rarely seemed like more than the sum of its thirteen individual movements. It's easy to sympathise with the performers. This is a difficult piece to bring off. Dvořák's music does not have the dramatic intensity of Berlioz's or Verdi's more famous requiem settings, and it cannot compare to the serenity of Fauré's. Dvořák's version, composed in 1890 and first performed in Birmingham a year later, conducted by the composer, needs a special patience and understanding if it's not going to sound like a pale shadow of its more famous romantic counterparts.

Yet you didn't need to make any excuses for Dvořák in the second performance, only a day later. This was an immeasurably more powerful experience than the Thursday performance. There were only tiny changes you could put your finger on and say were technically better: the transition to the fugue in the Quoniam was more seamless, the low strings and brass played with better togetherness in the violent outbursts of the Dies Irae, and the woodwind section's tuning and phrasing was more convincing at the start of the Offertorium. And yet somehow the atmosphere of the whole performance was completely different. From the first bars, when Dvořák lays out his snaking chromatic motto theme in the cellos and violas – a tune that perforates all 105 minutes of the Requiem – there was an extra level of concentration and commitment that rippled throughout the orchestra and the hall. All the colours in Dvořák's score were sharper, the balance between the voices and the sections of the orchestra was faultless, and there was that mysterious sense during the performance that this interpretation, this particular present tense of music-making, *was* the piece. Dvořák's unique commemoration of death and the afterlife no longer needed to hide in the shadows of the repertoires of nineteenth-century choral music, sneaking timidly behind Verdi or Berlioz. This performance in the Concertgebouw made Dvořák's vision into something essential and life-affirming, a combination of the grand and the intimate that only this composer could have conceived. It was, in short, one of those performances that Jansons described to me as 'cosmic': a term he reserves for that moment when a good performance becomes a great one, a coming together of the piece, the performers, and the audience that creates a positive feedback loop of continuous enrichment and enchantment. Or, to quote second oboist Jan Kouwenhoven, when he spoke to me immediately after the concert, '*Ja*, it was OK' – said with a smile and typical Dutch understatement. Principal double-bass player Dominic Seldis, who recently joined the Concertgebouw from the BBC National Orchestra of Wales, is less reticent. 'It just moved tonight, it just had – that thing.'

But in the adrenalin-filled atmosphere after the concert, just as half the orchestra prepare to pack up, to cycle off into the night, or go to the bars of Van Baerlestraat, they read a message on their noticeboard that postpones their post-concert revels. The performances are being recorded for the RCO Live label, the orchestra's own record company: like so many major orchestras in the twenty-first century, the Concertgebouw has set up its own label to make some headway in the marketplace after the end of the glory days of the big labels. The 'Live' part of the moniker isn't just some marketing nicety: the orchestra prides itself on the fact that what you hear on their CDs is as close as possible to what the audience have just experienced in the Concertgebouw. And so far, according to Jörgen van Rijen, the orchestra's principal trombone and head of its Artistic

Committee, they've only once had to do retakes after the concert to patch up their performances.

And they have to again tonight. On a whiteboard, the Dutch for 'possible retakes' has been replaced with 'retakes!' The 110-strong orchestra and 150-strong choir will have to reconvene on stage at the Concertgebouw after the audience have left. 'Is he serious?' Dominic says. 'I know this guy, he might be taking the mickey . . . You're not? I don't believe it!'

And so, from the cosmic realms of the end of Dvořák's Agnus Dei, the orchestra is plunged back into pragmatic, mundane work mode. It's the end of a long week of rehearsals, they are just about to tour the Requiem to Vienna's most famous concert hall, the gilded Musikverein, it's half past ten on a Friday night – and they're not finished yet. The players present an odd image to the handful of us who linger after the concert in the Concertgebouw's auditorium to hear the retakes. They amble back on stage, half of them in civvies, the other half in dress shirts and concert outfits in various stages of dishevelment. A gigantic red velvet cloth is suspended from the ceiling, a few rows back in the stalls, about ten metres behind Mariss Jansons' podium, to simulate the acoustic damping of 2,300 Dutch bums on seats, creating as much sonic continuity for the record producers as possible. The record-buying public, they hope, will never know the difference from an oboe solo played in full concert gear to a paying public, and one played in jeans and a T-shirt by a musician longing for a post-concert beer.

Apart from some light-hearted banter, there's no sense of annoyance from the musicians at having to work for another hour into the night. After the solo soprano,

Krassimira Stoyanova, is let off the hook by the producer, Jansons gets straight down to business in his shirt and braces. *'Drei kleine Stelle,'* he says to the chaotically assembled multitude in front of him – speaking in German to the Viennese choir, English to the orchestra. But it's not just a case of going through these 'three little places' in the Tuba Mirum, Offertorium, and *'Anfang Fuga!'* – the beginning of the fugue in the Quoniam. Jansons uses this patch session as a micro-rehearsal, entreating the choir – 'Don't sing into your parts, sing out!' – and making the Concertgebouw's violas play their entry to the fugue on their own three times. Happy at last, he asks the producer, Everett Porter, if there is more to do. Apparently the tenors were late in the fifth bar – a detail that escapes my ears – but on the third attempt, record producer and conductor are satisfied, and with a brisk *'Herzlich Dank'*, Jansons thanks the musicians and singers for their patience, and the Concertgebouw empties within seconds.

It's a total dissolution of the unforgettable atmosphere they created just a few minutes ago in their performance, and a brutal bump back into the real world. The miracle is how a performance like the one the Concertgebouw audience has just witnessed is put together in the days leading up to it. In rehearsal, the performance is fashioned from the complex ecology of the orchestra's personal and professional relationships, especially the chemistry between the players and Mariss Jansons. Somehow, this social and musical raw material has been turned into something transcendent.

The journey to the cosmic heights of Friday's performance started on a slushy Monday morning, a gloomy Dutch day when the grey of the buildings around the Concertgebouw melted into cold, snowy Netherlandish skies. In miserable weather like this, it's easy to imagine just how alien the Concertgebouw must have seemed to Amsterdammers in the late nineteenth century. Today, the building is at the heart of one of the city's most famous tourist districts, with the Van Gogh museum and its endless snaking queues of sightseers just around the corner, the glitz and glamour of diamond galleries not far away, and the lowering late-nineteenth-century facade of the Rijksmuseum over the other side of Museumsplein. But in 1888, the Concertgebouw was the first building to be constructed in what was a vast, open swamp outside the centre of Amsterdam. Contemporary paintings of the building show how isolated the concert hall originally was. The Concertgebouw's neoclassical pillars stand proud and lonely in the middle of the surrounding swamp-scape, defiantly proclaiming a victory for Dutch culture and symbolising the country's dominion over its watery topography. Getting there in the Concertgebouw's early days was an effort, and once they'd made it, the wealthy concert-going Dutch public had to put up with mosquitoes in the summer months.

That the building and its orchestra so quickly became the pinnacle of the Dutch musical scene was thanks both to its remarkable, burnished acoustic – still one of the best in the world – and the quality of its players. Right from the start, the building and its orchestra had a magical symbiosis, a phenomenon recognised in the orchestra's earliest years, when conductors such as Gustav Mahler and Felix Weingartner came to try out the new hall and its musicians. Willem Mengelberg was the orchestra's conductor for fifty years, cementing its reputation in Mahler (the

Concertgebouw gave the first ever complete cycle of his symphonies and orchestral works at Mengelberg's Mahler Festival of 1920), in Richard Strauss, and Anton Bruckner. Bernard Haitink was in charge for twenty-six years between 1959 and 1986, Riccardo Chailly from 1988 until 2004. The Latvian Jansons is only the sixth Music Director in the orchestra's 122-year history. The Concertgebouw's tradition is a story of long loyalties and steady, evolutionary change. A plaque inside the building, on the right-hand side of the balcony level, shows a list of those who have played with the orchestra for more than twenty-five years, ever since its formation. It's a long list. As first violinist Christian van Eggelen puts it, 'Once you get a job with an orchestra like this, you tend not to leave.'

But not once in that history have the musicians played Dvořák's Requiem – and not once in my concert-going life have I heard it live or even seen it on a programme, anywhere in the world. The last words I hear before the Concertgebouw begin their rehearsal are not especially encouraging. 'You'll be surprised how rubbish it is at first,' Dominic Seldis warns me. That seems like an unnecessarily demotic take on what should be, surely, a walk in the park for this hundred-strong ensemble of the world's finest musicians. Dvořák's piece may be unfamiliar, but it is not technically demanding for the orchestra. Surveying my score from just a few rows back in the stalls, to the left of the conductor's podium, the opening movement, Requiem aeternam, never moves faster than a leisurely Poco lento, and apart from the usual demands of making sure everyone is playing in tune and in roughly the same place, I can't see that there are any undue dangers for the orchestra.

A ripple of applause heralds Jansons' arrival. Last night, he and the orchestra played in Brussels, their third performance of a programme combining a sequence of bleeding chunks from Wagner's operas with Shostakovich's Tenth Symphony, one of Jansons' favourites. According to the orchestra – and the reviews – it was the best of all the performances. 'Thank you for last week,' Jansons says, in the Latvian-inflected English he will use with the orchestra all week. 'Yesterday was extraordinary. I ask for the same on Wednesday!' (In the middle of the week they spend rehearsing the Dvořák, they will bring the Wagner/Shostakovich programme home to the Concertgebouw.)

The opening phrase of the slow first movement, Requiem aeternam, is tentative, the winding pianissimo chromatic phrase a chiaroscuro of string sound in the Concertgebouw's cosseting acoustic. Jansons' concerns are mundane and practical – to the strings, 'the second phrase, pochissimo vibrato . . . try not to be too loud'; to the brass and woodwinds, who share one of Dvořák's characteristic rising phrases, 'now, try to hand over this note'; to the flute and clarinet players, 'Intonation! Be careful!' – the first time he has to stop the orchestra, making the players listen to each other. Jansons' arms extend hawk-like in front of him, his music stand is raised unusually high, and his head bobs between his score and the musicians as he makes eye contact with the players. He's engaged with maximum concentration in the three-dimensional activity of conducting. Inside his brain, there's a multi-layered musical chess game going on, as he compares the sounds he sees in his score in front of him with his sonic conception of the piece, prepared in hours, days, and years of study leading up to this rehearsal. At the same time, he has to deal with the reality of what he's hearing from his players. Later, I will see how Jansons marks up his score, the pencil notations and marginalia that are his personal mnemonic language for these rehearsals and performances. Unlike many conductors, Jansons rarely conducts from memory, using the score in front of him as a springboard for inspiration.

Every sound Jansons hears in this first rehearsal has to be understood relatively. Each note the orchestra plays at this stage has to be heard through a calculus of musical potential instead of as a fully realised idea. Nearly all the musicians are playing the piece for the first time, and none of them will really know how it goes until they feel it under their fingers, until their lungs have breathed life into the work's melodies, until their bows have charted the trajectory of the whole piece. One of the most important questions Jansons has to weigh up at this early stage is what he should do when he hears something that goes wrong – a fluffed note, a mistaken entry in the woodwind or the brass section, a phrase that doesn't sing the way he wants it to. How many of these musical minutiae will get better through simple repetition over the next few days? How much does he trust the players to sort out questions of tuning or togetherness on their own? And how much does he intervene, interrupting the flow of the rehearsal to focus on a particular detail of the score?

Reading the players' body language in these first few minutes is fascinating. I don't get the impression the orchestra is completely in love with this music. When the long first movement is over, a muted murmur goes round. Having just been playing a massively demanding but enormously rewarding programme of Shostakovich and Wagner, there must be a sense of anticlimax when the players confront the relative plainness of Dvořák's orchestration. The piece isn't helped by the fact that the choir don't arrive until the next day. Jansons' job today is as much about selling the work to his musicians as getting them to play it correctly. This faint sense of disappointment with Dvořák could be infecting some of their playing in this first rehearsal. I don't agree with Dominic's assessment that anything sounds 'rubbish', but I am surprised at some passages where the Concertgebouw sound as musically fallible as any mediocre provincial orchestra. A place where Dvořák writes a simple weave of string counterpoint momentarily foxes the violins and violas, and a bar in which the double basses play a pizzicato bass line with the brass is poorly coordinated. But Jansons lets all of these defects pass without comment.

The Dies Irae movement, Dvořák's fast, frenetic 'day of anger', is different. There's more for the orchestra to get their teeth into – and more that can go wrong. The opening ostinato rhythm in the cellos and basses, Dvořák's vision of galloping apocalyptic horsemen, takes a few attempts to get right. It's not an especially difficult rhythm, just a collection of quavers and crotchets that wouldn't frighten a half-decent youth orchestra, but what's harder to get right is the expressive intensity that Jansons wants from his players. Just a few bars later, when a rhythmic motive gets taken up by the whole orchestra, something strange happens. Each of the sections of the orchestra is ever so slightly out of sync with the other. It's a disconcerting effect, the aural equivalent of double vision, and it's ruinous for Dvořák's music. I'm surprised that Jansons rides the moment out and does not correct the orchestra. Instead, he plays through as much of the movement as he can. He shouts a few admonitory words over the cacophony: 'There is a decrescendo in the fourth bar – I know you have it – so do it! . . . This is not so difficult a text, technically, that you can't follow dynamics!' But one exposed passage for the first violins has Jansons pulling on the reins and stopping the orchestra. He's clear on the priorities for this first rehearsal. 'Tomorrow, when we're all together with the singers, we'll focus on musical things, so we need to sort out these technical things today.' At a slower tempo – a classic technique that any youth-orchestra conductor would use to familiarise players with a tricky passage – Jansons takes the first violins through Dvořák's difficult couple of bars. The problem is that the violins have to navigate a descent of an octave or more, at the same time as they have to change articulation within the phrase. On the second attempt, Jansons adds extra expressive energy to his demands, and on the third, he plays it up to speed again. It's still not right – but he goes on.

Yet that's not the most humbling place in the Requiem for the Concertgebouw's first violins. In the Hosanna of the Sanctus, the eleventh movement, there's a bar with a hor-rifically exposed and vertiginous two-octave descent, from the dog-whistle-like stratosphere of the violin's register down to the middle of its range. The speed of the music is fast, it's marked to be played loudly, there is no other instrumental accompaniment underneath the violins, and it's music that makes an important harmonic transition. This is no mere capricious ornament that the violin players can fudge. It's essential that every note is as clear as possible, and if a single player in the section doesn't play it correctly the whole audience will notice and the perform-ance will be scarred. It's all as if Dvořák was deliberately testing his violinists to the limit, and what it must have sounded like in Birmingham in 1890 is anyone's guess. In

2009, it's enough to reduce the Concertgebouw's violins to fits of nervous giggles and frank bewilderment. Jansons' approach is conciliatory. 'This is the most difficult place in the whole piece.' He runs through the passage six times. Slowly. 'The third note is C! ... on the string, maybe? ... spiccato? ... once more.' His suggestions, and the sheer number of repetitions help, and by the sixth time of asking, it has improved. But it's nowhere near perfect. 'OK, practise for twenty-four hours!' is the best advice Jansons can offer.

The atmosphere throughout this micro-rehearsal of a single bar is jovial and constructive, and the rest of the orchestra laugh and applaud when the violin section gets close to playing Dvořák's notes in tune. Dvořák's musical *cheval de frise* goes much better in the second rehearsal, when the violins attack the high notes with fearless intensity, risking a few smudges of less than perfect intonation. But in the final rehearsal, later in the week, Jansons has an announcement for the orchestra before they run through the Sanctus. 'First violins, I make a present to you – the second violins will play with you, an octave below.' They try it out. The difference is magical, and with their friends in the second violins now supporting them underneath their near-impossible part, the firsts suddenly sound much happier and more confident. Dvořák didn't write it, but, paradoxically, it's a solution that allows his music to come across more clearly. 'Bravo Mariss Jansons!' Jansons says – and the orchestra gives him a round of applause.

Jansons' solution to that small but significant problem in the Sanctus points to the way he handles his rehearsal, a process that's as much psychological as musical. When the pounding, thrilling rhythms of the Dies Irae movement come back in the Tuba Mirum, Dvořák indulges in a moment of sonic extravagance, using tubular bells and a thunder sheet to amplify the apocalyptic power of the movement's climax. And when you have a percussionist who hasn't played anything for an hour, and he's given a moment to play a set of bells as loudly as possible, all musical subtlety goes out the window. The rest of the orchestra disappears under a tsunami of tubular-bell resonance, and the effect is ridiculous – but thrilling. The strings laugh at one another; some make mock attempts to stuff their ears with their bows. It's a moment of levity and excitement that Jansons is happy to enjoy. 'Gustavo, of course it was too loud,' he says at the end of the movement, 'but I didn't show you – I wanted you to enjoy yourself.' It's a subtle way of making Gustavo the percussionist, and the whole orchestra, enjoy the music, creating a piquant memory of a particular moment, and forcing Dvořák's previously unknown Requiem into their imaginations.

Jansons only rarely reprimands his players, and he's careful not to criticise directly. If there's a problem with tuning or ensemble, the players are experienced enough to deal with it themselves. But sometimes he wants the players to hear a problem that he's aware of on the podium, which they can't hear so clearly from their desks in the orchestra. Another place in the Sanctus has some shoddy ensemble between the brass players and the low strings, the cellos and basses. It's a simple repeated rhythm, three crotchets and a dotted minim, which, on paper at least, is one of the least challenging places in the whole piece. I can't understand why the players should be so out of phase with one another. Jansons' baton is as clear and energising as always, the players are some of the best in the world, so what's the problem? Jansons asks them to play it again – 'It needs to be lighter, not so heavy' – and on the second run-through, the problem of togetherness is solved. Jansons confirms to me later that instead of saying 'You're not together, play it better!' he found another way of making the brass and low strings listen to one another, and realise what the problem was themselves. It was a psychological trick to achieve the result he wanted without making the musicians feel like naughty schoolchildren being brought into line by a strict headmaster.

But there's something else in the Concertgebouw, another reason the orchestra's ensemble has sometimes been shaky during this rehearsal: the acoustic of the auditorium. It's a common wisdom among musicians, listeners, and acousticians that the Concertgebouw is one of the finest places to hear music, and to play it, anywhere in the world. The first time I experienced the hall was unforgettable. This was another Jansons programme in 2007, and sitting in the balcony in the middle of the auditorium, Debussy's *La Mer* wasn't so much a piece of music as a tactile, sensuous phenomenon. I felt as if I could touch the sound the orchestra were making; it was as if the whole audience was doused in Debussy's marine onomatopoeia. Everything from the string writing to the percussion section was somehow transformed into liquid by the blending effect of the Concertgebouw's acoustic. Whatever the scientific reasons for the hall's acoustic perfection – its reverberation time, the precise proportions of its shoebox shape, the mix of materials in its reflective surfaces, from the wood of the choir stalls to the red velvet of its seats, the way different parts of the frequency spectrum are supported, sustained, and mixed in the space before the orchestral sound is diffused to the audience – the result is something you don't need any training in acoustics to appreciate. It's a place with the ideal balance of clarity and warmth for the vast majority of orchestral repertoire.

And yet all is not as it seems. Jan Kouwenhoven has been the Concertgebouw's second oboist for more than three decades, joining when he was just twenty-three. 'The sound of the hall an orchestra plays in is very important for the identity of any orchestra. But this hall has a problem. If you are playing on the left-hand side of the orchestra, and you have to play together with somebody on the right side' – a double-bass player trying to mesh with a horn player, for example – 'you always hear them much too late, so you can never play on your ears. You have to compensate. This means you have to have a special alertness for playing together.' I live in London, where the acoustic quality of the main concert halls, the Royal Festival Hall and the Barbican, is notoriously mediocre, so it's astonishing to hear one of the players of the Concertgebouw orchestra tell me it's a 'luxury to play in a dry acoustic' like the Royal Festival Hall. But everyone I talk to in the orchestra agrees with Jan. Christian van Eggelen, a first violinist, says, 'It's a difficult hall to play in, especially for certain repertoire. Even with pieces that really suit it, there are always a couple of places where you need somebody on the podium to get control of the whole sound picture to work it out.' Joel Fried, the Concertgebouw's Director of Artistic Administration, says, 'It's a well-kept secret that as wonderful as the acoustic is here for the audience, it's difficult for the orchestra. Whereas in another hall, they can hear one another across the whole stage, that might not be the case here. It's difficult for them to play orchestral music like chamber music.' And Jansons himself says, 'This hall is not easy.'

Dominic Seldis puts this criticism into perspective. Newly arrived from his previous job with the BBC National Orchestra of Wales – whose main performance space was St David's Hall in Cardiff, with annual forays to the Royal Albert Hall in London for the BBC Proms – he says, 'I find it astonishing how many people in this orchestra have problems with the hall! They've clearly never spent time in Britain or London, where they'd kill to have a place with an acoustic half as good as this. Talk about not being able to hear one another – you should try the Royal Albert Hall!' he chides Christian – with its huge, echoey acoustic, and auditorium that's nearly three times the size of the Concertgebouw, the Royal Albert Hall is one of the most challenging places for any orchestra to play in. However, on the Concertgebouw, Dominic says:

Even the greatest diamond needs polishing. And it's true that it's difficult to hear on stage here, but the hall corrects itself. If you sit in the audience, what you hear is a warm glow of sound. On the stage, the music might not sound together, but when it's projected out to the audience, it works. What's even more amazing about this band is that the Concertgebouw orchestra takes their sound and can reproduce it anywhere in the world. They adapt to any acoustic they're playing in, to recreate the sound they make here. If you hear them in the Barbican in London, they still sound like the Concertgebouw.

The interchangeability of the name of the building with the orchestra suggests the strength of connection between acoustic and orchestra. But to be able to reproduce that way of playing in completely different halls around the world is a musical phenomenon. And I've heard it happen. In London, playing two programmes conducted by Bernard Haitink, the orchestra managed to recreate the warmth of the Concertgebouw in the sharp, crystalline brilliance of the Barbican acoustic. Christian van Eggelen explains, 'We always have the ideal of the hall in our minds, and try and take that wherever we go. Which is either a kind of miracle, or it means we're so inflexible we can't change the way we play! No one knows how to describe precisely how it works. But it happens.'

There are some clues to the mystery. One is what Jan Kouwenhoven says about the special alertness you need to develop as a Concertgebouw player, to compensate for the difficulty of hearing across the orchestra. That alertness means the players have to concentrate on much more than the technical difficulties of their own part. They have to understand how their individual line works in combination with what the rest of the orchestra is doing. As a double-bass player, over on stage left of the concert platform, it's not enough just to play your bass line beautifully. You have to know whom you're accompanying, how far away they are on the platform, what kind of attack you need to use, how loud you should play, how the harmony is moving, what the poetic character of the music is at any moment. The musicians of the orchestra develop a sort of musical sixth sense to deal with the inbuilt imprecision of the Concertgebouw's acoustic. And that imprecision becomes an expressive advantage. That infinitely subtle time lag between instrumental entries gives the orchestra its colour, its warmth. It's part of the same acoustic phenomenon that explains why there are so many string players in a symphony orchestra. The same volume of sound could be produced by many fewer players: the point is not the precision, but the texture. If everyone played in exactly the same way, if each of the twenty first violins used exactly the same length of bow-stroke, precisely the same wobble of vibrato, played with identical loudness and softness, the effect would be as musically one-dimensional as a military pipe band. It's the tiny differences between the way players and their desk partners interpret the notes in front of them that gives an orchestral string section its flexibility, its identity. The Concertgebouw simply extends that principle over the whole orchestra.

This sonic differentiation has important musical and aesthetic consequences. Dominic Seldis explains:

When you play precisely together, the result isn't always musical. But with this orchestra, they have an entirely musical approach. It's not a technical approach, about just getting things right. It begins and ends with the music here. I wouldn't like to try and play a very mechanical kind of modern music, like John Adams or Philip Glass, with this band. And I can't imagine what they would be like with a click-track, for a film score, say, where you have to play exactly in time. It just wouldn't work. But when you have ten violinists, all with a slightly different tempo in their brain, but they're approaching the emotional and expressive qualities of a phrase with the same intensity – well, it's an amazing sound. It's not a robotic sound. As a bass player, I've not played a great deal of chamber music, but it feels on stage like we're playing chamber music. I hate it when conductors say that – it's such a cliché, you know, 'Play this like it's chamber music' – but sometimes, in a great chamber-music concert, the players of a string quartet aren't playing precisely together. I find that endlessly fascinating. If you're of the mindset that everything has to be right, this isn't the band for you. The sole purpose of this orchestra is to work off vapours, to give themselves to the vibes of the moment. And to do that, they bypass what can sometimes be called orchestral discipline or accuracy.

Christian van Eggelen, who used to play with the Berlin

Philharmonic, agrees that the Concertgebouw's priority is musical truth rather than technical perfection.

We give the best concerts when we have a conductor who is here to rehearse and to work on the music. We're not so focused on whether it's together – a place can be not together one time, and we're not so bothered – we'll get it right next time! What's more important is to feel during the rehearsal week that the conductor has the potential to be in the moment of the music, to make something special happen. The conductor Sergiu Celibidache said that if you have three concerts in a hundred that are the really special ones, you're lucky. Well, with this band, you're always trying for that. Ninety-seven out of a hundred times, it doesn't happen, but even if ninety-seven per cent of the time we won't get there, we're trying for it a hundred per cent of the time.

Dominic, leading the double basses, is both inspired and overawed by the experience of playing with his new orchestra. 'When Jansons is really on form, and you've caught him on a good week, I can feel the orchestra just raising to a level and leaving me way behind. I feel like I'm constantly trying to catch up to where everybody else is. With this orchestra, when they fly, they're uncatchable.'

But these transcendent creative goals need practical realisation. For Dominic and Christian's lofty musical idealism to become an everyday reality, there needs to be a social and professional context in which it can flourish. The secret lies in how the Concertgebouw is run. The orchestra is a Dutch institution to its core, and that means it has a spirit of egalitarianism bound into every aspect of how it functions. Take the audition process. New players are elected to the orchestra by playing an audition in front of a panel of around twenty-five of the orchestral musicians and the chief conductor. To get the job, a musician needs a majority of sixty per cent or more, and if they're successful, they are given a year-long trial with the orchestra, and are subject to more meetings by the orchestral committees. No one's voice or vote is privileged above anyone else's in this process – not section leaders', not Mariss Jansons' – and there is a strict rule of one person, one vote. And if no one has a clear majority, no one is appointed. It's a process that's just about as fair and transparent as it's possible to imagine, but there are problems. Jörgen van Rijen is the Concertgebouw's principal trombonist, and chairman of the orchestra's artistic committee. 'We were trying to appoint a new principal horn player, and we had three fantastic players come, but because they all got a third of the vote, none of them was given the job.' That's real egalitarianism in action – even if it seemed crazy that none of these three brilliant players could play with the orchestra. (In the end, the post was re-auditioned, and one of the three was eventually appointed.) The same principles apply to the orchestra's artistic policy and their pay structure. The players on the artistic committee ensure that every programme and every conductor the orchestra works with in the season is vetted by each player. Unlike in the vast majority of orchestras, every member of the Concertgebouw has a meaningful say in the artistic direction of the institution. All the players I talk to tell me about how good for morale it is that section principals in the Concertgebouw are paid only a tenth more than the rest of the orchestra, meaning there's far less of a hierarchy between the player sitting at the back of the second violins and the leader than in most orchestras. But all of them also complain that they are paid about half as much as their colleagues in the Berlin or Vienna Philharmonics, the orchestras the players most often compare themselves to. If they're the best orchestra in the world, shouldn't they be paid that way, too?

Nonetheless, the Concertgebouw is, psychologically speaking, a happy place to be. There's a lot you can tell about how an orchestra sees itself through the atmosphere of the canteen during breaks and lunch-hours. Downstairs in the Concertgebouw, there is a continuous thrum of laughter and conversation in every break during rehearsals, a sense of close relationships and friendships being developed and deepened. The players know they are at the top of the orchestral tree in Holland, they know that they are well supported by one another, and instead of feeling like drones in a musical bee colony, they are valued as individuals as well as part of the group. Principal flautist Emily Beynon's first job was with the BBC National Orchestra of Wales; her second, three weeks after signing up with the BBC Welsh, was the Concertgebouw position, an astonishing achievement for a player who was then just out of music college. She describes the orchestra's DNA as musical risk-taking.

You can only do that when you feel supported by your colleagues. There is a great atmosphere here, it's sincerely friendly and socially incredibly supportive, and that allows you to dare, to explore. There's an incredible sort of freedom you can play with here, which you can only do if you feel safe. I can remember very clearly being totally terrified before I walked on stage for my first rehearsal with the orchestra, and by the first break, my shoulders had dropped about four inches because of this tangible feeling of support and trust in one another. That's very special, in my experience. The point is, this really feels like *our* orchestra.

There might be a decision you disagree with about programming or whatever, but that's fine, because it's a majority decision. And the fact that every appointment is made by so many players in the orchestra is wonderfully democratic. The fact that a humble wind player has the same rights as the chief conductor is fantastic!

And yet all this easy democracy has a clanging great paradox at its heart. The most important musical relationship of all is the one they form with their chief conductor – the person to whom they willingly subjugate their authority, the person they elect to lead them. Jansons was appointed to his job just like any other Concertgebouw musician. In 2005, he was the conductor the majority of the players wanted to succeed the Italian Riccardo Chailly. Chailly led the orchestra for sixteen years, and was voted in after just two appearances as a guest conductor. This was musical love at first sight, after the orchestra's quarter-century relationship with Bernard Haitink had started to go off the boil. Jansons, on the other hand, had been visiting the Concertgebouw for more than twenty years when he was appointed, so the players knew what they were getting. There could hardly be a bigger difference between Chailly and Jansons. They have completely different styles and approaches, as Jan Kouwenhoven explains.

Chailly is a more intellectual conductor. He always wanted clarity, he wanted to hear everything in a score, so he always chose tempi where every detail of the score was audible. But that was not always nice: there is a natural tempo that a piece of music needs to go at, which he sometimes compromised. Jansons is a more strongly emotional man and conductor. He is a marvellous conductor, technically speaking, in his gestures. But it's his integrity as a person we all admire. He doesn't behave like a star conductor. Of course, he *is* a star conductor, but he doesn't act like one with the orchestra. He is really willing to cooperate, to work with us. He's one of the few conductors who wants to work for a result. He works us like hell sometimes.

He works himself like hell, too. Jansons had a heart attack on the podium in 1996, when he was conducting Puccini's *La Bohème* in Oslo, a concert performance with the Oslo Philharmonic, the orchestra he had turned around in a twenty-one-year tenure. He was still conducting as he fell to the stage. After taking time off to recover, and occasional periods since then when he has had to curb his workload, Jansons is now in charge of two orchestras. As well as the Concertgebouw, he is music director of the Bavarian Radio Symphony Orchestra, rated sixth in the same *Gramophone* poll that the Concertgebouw won. The players in Amsterdam claim him as their own, and he spends twelve weeks a year with them in Holland and on tour, but Jansons has to split his time carefully between the two orchestras, as well his guest conducting with the Berlin and Vienna Philharmonics.

After a second day of rehearsals of even greater intensity than the first – the singers of the Vienna Singverein have arrived, as have the four soloists, the two off-stage trumpeters, and a whole troupe of recording engineers – I meet Jansons in his dressing room. The conductor's room at the Concertgebouw, a place in which musicians from Gustav Mahler to Carlos Kleiber have taken up residence over the decades, has a padded leather door. You don't have to be mad to work here, but . . . there is a psychological peculiarity about anyone who can stand up in front of an ensemble of some of the world's most talented and democratically self-confident musicians and try and cajole them into doing what they want. How different is his approach with this orchestra to that he takes with his other band in Munich?

Not at all. The principle is the same with any orchestra. You have to be – like you are. You can't say, with this orchestra I will be this person, with that orchestra, another person, another personality. No – I must be Mariss Jansons. To always try and artificially adjust myself to be a new person for each situation is not natural. And so, I must rehearse as I am – either you take it so, or you do not, what can I do?

But Jansons is alive to the different personalities in front of him, and to the atmosphere of the Concertgebouw players in rehearsal.

The important thing I must understand is that I'm working with musicians and with colleagues, not with machines, but with people. Of course, there are things that you have to respect in each country, some things to do with mentality you have to understand. And as chief conductor you cannot be very stubborn, you must feel the atmosphere and temperament, how the people think here. It's different here in Holland. Even their lifestyle is different here, from the way it is in Germany or England. And this you have to know and understand and work with. There is no point beating your head against the wall.

In this second day of rehearsals, Jansons has had two cultures to deal with, the Austrian and the Dutch, and he speaks German to the singers and their chorus master, Johannes Prinz, and English to the orchestra. Dutch, he never attempts. With more than three hundred people in front of him, this second day of rehearsal was occasionally as much about crowd control as it was music-making, even with players and singers of this quality and professionalism. Near the start of the rehearsal, he says, 'Please may I ask you all not to talk today. There are so many of us, it will be very tiring and difficult if we are all talking.' The effect is immediate. After years of working with these musicians – he has often conducted the Vienna Singverein, ever since he studied conducting in Vienna in the 1960s – Jansons has earned their respect.

His priorities are subtly different today. The violinists aren't asked to retake their most difficult bars, and many infelicities of ensemble have been ironed out by the players themselves. Dvořák's Requiem is getting into their musical bloodstream. Instead, what Jansons is doing is showing the music's expressive power to the orchestra and to the choir. 'It has to be the right rhythm: it's not together, but not just that, it's the character,' he says to the low brass and basses, as they play one of Dvořák's ominous, tolling rhythms in the final movement, the Agnus Dei. The singers are asked for more words, to make more of the harmonic changes in the slow music, and the orchestra have to ensure they're not drowning out the singers. In the Recordare, he has to admonish the players: 'If you can't hear Herr Quasthoff, then it means you are too loud – listen to the bass!'

Where yesterday, in the Confutatis, Jansons had to go through a place no fewer than twelve times with the first and second violins, a tricky bit of rhythmic coordination between the parts, today his focus is on the singers, and bringing out the colour of the meaning of their words. Jansons' concentration is total, but he is not as physically demonstrative as I am used to seeing him be in perform-ance. It feels to me that he is deliberately holding back his gestures in order to maximise their power: so when, in the Offertorium, he suddenly implores the choir to give him more in their repeated cries of *'Rex gloriae'*, the impact is immediate and visceral. Just by looking up from his music stand, glaring at the choir, and using a typical Jansons gesture of flicked baton and cajoling left arm, he transforms the sound the singers make. In the big fugue on the words '*Quam olim Abrahae*', the most joyfully explosive music in the entire Requiem, Jansons sets the tempo – it takes a few attempts for the tenors, violas, and cellos to play at the same speed – and gives occasional flashes of inspirational eye contact to clarify an entry in the choir, or a subtle but thrilling quickening of the pace just before the end. But apart from those moments, he is a picture of restraint, a cool eye and ear at the heart of the storm, as Dvořák's contrapuntal tumult builds to a huge peroration, the loudest music in the piece. The singers and the players don't need to be told that '*ff*' means fortissimo, that the character of the music ought to be triumphant: what they need from Jansons is something else, something that will be reserved for the performances.

This is all part of Jansons' rehearsal strategy. It has taken him decades to work out how best to rehearse, how to prepare the musicians and singers enough that they feel confident that they know the piece, but with sufficient gap for the spontaneity, life, and improvisation to come in the performances.

My approach has changed. When I was very young, my priority was more the technical side of things. But now, it is more musical. This can be because I am now conducting better orchestras, who are already strong in ensemble and rhythm, but when I was young, that was not the case. But generally, with rehearsal, there are two dangers: that you over-rehearse or that you don't rehearse enough. Both are not good. But it is hard to find the right middle.

I ask Jansons which he has been guilty of in the past, over- or under-rehearsing. 'Not enough I think, when there was not enough time. Over-rehearsing? In my opinion, not, but perhaps in musicians' opinion, yes!'

Jansons' goal is to prepare the players to the point where they feel supported enough to allow the piece to take wing in performance.

If everyone feels the piece is under-rehearsed, the music doesn't sit so fully in your blood. Musicians need to feel that they are sure that everything technically is fine, and then they can be free to make music. It's a very good feeling. So you need to prepare the orchestra technically and musically, but also leave room so that something new, something fresh can come out in the performance. I would say for preparation is not only how many days you have, but how many nights you have with the music.

Nights? Hard-working as they are, the Concertgebouw Orchestra has not this week pulled any all-nighters working on Dvořák. Jansons explains.

During the night, when you are sleeping, the music settles. It is not the same to rehearse one day for twelve hours as four hours over three days. When you don't have enough time to live with this music, then you can only manage some kind of immediate reaction to the music, you cannot emerge into the atmosphere of the piece. For that, you need to rest with it, you need to be reminded of the piece day by day, especially with a work like the Dvořák, which this orchestra does not know. You need special time for this to happen.

Jansons outlines his plan for the journey from first rehearsal to performance with the Dvořák Requiem:

Before the first rehearsal, I prepare my interpretation, my sound-model, then I play through, and see how the situation is. And then I start immediately to decide what I need to do. After the rehearsal I always analyse what happened and prepare for the next day, what I need to do. Yesterday, I did not correct too much – apart from places like this crazy passage for the first violins! But today I started to think about character, and very much with balance. With the choir and the soloists, it's always hell. The piece is new for the choir too, so for this you need a lot of work. And you saw how I worked: there are many tricky places for intonation, so you play a passage, like the start of the Offertorium for the woodwinds, and then I repeated it, always correcting some things. And today after the rehearsal, four of us were sitting for an hour and fifteen minutes, looking through the whole piece: me; the chorus master, Prinz; the record producer, Everett Porter; and my assistant, Ivan Meylemans [the Concert-gebouw's former principal trombone player, now a conductor]. And we decide what should be done tomorrow. We are like a group of plastic surgeons. But there is not big surgery to do, only small places.

Jansons' relationship with the chorus master and his assistant is genuinely open and collaborative. He needs and accepts their advice during the rehearsal, often asking *'Herr Prinz, alles gut?'* and inviting Ivan to give his opinion on particular places. Which he does. 'We have a big problem with the balance in the Tuba Mirum – the orchestra are far too loud, brass, organ, low strings,' Meylemans says. I wonder how Jansons is going to take this direct criticism. 'OK, we try again.' Ivan is still not happy. 'It's better, but now it's all not powerful enough.' Jansons draws a line under any further discussion. 'Well, the best is that we have the right balance.' No one takes any of this personally, least of all Jansons, whose model of leadership admits being open to other opinions – but also knowing when to exert his authority.

These small technical issues are meaningless in them-selves. What is more important is what they reveal about Jansons' musical priorities, and his philosophy of the rela-tionship between rehearsal and performance.

All of these technical things are connected to the musical goal you want to achieve. They are the means to support your artistic direction. What is a very big mistake is to make this technical perfection the goal of your performance. If the end point is only that everything should be together, that everything should be the right note, that the intonation should be perfect, and then you are happy – it's nonsense. If you are satisfied as a conductor only that they play together and not out of tune, it's a very low level of performance.

He shows me his score of the Requiem, with the mark-ings he has made during his preparation. And there aren't many of them, just a few pencil annotations, reminders of which instrument has the main musical line at any point in the argument, extra-large hairpins that reinforce Dvořák's crescendos and decrescendos. It's all much more sparse than I had imagined. I expected a Jansons score to be full of a detailed commentary on Dvořák's notes, given the level of refinement he works on in his rehearsals. The score is open at part of the Dies Irae.

You know, what is this? B–A–F–B–B flat–F sharp. These notes are nothing. The symbols are like letters. It is only when they are combined that they make sense. From letters you get words, with many words you get sentences, and with sentences you can express something. It is the same in music. Many notes make a phrase, and a big phrase of music is already an episode of one of the movements of Dvořák's Requiem. And this creates atmos-phere, it creates content and some expression. So what you must find is what is actually behind these notes, these signs, what kind of image and atmosphere is there. Then you will perform better. If you are only concentrating on interpreting the signs correctly, making sure this crescendo is right, that note is in tune, then you make a limit on the music.

Jansons speaks with passion, with the same intensity and focus I have been watching on the podium, and his words are accompanied by miniature versions of the downbeats and sforzandos he uses in his conducting. He is performing, in effect, giving his words expressive force and power.

You have to look at what the composer wanted to say with this phrase. So at this point [a fortissimo explosion in the Dies Irae] let's say, he wanted to express anger, because that's where the Day of Anger comes from. You must know that to be able to play this. If you just play these notes shorter or longer, that's not enough. You have to be thinking – what does this mean? You are anxious! So you have to play that way. This is the goal of how I see music. And therefore the job is trying to get to this level of expressing what is behind the notes all the time. This level I call the cosmic level.

The cosmic level. That's what Christian van Eggelen means when he talks about the three per cent of performances that reach the extraordinary spheres that Sergiu Celibidache wanted to reach, that Dominic Seldis means when he talks of the Concertbegouw 'flying'.

Why do I call this a 'cosmic' level? Because when you leave the earth, when you escape the earth's orbit, magnetism, and gravity – then you are in the cosmos. And it is the same in music. There, the questions of things being in tune, being accurate, being too short, too long, whatever – they are gone, finito. Instead, there is only atmosphere and imagination. And if you can get there, you are in heaven, you are in the cosmos. But to get to this place is very difficult, because you have to go through gravity, and gravity is always holding you back.

Jansons can tell when one of these concerts has taken place. 'If the public says to you after the concert, "Oh my God, I was in heaven for two or three hours" – then you know it was one of those cosmic concerts. But if somebody says, "It was a very good concert, the orchestra played very well, there were nice tunes, it was very polished," then it is not right. That is the difference between a very good concert and one of those excellent concerts. But of these excellent concerts, there are not so many.'

The gap between the very good and the cosmic describes precisely what happened between the first and second concerts of the Dvořák Requiem in Amsterdam that week. The question is: how? The first explanation is the deliberate expressive gap that Jansons leaves between rehearsal and performance. His teacher and mentor growing up in St Petersburg, Yevgeny Mravinsky, the marmoreally stern disciplinarian of the Leningrad Philharmonic Orchestra for more than fifty years, would not have approved. 'His principle was that everything should be done in rehearsal, and then, in the concert, all you do as a conductor is give them the signal and they play. He said that the best situation of all would be that if the public did not see the orchestra and conductor at all.' Jansons worked under Mravinsky in the 1970s, and there is a famous bit of musical apocrypha that has Mravinsky cancelling a concert because he had already achieved the best possible result in the rehearsal. What would be the point of a concert if the highest level had already been attained? 'Musicians were terrified of him. You can't imagine the kind of fear he produced in people. Terrible! Those were different times. And this idea of making music in the moment, like Carlos Kleiber did, would not be allowed by Mravinsky.'

Jansons' need for a public, an audience, would not fit Mravinsky's strict aesthetics. And neither would Jansons' musical risk-taking. He has a marvellously mundane metaphor for this process. 'With Mravinsky, it's as if he gives you a gift in the performance, a cake he has already cooked. And you eat it, you say – this is unbelievably delicious. With me, I prepare the cake a little, but in the evening I put a little cream on, or some decorations; I am also making the cake during the concert!' More ethereally, you could say that Jansons consecrates the potentially cosmic moment of the concert to chance, where Mravinsky would rather have mapped the heavens beforehand.

Jansons' is a deliberately dangerous strategy. There are infinite factors that go into any concert experience, and remarkably few of them can be controlled beforehand. Jansons talks about unknowables like how tired the players are, how happy they are, even what they have eaten. From a personal perspective, he says things depend on his mood, whether he is in a good or depressed state, whether he has a headache. 'So it happens that one day you are on this level, today you are a stage higher, and tomorrow you may be up there. But you search. And you must strive always for the highest level of experience.'

And that's just the people on the platform. The audience is part of the concert, too. Perhaps it's just me, but the Concertgebouw crowd for Thursday's premiere seem underwhelmed by the prospect of hearing Dvořák's Requiem. This is something less quantifiable even than the dynamics between the players on stage, but the audience doesn't buzz with excitement, even when Jansons and the soloists make their sedate progress down the Concertgebouw's thirty-seven steps at the back of the stage that lead to the concert platform. (It's one of the most dangerous walks you can make in classical music – when Andrew Davis made his debut with the Concertgebouw, he came on too fast, and tripped before he made it to the podium.)

But the differences from Jansons' rehearsals and the extra intensity he gives to his performances are immediately apparent, in his gestures, his demeanour, and the sound the Concertgebouw players produce, even in the first performance. All of those details of phrasing in the first movement that he needed to correct in rehearsal are magically in place; Jansons turns the pages of his score as if on automatic pilot, only rarely glancing down at Dvořák's notes, meaning he makes nearly constant eye contact with the players, the choir, and the soloists. Those places where he seemed strangely restrained in rehearsal are released with new energy and drive. He takes the big fugue at a different tempo to any he has tried in rehearsal, and dives into Dvořák's counterpoint with a ferocity that seems to take the musicians by surprise – it's only by the fifth bar of the fugue that the tenors, cellos, and violas have picked up the tempo he wants. Jansons' body language is an amplified version of everything he has done in the days of preparation leading up to the performance. He places himself within the music, sometimes hunched over the score, mixing the orchestral palette in real time, making the dynamics more extreme – softer, louder – and sharpening the responses of his players with the swift flicks and ticks of his baton. More often than not, Jansons embraces the music and his performers, extending both arms over and around the music stand, as though he is holding the entire ensemble and the piece in his grasp.

Dvořák's Agnus Dei ends the Requiem where it began, with the repeated lamentation of the chromatic motto theme, and in the same tenebrous key of B flat minor, with a slow tempo that slides into silence in the final three bars. This is not a victory over death, or its transcendence, but a fatalistic acceptance of the inevitable. Jansons holds the silence in the Concertgebouw for a few seconds before turning to the audience, and looks at us with the quizzical stare with which he always fixes his audiences – partly imploring us for praise, partly challenging us to respect the emotional journey through which he has led his listeners and his performers. The audience does the right thing, and responds with tumultuous applause.

He looks drained, physically and mentally.

For me, the most difficult thing is, since I'm giving to every concert so much energy, so much inner energy, I am always burnt out after the concert. So for me it's very difficult when I repeat again the same programme to get the same fire. This is for me the question number one now – how do I keep that energy for the next performance? Before [my heart attack] every concert was not so much an event – of course, I could conduct emotionally and intensely, but now for me every concert is something special. And you want tonight to be special and tomorrow night to be special as well – you want, but you can't have that always! Therefore I always try to mobilise my energy to find new things, to be at the same stage like you were performing the piece for the first time. So I get some new ideas, and I do things differently.

This is another of Jansons' secrets for maintaining the possibility of travelling to the cosmos in all his concerts

– deliberately doing new things with the same piece of music in each performance.

I remember when I did my first tour with the Oslo Philharmonic, and we played in Leeds Town Hall, Sibelius's First Symphony. In the rehearsal, I did one thing, and in the concert, I did something different, a different tempo. And one contrabass player came in much too early. And then I said to the musicians: be careful with me, there will always be new surprises in every performance. So then they knew and were alert. And this is one way to get fresh, interesting performances.

Jan Kouwenhoven confirms that Jansons is still up to his tricks with the Concertgebouw.

When you play a piece several times, you see that he never does all performances the same, but some aspects are really different. He communicates with you a bar before that something is coming up, or gives you a different facial expression that alerts you to the fact that something will be different. Sometimes he says in rehearsal, I want to make a ritenuto here, but maybe in the next performance I will do it differently. It's a way of avoiding routine.

There could be something cynical in this – change for the sake of change, for the sake only of keeping players on their toes rather than for any deeper musical reason. 'No, it's not like that,' Jansons says.

You come again with your emotions. It is about listening to your emotions in the moment. So in one place where you always do a ritenuto, and it is becoming boring, you change it – because you are full of ideas and fantasy. If it is done in this spontaneous way, then it is very convincing, and the orchestra will follow you. But if you prepare something at home, then it comes artificially, and it's not natural.

The second performance, on the Friday, is full of small details of texture, of tempo, of rhythm, which make it a different experience from the first performance. But it also reaches Jansons' 'cosmic' level of atmosphere. Jan Kouwenhoven says that the conductors who work best with the Concertgebouw are those that 'have more qualities than just being good in their movement. You have to tell us something about the music: what is your story, what is your feeling, and you have to express that. This is the deeper level that this orchestra is looking for.' With Jansons on that wet, cold night in early February, they find that profound connection with Dvořák's music that communicates with unforgettable power to the Concertgebouw audience. The whole performance is a single, drawn-out moment of musical inspiration. But this is no musical fluke. This performance is a hard-won prize made from practical mundanities and philosophical ideas about performance – and everything in between. It happened because orchestra and conductor collectively believe that every performance they give ought to aspire to the condition of transcendence; because each player feels supported by the institutional and personal relationships within the orchestra; because they felt sufficiently prepared over the week of rehearsals to be spontaneous and free in the performances; because the players and the singers trust Jansons' musical instincts without question; because the Concertgebouw players believe they deserve the title of the best in the world; and because whatever misgivings they may have had about Dvořák's Requiem at the start of the week, on that Friday evening, it was the only music in the world that mattered to them. The audience, already rapturous the night before, gives Jansons, his orchestra, and the singers a quarter-hour or more of standing ovation. This was a gravity-defying performance that transcended musical limits, but only because it was built on solid, Dutch, democratic foundations – and the Latvian inspiration of its conductor.

3

Jonathan Nott
Bamberg Symphony Orchestra

Bamberg is the definition of a sleepy Bavarian town, a picture-postcard agglomeration of castles, cathedrals, and cobblers' houses that could come straight out of the imaginings of the Brothers Grimm, or a chocolate-box production of Wagner's *Die Meistersinger von Nürnberg*. Walking around the city's late medieval heart, the so-called 'Little Venice' of perfectly preserved boating houses that perch along the banks of the river Regnitz, you half expect Hans Sachs to peer around every corner, bursting into boastful song about the supremacy of German art, music, and culture. The jewel in Bamberg's historical crown is the fifteenth-century Town Hall that seems to float on the Regnitz, built on an island in the middle of the stream, whose gilt-panelled rooms once housed the municipal administrations of the good burghers of Bamberg. Today, this magnificent palace of medievaldom, like the whole of the centre of Bamberg, has the atmosphere of a living museum. To walk from the river to the cathedral and castle on a sleepy Sunday, when all of Bamberg's shops are closed, the houses shuttered by wooden panels, its seventy-thousand-strong population dreaming, you want to imagine, of lederhosen and bratwurst, is to experience the closest possible simulacrum of an idealised Germany. Bamberg is a domesticised Neuschwanstein, a town from a theme-park Bavaria whose greatest mystery is that it's not the lurid fantasy of a mad king, but a real place, somehow part of Germany in the early twenty-first century. The untranslatable German word *Gemütlichkeit*, which denotes all the following at the same time – comfort, contentment, small-c conservatism – could have been invented for Bamberg.

It is not the sort of place where you'd expect to find an internationally renowned orchestra with one of the most imaginative approaches to programming anywhere in the world. And yet, further down the Regnitz, past another suite of mock-Venetian Bavarian houses, along pavements unadulterated by even a single smear of chewing gum, there's a big, ugly concrete building. It's a typical early-1990s nondescript municipal lump, not self-confidently abstract enough to be called brutalist, but without any compensating postmodern flair, which throws a dissonant, angular modernity into Bamberg's architectural mix. Until recently, there was no external indication of which institution this building housed, only the lugubrious moniker of 'Konzert- und Kongresshalle' offering any real clue as to what might be going on in there.

In fact, this is the home of the Bamberg Symphony Orchestra, an ensemble that's been going through a musical revolution since 2000, when their new music director, the then thirty-eight-year-old Jonathan Nott was appointed. Nott, who was born in Solihull, near Birmingham, has dragged this well-respected but provincial orchestra, famous in German musical life for its dark, warm, and heavy *Böhmischer Klang* ('Bohemian sound'), into the present day. He has instigated bold choices of repertoire and interpretative style, and made the Bamberg orchestra a force to be reckoned with on tours from New York to London, from Edinburgh to Tokyo. The story of their relationship proves how an internationally successful orchestral partnership can be created in the midst of provincial conservatism – with the necessary conflict and turmoil that contrast suggests. But it's also a personal drama, fuelled by Jonathan Nott's continual intellectual, psychological, and emotional exploration of what it means to be a conductor. He has pondered long and hard on the relationship between his private personality and who he is on the podium, and he is open and honest about the battles he fights within himself every time he steps out on to the stage of the Konzert- und Kongresshalle to rehearse or perform with his orchestra.

When I first meet them in May 2009, Nott and his orchestra are rehearsing programmes for a tour to Avery Fisher Hall in New York. They will give concerts that include all three Bartók piano concertos with the French pianist Pierre-Laurent Aimard, as well as the works I hear them rehearse and perform in Bamberg just before they get on the plane: Debussy's *La Mer* and *Prélude à l'après-midi d'un faune*, Stravinsky's *Symphonies of Wind Instruments*, and his epoch-making ballet *The Rite of Spring*. It's an uncompromising line-up of mostly early twentieth-century masterpieces, designed to show off how far the Bambergers have come with Nott since the last time the orchestra played across the Atlantic. The central idea is to show a jaded New York public that it's not only their home orchestra, the New York Philharmonic, who can produce the goods in *The Rite of Spring*. *The Rite* has undergone an astonishing transformation in musical culture: the score was heard as a riot-inducing pile-up of dissonance and rhythmic complexity in Paris at its premiere in 1913, but nearly a century later, the piece is a byword for orchestral virtuosity that every ensemble worth its salt needs to have in its repertoire.

Nott has a clear game-plan with his interpretation of the piece. 'I've told the orchestra that our performance has to be even better than the last time we played it in concert' (which was very good indeed: I heard a performance at the Lucerne Festival in Switzerland, in which Nott and the Bamberg players opened up new expressive depths in *The Rite*'s atavistic dance to the death).

I said, 'Why are we going to New York?' and here's the answer: 'We're going because you make a sound that the New York Philharmonic don't. Lorin Maazel [the New York Philharmonic's outgoing music director, master technician of maestros] conducts *The Rite of Spring* off by heart, and so I'm going to as well. And you're going to show them what they're missing in the way they play the piece!' We had a bit of a laugh, but then we got on with working on it. Because this orchestra doesn't think about how it's going to feel in three weeks' time, when they're on stage at Avery Fisher Hall. Bamberg is a bit of a sleepy place, so I have to wake them up. That sort of psychology is all part of working here.

Nott starts the first rehearsal on *La Mer* – 'Three Symphonic Sketches', as Debussy described the work – with an announcement whose timing may also have something to do with a bigger psychological strategy. In his near-perfect German, Nott tells the orchestra that he has just finalised negotiations with the orchestra's administrators to stay as their chief conductor for another three years. 'I'm looking forward very much to planning the next three seasons, and to playing with you.' There is warm, but efficient, applause: it's not unexpected news for the Bamberg players, but it means that the New York trip will not be a last hurrah for their music director, but rather the start of the next stage of their partnership. And then they get down to work.

If every concert is just the tip of an iceberg of individual and collective musical work, then so too is every rehearsal. Before Jonathan Nott walks out on stage to lead his orchestra through *La Mer* or *The Rite of Spring*, there are hours of private work that need to have been done. The ambition to conduct both these huge musical masterpieces without a score requires a freakish feat of memory and concentration. How is it possible to know what every instrument of a 120-strong orchestra should be doing at any point in the thirty-five minutes of *The Rite*, to know not just which note they should be playing but for how long and how loudly? This is a piece whose chaotic jump-cuts from one time signature to another, from one tempo to another, are difficult enough to fathom even when you're following the score with a favourite recording. The idea of memorising each instrumental line, and having each twist and turn of the music in your brain, your body, and your hands requires superhuman levels of concentration and focus – not to mention a massively developed memory. Nott plans to conduct *La Mer* without a score as well, which may be an even more formidable task. Debussy's quicksilver music moves with all the fluid unpredictability of a cluster of cumulus or a shoal of fish in the tide. A simple question, then, in the spacious conductor's room backstage: how does Nott prepare himself for his rehearsals, and hone his ability to memorise these huge pieces?

JONATHAN NOTT: I find learning from memory is always a mixture of two elements: the mathematics of knowing what happens when, and then trusting that the music is in your head, that you know the music. You have to analyse these pieces, like the second movement of *La Mer*, where it's very difficult to find a structure. Or a Mahler symphony, when you can at least say, it's in sonata form: once you've done that, you can parse the thing into little blocks, and memorise it like that.

The Rite of Spring, though, is something else. *The Rite* is full of sandwiches of little cells, little blocks. So you might have one bar of 3/4, four bars of 4/4, and then one 3/8 bar. If I'm in the middle of the block, I don't have to worry about it, I know what's happening and where I am. But the trouble in *The Rite* is that the blocks come so fast. When I tried to conduct it from memory at first, the problem was that I was concentrating so much on the blocks that I wasn't conducting it any better than if I wasn't doing it from memory. But basically I feel I can always conduct a piece better without a score, because there's nothing physically between me and the music, between me and the musicians.

TOM SERVICE: *But I don't understand how the music actually goes in to your head: how do you make the mathematics of a piece stick in your brain?*

JN: The analysis I do of each piece isn't just looking at a score. I mean, I'm no genius from that point of view. I can read a score moderately well, but not so well that I feel I could just look at the thing and hear it in my head. OK, if it's a piece of Mozart, we're all right with that, but if it's more complicated, I need to play it at the piano. And that's an interesting point about memory. I have to have some kind of physical experience of the music to memorise it. I can remember a long time ago playing the slow movement of Bruckner's Seventh Symphony on the piano before I conducted it for the first time. And everything about the piece stayed with me, because it was in my fingers. That's the best way to do it.

But sometimes you don't have time. If I've somehow let myself get in a position where I'm required to know all of Schubert's symphonies as well as Pierre Boulez's *Pli selon pli* [one of the great modernist masterpieces, a symphony of half-lights and shadows and slinking ambiguity], that's just too much repertoire to learn the pieces from memory. Instead, I have to mark up my scores. Which means I will colour things in on the score, and write in notes of all the things that have interested me. If I'm conducting a Mahler symphony, that means there's a huge amount of biographical information that goes on to the page: what Mahler himself said about this music, how he conducted it, what other people have said about the piece. I find that my scores become a collection of all my thoughts about the music. It gets to the point where if it's a piece I've done a lot, I can't see the notes any more.

TS: *You mark up all your scores like that, not just pieces you know well?*

JN: Yes. You could be in a situation, especially with a piece of new music, where there's not much time to feel really at home with it. But I have to be sure as I can be: I have to know to wake up the trombones, otherwise they may not play. So I will write in rhythms, colours, beat lines, anything that helps. Quite honestly, I have to make this composer's music my own, by doodling on it, by scribbling on it – and I think that's fair enough. Think of [György] Ligeti: his scores are full of colours and mathematical markings. He needed all those extra markings to compose, therefore I don't mind doing all that as a conductor. And unless you've got a lot of time – or you're a genius – I can't see another way of doing it. I'm not ashamed of colouring in my scores.

Nott finds a score to show me what he means, an old copy of *La Mer*. Each bar has a coloured pencil marking somewhere in its strata between the double basses at the bottom of the page and piccolo at the top. The already jam-packed space-time of the music's notation has been turned into a rainbow-coloured palimpsest: pinks, greens, blues, reds are used to emphasise the moments when particular instruments enter, and when they have a prominent part to play. To anyone who isn't Jonathan Nott, it looks confusing and just a wee bit psychedelic. These are his particular aide-memoires, the physical remnants of his private learning processes, as he tries to commit the music's mercurial structure to memory. They are also essential to his rehearsal sessions on this music (he will use a score throughout the rehearsal process), when he has to know in an instant what is going on and what mistakes the orchestra is making, just by looking down at the notes in front of him on his stand. There is method to this colouring-in madness.

TS: *So do you have a system for all these crazy colours?*

JN: Yes. For example, the horns are always pink, for some reason, the trumpets are blue, and the trombones are green. And I will always tend to colour important lines red – you see these longer lines over the whole page rather than smaller signs for individual entries – and the less important lines blue. I've been using this particular make of pencil for years, which I think are no longer made. So I'm going to have to change my colours. Which will be traumatic.

TS: *This is already a pretty sophisticated analysis of the piece, because it tells you so much about the music's architecture, as well as being a practical necessity.*

JN: The most important thing is that if I look at this page, I know what's happening in each bar. So that when I'm in the middle of this movement ['*Jeux de vagues*' ('Play of the waves'), the second panel of *La Mer*], I can instantly see I have to give the fourth horn a cue, a physical gesture, to play. And I can rehearse the instruments that are playing together at any one point. Look at this bar: I can see immediately, because of the way I've coloured it, that the second clarinet and bassoons are playing the same line, so I can pick them out and quickly rehearse that passage if I need to. The more I write, the more I doodle, the more it goes into my memory.

TS: *But how does all this help in performance?*

JN: Well, what you can do is to prevent disasters. When I was in the middle of a live recording of Ligeti's *Lontano* with the Berlin Philharmonic, a piece I conducted from the score, one of the trumpets came in at the wrong time. And I put my hand up to say, 'No, I'll give you your next cue.' That's part of one's job as a conductor, to put things right. And you need to be able to do that when you're doing a piece off by heart as well: you have to know it so well that if somebody comes in wrong, you can put it right. If you're doing an opera, and you don't know all the words, then you shouldn't be doing it from memory. You can't help when it goes wrong.

And that's the thing about trying to perform as much as possible from memory: the reason to do it is to help the music-making, to create the best interaction between me and the players that is humanly possible. When it works without a score, nothing gets in the way of me communicating with the orchestra: you have the music, and you have my gestures. And that means I can improvise much better when I've memorised the music, because you're just one step away from the piece, from the composer.

TS: *But it's much more difficult, surely, to learn as many pieces as you can by heart, rather than have the score with you.*

JN: Yes, it's a risk. That's why I do it. It's part of a journey of self-discovery, of challenging myself. This gets into a much bigger question that I've been asking myself recently: why do I want to be a conductor? What's the point of it? And one reason is the fight inside myself, the fight to be a better musician, a better person. Yes, there's a risk involved in doing things off by heart, but that risk helps me to push myself to somewhere I haven't been before. I detest plateaux. The mountain gets higher and higher – it doesn't get lower. This challenge of doing the pieces off by heart is part of that. It forces me to discover the next boundary. And if you're constantly pushing the boundaries of what you do, there's a chance you will do a better job, that you will discover the piece better, and you might discover more about what you're capable of doing.

What's the alternative? If you don't try to break boundaries within yourself, if you say, 'I've done this a thousand times before, it will be fine,' if you don't try to make each concert the best you can, then you're not being true to why you should be conducting in the first place. And those moments when you do go through a boundary – playing *The Rite of Spring* from memory, or the last page of Mahler's Ninth Symphony [music that traverses a sonic and emotional journey from sound to silence, life to death], then you feel you're being true to the real reason for conducting. You feel that you're a purveyor of the elixir of life. In moments of self-doubt, I still have those thoughts that maybe I should be a train driver or a bus conductor or something instead. But really – I can't avoid this destiny. I can scream and shout, I can say at low moments that I don't want to do it again – but somebody has to. It's such an amazingly important job to do, to channel this music. And to conduct from memory, for me, is to get closer to the earth energy, the divine speech, or whatever music is! I have a better chance of being a vessel through which that energy is passing, rather than a wall that's getting in the way of making the music speak.

I was reminded of all this when I went to Bali on holiday, and saw these enormous waves and people trying to surf them. And I thought, that's such amazing power that the surfers are dealing with. It's a good analogy with conducting. First of all, you've got to be prepared to get wet, you have to decide to get out of the comfort zone of what you know and chuck yourself into the water. But it's also the skill and the quickness of thought required to surf the wave's gigantic momentum. Like in conducting, you have to be one step ahead, you have to anticipate where the wave is going and how it's moving. And the size of the wave is also an analogy for the responsibility you feel to the music, to this elemental power of whatever piece it is you're conducting. The more you discover, the more awesome it becomes. And of course, once you've jumped in the water, once you've started the piece, you can't stop the wave. You've dived in, and you've just got to go with it and deal with it, come what may. That mirrors exactly what I feel about conducting.

If you can pull people through this fantastic experience, make them part of this wave of music-making, it's one of the most powerful feelings you can have and that you can give to another human being. That's what I feel the whole point of this conducting thing is. When music-making is that intense and all-embracing, it's one of those things that can unite everyone on this planet – and help them. We the musicians are so emotionally involved, if we communicate that intensity authentically, then these musical experiences can help people get through things they wouldn't be able to without them. And so that's why I'm the one going into the water, into the trenches, into no man's land. It's got to be done.

And all of that philosophising is just an upbeat to the immediacy of Nott's encounter with his players for these rehearsal sessions on *La Mer* and *The Rite of Spring*. Nott works his orchestra hard. There are moments when it's difficult even to follow the score with the minutiae of his requests, let alone pick up the precise import of his instructions, delivered in his speedy, but faintly Midlands-accented German, and act on them as an orchestral musician. The forensic detail that Nott finds is fastidious, relentless, and extraordinary. He plays through the third movement of *La Mer*, Debussy's 'Dialogue of the Wind and the Sea', and then spends three quarters of an hour on just the first few pages of the piece, taking apart nearly every harmony, every line, every texture. The first real tune in the movement comes after a minute or so. It's a moment that you can't miss when you hear the work. After a tempestuous opening, in which the inchoate clouds and waterspouts of a Turneresque seascape seem to spring to life, the music comes into focus on a single object, like a boat or a bird on the sea. It's a keening woodwind melody, suspended above a roiling, repeated figure in Debussy's string writing. The expressive power of this music is essential to the trajectory of this whole movement and to the shape of the entire piece. It's a passage that Nott works over obsessively. 'There is still not enough space between the melody and the non-melodic parts in the woodwinds ... I'm still not hearing enough "wind" in the string parts – play it on the D string ... I need more!' And slowly, when he puts the individual parts back together again, the instrumental lines coalesce into a visceral marine symbology, where before the passage had sounded merely like a woodwind melody played over some string figuration. It's a transition from technique to poetry.

He forces the same transformation from his players throughout *La Mer*. The unforgettable solo for the cello section in the first movement, where Debussy divides the cellos into four separate parts that move with silvery, leaping unpredictability, undergoes a similar sea-change. Nott begins by analysing what his cello section have just played: there needs to be a pause between the third and fourth notes of the phrase; a crescendo in the third bar, but only on the second note; a diminuendo in the following bar, to prepare the up-swelling of the bar after that; and the players have to make sure they have allowed themselves enough bow to make the whole eight-bar melody flow as it should. All that, and still more technical details. This is a cello section that makes a thrilling, full-bodied sound in any case, but at the moment, they seem focused more on making a beautiful noise than on giving Debussy's music the subtle light and shade it requires. Nott sings to them how he wants the phrase to sound – there's a point at which words, whatever their exactitude, can't hack it if you're trying to tell ten cellists how a tune goes. Nott trained as a choral scholar at the University of Cambridge, with the choir of St John's College (second in fame only to that of King's), and his practised tenor helps him now. He obeys all the technical instructions he has just issued his cellists, but makes music from them, and sings with inspirational naturalness. That's what his musicians respond to, and when they play the passage back to him, they are a cello section transmuted into a shoal of musical fish.

After a day of rehearsals, we are in Nott's luxurious flat in Bamberg, just a stone's throw from his place of work. It's impossible for him to escape his work in this city.

TS: *Did you have a strategy when you came to that solo for the cellos in the first movement today?*

JN: It's just a question of efficiency and how quickly you can get the piece to sound like it ought to sound. That's the point of rehearsal. If they play that passage like they always play it – they're always too slow, they're thinking about their sound: actually, I don't know what the hell they're thinking about! – then I have to get them to do something different. So sometimes I sing, sometimes I explain what's going on, sometimes we play the place through a few times. Debussy himself was pedantic about the articulation in those bars, and so I can say, 'Look, it's just a question of how much weight we're giving to each note – I'll show you what I want.' But then, you have to be able to show that with your gestures as well as with your voice. It's funny, orchestral musicians often say, 'Don't tell us with words, just show us what you want!' – but if I did do that, sometimes they wouldn't take any notice. They've got to be a great orchestra just to rely on gesture.

TS: *And the way the whole day of rehearsals progressed – was that pre-planned or improvised?*

JN: There are practical things you have to decide, which dictate which pieces you play when. I started with the third movement of the Debussy because it's the only one with cornets in it, and I don't want people hanging around the rehearsal who don't have to be there. I haven't got a right to take over the rest of their lives, as well as their musical duties. It's the same thing with *The Rite of Spring*, because you have a bass trumpet player in the orchestra who doesn't do anything until the penultimate movement. And I don't like to have too many people just sitting around in the hall, it creates a dead energy that can suck the life out of the rest of the rehearsal. I can feel that happening in the room.

Today, there were some basic ground principles that I wanted to instil in them in the Debussy. The idea was to play the piece through, speak about some general principles by looking at a few particular places, and then hope that they will then figure out how to apply those principles in the rest of the piece, so that they can play it automatically without me stopping them after every phrase or every bar. It's a bit like bringing up children: if you let them off once, you then have to make them do their maths homework, and them give them some slack again. My calculation was: depending on how they sounded the first time, that would tell me what to focus on and how to communicate it to them. All the time the rehearsal is going on, I'm thinking, I've got two rehearsals and a general rehearsal [a run-through of the concert] to create this performance. So that means I've only got time to concentrate on a few things and hope they understand. I decided to spend a whole hour on the third movement because then they would see how seriously they have to take every bar of this music. And I knew that when we came to play the first movement, it should be much better than if we were just playing it through the first time, if they have properly learnt from the rehearsal. If I've rehearsed one line in particular, that place should be together the next time we play it, so that's one box ticked off, and I can concentrate on something else in the next rehearsal and performance. It's a combination of practical things, and moments where you improvise.

TS: *But you must have some clear ideas about what you want to do with* La Mer *and* The Rite of Spring.

JN: It's a question of reversing the usual polarities of these pieces for me. I want *The Rite* to sing, to have lyricism as well as rhythmic power. And *La Mer* is not this impressionistic wash of colour. It's much more elemental than that. With this orchestra, there's the chance to connect *La Mer* with other traditions of contemporary orchestral writing. It should have – or it can have – the same visceral, violent power as the orchestral works of, say, Berg or Mahler. As well as, of course, being infused with those unique Debussyan colours. But these aren't generalised brush strokes of sonic onomatopoeia. They're precise, particular – and difficult for an orchestra to find.

TS: *Has your rehearsal approach changed since you got this job, nearly ten years ago?*

JN: It's transformed in that time. We've developed a lot together, and there's been a great deal of personal development on my part. I now find that they're not as far off the sound that I want as they were before. At the beginning, I wasn't sure what the possibilities were with this orchestra, but as we've learnt about each other, that's changed for the better.

* * *

Such immediacy of communication is the hard-won prize of Nott's ten-year relationship with the orchestra. A decade ago, few in the musical world would have predicted that this thirty-something *Engländer* would be running one of Germany's most respected orchestras. His history with the orchestra began under unusual circumstances. At the end of the 1990s, the Bamberg Symphony was an orchestra in crisis, both financially and artistically. They needed to renegotiate their terms with the federal government (at the time, they were the only German orchestra whose money came direct from central government, as opposed to the separate budgets of Germany's individual *Länder* – in Bamberg's case, Bavaria). Their reputation as a solid orchestra, a purveyor of the standard repertoire, especially Brahms and Bruckner, had been forged in the fifty years of their history with conductors like Joseph Keilberth, Eugen Jochum, and the incumbent in the 1990s, Horst Stein. Throughout the 1960s and 70s, before the orchestra moved to its architecturally nondescript but acoustically outstanding new concert hall, the musicians played in the cloister of a church in the old town. 'It was a terrible acoustic,' Bamberg's new Intendant, Wolfgang Fink, says, 'but it had a huge amount of charm. And it and the orchestra attracted great names over the years: pianist Martha Argerich, cellists Mstislav Rostropovich and Yo-Yo Ma.' But however international their roster of concert soloists, Bamberg's conductors remained stolidly German.

And that's no surprise, given the orchestra's origins. The Bamberg orchestra was founded in the embers of the war, from German-speaking refugees who had been evicted from the newly communist Czechoslovakia, regardless of whether they had a Nazi past. The orchestra's famous 'Bohemian sound' comes from this first generation of players, whose warm, dark, velvety playing you can hear on recordings from the 1950s and 60s. The orchestra became Germany's most-travelled orchestra, an ambassador of German repertoire to the rest of Europe and the world.

Yet it's still a minor miracle that the orchestra found more than a foothold in Bamberg. 'There was no musical tradition before the orchestra,' Fink explains.

There is no opera house here; and the only musical story that the town is famous for comes from E. T. A. Hoffmann, who tried to set up an opera company here in the early nineteenth century. But he nearly didn't survive the five years he was here: the court didn't pay him properly, the singers were terrible, it was a disaster. This was the musical heritage of Bamberg before the orchestra! It was very unlikely a big musical institution could ever root itself here.

But the orchestra's success in Bamberg today is thanks precisely to the fact that it's the only major cultural show in town. Extraordinarily, of the town's total population of seventy thousand, nearly seven thousand are subscription holders for the symphony orchestra. Ten per cent of Bamberg's entire population are regular ticket holders. That's a statistic that's pretty well unique in musical culture (only the small town of Lahti in Finland with its symphony orchestra can compare). Orchestral managers in bigger cities can only look on with envy.

That means that the conductor of the orchestra is the most important cultural figure in the city. And Jonathan Nott's name was not on most Bambergers' lists of potential successors to Horst Stein in the late 1990s. By that time, the

German conductor, 'the last of the German *Kapellmeisters*', as Fink describes him, was ill and unable to fulfil the position. Finding his replacement became a practical necessity. 'Nonetheless, I think Jonathan's appointment was the most unlikely in German music in recent years,' Fink told me. 'It was an extremely courageous choice on the part of Matthias Weigmann, one of my predecessors.'

And this is how it happened. Nott was asked to come to the orchestra to try out with them. All there was time for was to rehearse Beethoven's Seventh Symphony. And yet that was enough for the orchestral management to feel he was the right person. It was like a musical arranged marriage. The most important single relationship in the musicians' working lives for at least the next few years was decided on the briefest of encounters. But even if Weigmann had made his mind up, Nott needed more.

I needed the orchestra to say that they wanted me. I didn't want to come if I was just imposed on them. A majority must have wanted me – but that doesn't mean that everyone did. I mean, there were some older guys in the orchestra, whom I had to be terribly wary of when I came. They had been in the orchestra for decades, and had played their first Bruckner symphonies with Eugen Jochum and Günter Wand [both Brucknerian legends of the old German school]. And here was me, this thirty-eight-year-old who was supposed to tell them how to play these pieces.

Nott had new ideas for the orchestra. His years at the helm of the Ensemble Intercontemporain in Paris (the crack ensemble set up by composer/conductor Pierre Boulez in 1976, which exists to play music at the bleeding edge of avant-garde experimentalism) gave him unique experience of the whole spectrum of contemporary music. Yet Nott's love for new music was combined with his training in Germany's opera houses, the breeding ground of so many of the great conductors of the last hundred years – including, ironically, Nott's Kapellmeisterish predecessors in the job at Bamberg. Rather than confining contemporary music to a ghetto of specialist performers and specialist audiences, the opportunity in Bamberg was to combine his love of the new with his exploration of the old, to create a conversation between the music of the past and the present, and illuminate both with inventive, imaginative programming.

It was a chance that Nott grabbed with both hands. The first time I saw him conduct the Bamberg orchestra was a startling collision of the familiar and the unfamiliar at the Edinburgh Festival: a programme of Helmut Lachenmann's *Nun* and Richard Strauss's *Alpine Symphony*. It's rare to hear an orchestra of Bamberg's pedigree explore the strange world of Helmut Lachenmann's music. His is a music that finds beauty in the usually unloved sounds of instrumental possibility, the scrapes, whistles, and knocks that string players can make from their instruments, the hoots, breaths, and clacks that woodwind and brass players have at their disposal, the whispers, shrieks, and cries that the human voice can muster. The Bamberg players performed Lachenmann's gigantic fresco, which depicts the violence of natural phenomena as well as the dark internal struggle of human creativity, with the same care, attention, and love that they usually lavish on Beethoven or Mozart.

Or Richard Strauss: the effect of hearing the *Alpine Symphony* after *Nun* was shattering. After Nott and the Bamberg players had opened up a new world of sound, inviting the audience at Edinburgh's Usher Hall into Lachenmann's realm of heightened musical awareness, you heard Strauss's late-romantic mountaineering expedition with new ears. What struck me was the strangeness of Strauss's music, the moments when he creates a weird, modernist dissonance right at the opening of the piece from the notes of a descending minor scale. Strauss freezes these pitches through the orchestral texture. Each note is sustained rather than resolved, as if the orchestra were being held in suspended animation, fixed in time like a boulder in a glacier, one instrument at a time. This icy imagery was just as strange, just as surreal, as anything in Lachenmann's score. The storm that engulfs Strauss's party of climbers as they make their descent from the summit was equally disconcerting, as was the work's coda, returning the piece to the icy strangeness of the opening. This music, at the centre of the Bamberg orchestra's repertoire, had never sounded so modern – just as Lachenmann's music, played with such sensitivity and love, had never sounded so connected to the long traditions of German music.

Nott made the same alchemy happen in programmes that juxtaposed Ligeti with Mahler, Jörg Widmann with Mozart, Rachmaninov with Bach. Meanwhile, his performances and recordings of Schubert's or Beethoven's complete symphonies have found a style that is informed by the patina-stripping practices of the early-music movement without losing the earthy power of the native Bamberg sound. Another performance I heard in Edinburgh, of Bruckner's Third Symphony, came close to establishing a new ideal for late-romantic music. This was an unmistakably German Bruckner, but a Bruckner connected with the earth as well as the heavens – no longer simply a grandiose monument to musical piety, this massive symphonic structure had a human dynamism as well as spiritual grandeur.

But in this journey from German provincialism to cosmopolitan modernity, from core symphonic repertoire to contemporary relevance, there may have been costs. For an orchestra whose calling card all over the world has been their tradition – their unapologetic, high-cholesterol, meat-and-potatoes performances of Austro-German repertoire – such a transformation has not been without its problems. I convened a panel of players from the orchestra, with some of its oldest and newest members. Christian Dibbern is a second violinist who has been with the orchestra for thirty-two years. He explained that 'there have been two big generational changes in the lifetime of the orchestra. The first was in the 1960s and 70s, when the original members of the orchestra began to retire; and now, you have those players who came in around that time who are also leaving. The question is, what these changes have done to the sound of the orchestra.' Szabolcs Zempléni, a Hungarian horn player brought in by the orchestra in Jonathan Nott's time, says that the people who have come in since he took over the job have been naturally to Nott's taste. 'The flutes are a good example: they play with less vibrato now, with a straighter tone.' Nott has a power of veto over whom the orchestra choose as their new colleagues. So far, he has never used it, but much of the orchestra's personnel, about thirty positions, have changed under his leadership. Peter Rosenberg, the orchestra's leader, who is soon due to retire, gives his assessment of how things have changed in the Bamberg orchestra.

There are two important things that this orchestra is famous for. One is the sound we make, and the second is the repertoire we play. Both things have changed. The sound principle is not the first thing any more. Since Herr Nott came, it is about virtuosity, transparency, and flexibility. And he has introduced new repertoire, the sort of music he played with the Ensemble Intercontemporain in Paris. We didn't have that in our repertoire before. We had lots of Brahms and Bruckner, and there's less of that now.

There's more than a hint of nostalgia in Peter's words. 'There is a musical globalisation happening everywhere. Even with the Berlin Philharmonic: if you listen to their recordings with Furtwängler from the 1940s and 50s, they were a different orchestra then.' Christian Dibbner confirms:

It's hard to hold on to the individual sound that makes you special. But one should! And actually, that's the reason Nott wanted to come to us. He said he wanted to play contemporary music with us because of our German sound. And it is very beautiful to play new music in this way for us. So I think it should develop, this combination between new players, new repertoire, and our sound.

Szabolcs Zempléni explains:

It's not just that we have our sound in German music or that we can play contemporary music well, we have to make a French sound in French music, and have appropriate styles and approaches for other repertoire. That *Böhmischer Klang* isn't enough on its own. When I came here, friends said, 'Watch out, the Bamberg orchestra plays very loud, very dark.' And yes, they can be like that in Bruckner and Brahms, but with Herr Nott, you can hear lots of other colours in lots of other repertoire.

One of the orchestra's newest members, double-bass player Alexandra Henstebeck, feels that the essential identity of the Bambergers remains: 'The sound is still there – that's why young people want to play with this orchestra.'

Nott has had to work hard to win his orchestra over. So much so that a few years into his tenure, he asked for a series of individual meetings with every member of the orchestra who wanted to talk to him about any issue or problem they were having. This was an astonishingly brave thing to do for a conductor, potentially opening himself up to criticism from all quarters. 'I feel a responsibility for their lives, for their working lives. I want them to feel fulfilled. If somebody is in a bad mood, I find that very difficult to ignore. And I can't allow myself to be second-guessing what they're thinking about me.' But there comes a point where the listening has to stop, and where leadership has to take over.

It's a very strange thing. You have to have a certain amount of vanity to say, 'Sorry, I'm the one who's doing it. I'm paid to do this, to be up here on my own, and you're paid to do it how I want to do it.' You need enough confidence to make that work. But I don't force myself to be like that any more. After so many years conducting, I should do what I feel is right, because I'm probably going to make the right decision. If I've made wrong decisions in the past, it's because I didn't have the confidence just to do what I wanted to do.

It's not just confidence that Nott radiates in his rehearsals in Bamberg. There's a furious intensity and energy he communicates at all times to his players. It's an atmosphere of urgency, risk-taking, of taking nothing for granted, that's deliberately at odds with the über-comfortable surroundings of the city and the luxurious civic and financial situation of the orchestra. During the final day of rehearsals before the concert in Bamberg, Nott's work-rate goes up yet another notch. He is rehearsing the opening of the second part of *The Rite of Spring*, music that sounds strangely unlike the rest of the piece. Instead of the fast-paced rhythms and unpredictable jump-cuts of the first part, there is a weird stasis at the start of the second half, 'The Sacrifice', an atmosphere that can bring an unwanted sagging in structural tension. But not after Nott puts his orchestra through its paces. He teases Stravinsky's lines apart, showing the orchestra how chords that sound like pile-ups of random dissonances are created from the superimposition of the simplest of common triads. He builds the chords up through the orchestra, so that woodwind players know which part of the string section they're in harmony with, so that brass players know to tune their parts with the violins. It's a rehearsal technique that gives the orchestra a new way of listening to this music. And a new way of performing it, too: when they play the passage through, the Bamberg musicians find a lyricism and warmth in the music that illuminates the harmony from within. It's a typical Nott combination of focusing on a microscopic detail in order to have far-reaching consequences.

There is another example at the very end of *La Mer*, as he subjects the tumultuous final bars to analytical scrutiny. Nott asks individual sections – the double basses, the bassoons, the trombones – to play their parts individually, building up a mental and musical map of Debussy's work, and giving them access to the richness and complexity of the music, making them realise how their independent parts combine to create Debussy's musical tempest. He rehearses the accelerando in the second movement of *La*

Mer obsessively, trying out different ways of speeding up his orchestra, finding the right technical balance of beating patterns in the shapes described by his baton and the movements of his body to cajole the hundred players to come together as a single organism, to pick up telepathic impulses of changes of speed, direction, dynamic, and to translate them into music. After six hours of rehearsal, orchestra and conductor have been on a journey inside these pieces, and are better prepared for whichever of the infinite number of possible traversals of the musical labyrinths of *La Mer* and *The Rite of Spring* tomorrow's performance will bring. It's a feat of massive mutual concentration from both sides of the podium.

JN: It was a big day. I'm a bit knackered. And there was plenty of strategy in the way I planned it, based on the things I knew I wanted to get right, and other details the musicians asked me to do. But I'm happy. I knew I had to do the end of *La Mer*, because usually everybody just gets louder and louder and nobody gives a hoot what's actually happening. But that's not fair to the music: we have to find out how to create different colours, to make some people less dominant than others. And in fact, that meant changing what's in their score to what's in mine, the latest edition of the piece. It's a question of working out whether those changes are worth the destruction you're going to wreak on their normal way of playing that passage. But it was worth it. The funny thing is, the beginning of the third movement of *La Mer* still isn't as good as when we first played it. Is that because they're bored of it now? Because they're talking in the rehearsal when they're not playing? But I was pleased with the rest of *La Mer*. And with *The Rite*, I didn't want just to play it through. I think some of them were surprised by what I did. I knew we would get much more out of the time if we still rehearsed properly, as long as I didn't annoy them by only doing tiny chunks of the piece. And

Debussy's *Prélude à l'après-midi d'un faune* was also working much better today.

TS: *Something happened today when you played the* Prélude. *At the climax, you found a new level of intensity and volume from the orchestra that wasn't there previously.*

JN: It's marked fortissimo at that point, and today I really wanted to try that. But I didn't tell them I was going to do that crescendo, I didn't warn them to watch out for that moment.

TS: *No – it happened in your hands, because they were watching you and interpreted your gestures – and because they were paying attention!*

JN: That has really developed in my time here. They are now such a warm, giving orchestra. Earlier on, I would make a movement, a new gesture, and nothing would happen. It sometimes felt like the orchestra was a lump of cold plasticine, which I could dance merry hell in front of, but which I couldn't get through to. I discovered that wasn't the solution with them. In fact, when I took a step back, when I became less forceful, I could control them more. Instead of thrashing at them, I had to gently drill a hole into the plasticine, and gently warm them up, and then I found I could bend them and mould them in performance. That's where we are now. As a conductor, you have to think of your gestural language like a rubber band: if you stretch it too far, it snaps, but if you just move it a little, you can change the shape, you can make the orchestra move. And now, if I do something they're not expecting, at least half of them will follow me!

TS: *And that's really the question: what do you expect to happen in tomorrow's performance? What is the relationship between the work you've been doing in rehearsals and what you want from the concert?*

JN: The fun with this orchestra is the sheer striptease of performance.

TS: *Striptease?* . . .

JN: . . . the ability to twist things in a slightly perverse light, in a way that they're not expecting, and to be able to create unpredictability within the framework you've built through the rehearsals. Especially after the general rehearsal tomorrow morning, when I'll have learnt more of what I want to do, I'll be able to make things happen. You can even make them laugh in performance: if suddenly I go crazy at the cellos, and they're thinking, what the . . .? – but they know it's what I want, and so they're there for me, and they enjoy it. And then it's in their heads for the next evening, the next concert. It's such a glorious feeling!

The striptease is about a sense of risk-taking, of not being programmed. It's almost that I do whatever I can with them, up to the point where things might go wrong. A change of tempo, or loudness, or intensity. Of course you don't want to push them that far so that you break them, because you don't want them to look stupid. But the worst possible thing you can do is rehearse to a point of utter, stupid boredom and complete lifelessness. Then there's nothing else to do. If you do that, you don't need an audience. But this orchestra and I need an audience: we channel all their energy.

TS: *But there was a time when you deliberately pushed the orchestra to its limits – and beyond.*

JN: That was earlier on in our relationship. We were giving some concerts in Cologne, and we had played Bartók's *Concerto for Orchestra*, and only just held it together. Some people were playing so far behind my beat, I had to drag them physically through the music. And then we played Strauss's *Alpine Symphony*, a piece we had already performed a lot together. One of the horns came in at the wrong time, just a small mistake. But for me it was a symbol of what they thought of themselves. Sometimes this orchestra isn't self-disciplined enough to realise how good it really is, and it doesn't do itself justice. After that mistake,

I got so cross at them. I was conducting the music off by heart, and was just scowling at them, and pushing them through the piece, forcing them to be uncomfortable – to the point where this nice trumpet player cracked halfway through one of his solos. I thought, 'Right, I've got my revenge on you lot being so stupid and undisciplined.' It's a little bit childish, but that's what it's like sometimes. In every marriage there are moments where you scream and swear at one another, and the next day, you're fine together. And now, the orchestra is much better at playing on the big occasions, like the concerts at the Lucerne Festival a couple of years ago. They played fantastically there, especially that performance of Wagner's *Das Rheingold*.

TS: *Back to the striptease: there must be dangers if you're under-prepared as well as over-prepared?*

JN: Yes. You could do each performance so that it was completely improvised, with no rehearsal at all. If you said, 'Ladies and gentlemen, I am never going to rehearse, and I'm going to play the piece differently every time we do it in concert,' the feeling from the players would be: 'Jesus Christ, we've never played this piece before,' which is completely unfair to them. You might end up with a mediocre performance of *The Rite of Spring* – but even a mediocre performance of that music has a certain amount of strength – but it would be a disaster with *La Mer*. In the Debussy, you have to get people to breathe together, to listen to the resonance of their notes melting into other people's parts, making sure there's just the right gap between one phrase and the next. And you have to do that in rehearsal. The idea is to do enough so that no one is going to go crazy when you decide to take a different path through the piece, so that they feel prepared enough, and free enough, to follow you.

In the concert, I hope that my job will be to play with the music; that they're so sure of the way the pieces move, that I can wave my arms around any way I want, and *La Mer* and *The Rite* will still work! I hope that they can each feel the structure of the music before each piece starts, where their piece of the jigsaw fits in. And that I can bend the performance within those limits, and surprise them with some gestures. For example, in the second movement of *La Mer*, they know how the accelerando at the climax works in terms of the architecture of the movement, but they don't quite know exactly what I'm going to do within that structure. I can play with it. And even in *The Rite*, I expect to be able to play with it, too. If I can, it should stop an audience thinking, 'Yeah, we know this, we've heard it a thousand times before'; or in New York, stop them thinking, 'We know how this goes with Maazel.'

That's the worst-case scenario with music that's extremely familiar, like a Brahms symphony. The audience just shuts out from it, because they know exactly how it goes. So what do you do? Give them what they want, in which case nobody's getting anything from the experience, or do you do something deliberately surprising just for the sake of it? That's unmusical, in my view, but you have to accept that the limits to surprise an audience are getting smaller and smaller in repertoire they know very well, like Beethoven, Brahms, even Mahler.

TS: *It's a question of trying to find an individual interpretation of these pieces, and being true to the moment of performance.*

JN: You have to live that moment. And I love it. Perhaps it goes back to my early days of being a choral scholar at Cambridge, and having to give worthwhile performances of pieces of music as you're sight-reading them – the thrill of doing the unknown in public! Or maybe it's the British delight in breaking rules, or rather, the vehement fear of rules. There shouldn't be any rules about what a piece of music is, about what we expect from it. Take the start of the second part of *The Rite*: I don't want people to be bored. It's slow, it's damn slow, but I can make that music lyrical, I can make it sing, I can breathe with the phrasing, which some conductors won't do, through colour and through intensity. Conducting without a score, I've already got the upper hand, because there's nothing in the way of me living that moment completely with the players. And that means you're not stuck to rules.

TS: *How important is it to give yourself to that moment, that now of performance?*

JN: It's absolutely unforgivable not to be absolutely committed to the moment. And I see a lot of conductors and orchestras who aren't. And if you're not doing that, you're simply not doing your job. You've got to give yourself to each performance as if it was the last thing you're ever going to do. And I've been in the middle of conducting certain pieces – Mahler's Ninth Symphony comes to mind – where I think, if I die now, it will be OK, I've tried my best. And if you can't do that in performance, there's just no point doing it. If you're not doing that, what have you got to fall back on? As a conductor, all there is apart from that is showmanship and vanity. There's a big danger you believe your own hype as a conductor, and act as the centre of attention, that you play up to that role.

TS: *There is a moral dimension to all this, to being true to your vision of what a conductor should be, in a social as well as musical sense.*

JN: Maybe it's because I'm one generation away from the British working class. But I simply can't feel as though I'm more important than any other human being. Obviously, I'm being paid to be a leader, and they have to come along with me, and I have to inspire with sheer volume of energy – and sheer bloody-mindedness. But if you can't be a normal person at the same time, and treat other people how you would like to be treated yourself, then you're not being a very nice human being. And I don't believe being a conductor should stop me being a nice human being. But that makes being a good conductor so much more difficult. Because you have two lives: a life as a person with a family, with your relationships, and then you have the life up there on the podium. And what right do I have to stand up in front of these people and tell them what to do?

TS: *But all of this goes into your relationship with the orchestra. In other words, surely the reason they follow you in performance is because of the integrity of the relationship you have built up with them.*

JN: We have built up a close bond, for sure, and I hope I have real personal and musical relationships with really every member of the orchestra. We've experienced so many different emotions together. What I admire so much about them is their commitment to playing music. That sounds self-evident, but this is an orchestra who can't wait to play, who can't wait for me to shut up in rehearsal so that they can play again, and who give themselves to everything they're doing with complete focus and dedication. With some orchestras, like the Concertgebouw, I have to ask them to show me a little of what it's going to sound like in the concert, because they never give themselves completely to the music in the rehearsal. But here in Bamberg I never have to say that. They're almost unstoppable in how much energy they give all the time.

TS: *Can you account for the difference between a 'normal' concert, and one where everything just lifts off, and goes to that next level?*

JN: I think I can. The performances that have worked really well are those where I'm so immersed in the moment that nothing can distract me or the players, but also where the sense of architecture is second nature. In a performance like that, there's no question that we are going to land in all the right places, to make the larger shapes of the music as well as have the intensity of the moment. We played Mahler's Second Symphony recently: in that piece, I know that we need to land together with that chorus coming in an hour's time, but I've also got to hope that the cellos and basses are together right at the start of the piece. I need to create a continuous line that connects all of those parts of the piece together. It's a question of living the moment in one half of my brain, but pacing it in the other. And when that doesn't work, it's because I've got in the way of the music somehow, either by making gestures that stop the flow of the music, or by consciously counting bars instead of going with the energy of the performance.

TS: *Can you feel when that connection is there – and when it's not?*

JN: Absolutely. This afternoon, when we first went through Stravinsky's *Symphonies of Wind Instruments*, even though I was very tired, somehow my gestures kept the flow of the music going right through the chorale at the end. But if you start to interrogate that process, if you become too conscious of it, you can lose that secret circle. If I worry about what I'm doing and what they're doing, it starts to go wrong. Physically, my beats change. If I'm worried about keeping the ensemble together, I start to emphasise each beat to try and be clear. And ironically, that makes it less likely they will play together. It's better to be less correct and more vague in your gestures, so that the music moves between the beats instead of being limited by them.

And something else happened in that chorale in the *Symphonies of Wind Instruments* today. There's a bit at the end where the first horn comes in with this really high note. He just plays 'bah', and it's very high and very exposed. And I swear to you this is true: if I hear that note clearly in my head before he plays it, there's absolutely no way he can make a mistake, but the two times I didn't hear the note in my imagination, it didn't work. It's quite amazing.

TS: *That's telepathy . . .*

JN: It's force of concentration. And that's when the heights of performance come, those moments of absolute connection.

The concert hall on the Regnitz is full – this is Bamberg, after all – with an audience of students. One of the orchestra's occasional *Studentenkonzerte*, with cheap tickets for the town's twenty-somethings, this concert shows how seriously these young Germans take their classical music. When the orchestra first experimented with these events, they wanted to create an informal atmosphere, and performed in normal clothes rather than concert regalia. The students disapproved, wanting a proper concert experience rather than anything that sniffed of a patronising, watered-down experience. The students dress up for this concert in blazers and suits, smarter than an opera-house audience in London. It's surprising to me, but also touching: they want to make this concert an event, and feel proud of their local symphony orchestra and privileged to be there. The cheap beer and pretzels afterwards in the foyer, which the orchestra enjoys too, only helps the sense of occasion.

And in the concert, all of those moments on which Nott and the players have worked so hard are transformed by the adrenalin of performance. The cello passage near the start of *La Mer* sings with a sensual abandon, the accelerando in the second movement has all the naturalness and inevitability of a tidal surge ('I didn't have to do anything – it just happened!' Nott tells me afterwards), the opening of the third movement sounds not like a collection of notes, of crescendos, diminuendos, attacks, and accents, but rather like the first portents of a storm, a darkening cloud on the horizon. 'I only gave them the first and last notes with my gestures,' he says, 'but it just had that freedom.' Nott animates his players still more in the Stravinsky. His gestures are simultaneously more concentrated and more extreme than in rehearsal. Leaning into the orchestra, he grabs his stomach as he looks over at the double basses. He explains to me that he 'wanted them to feel the entrails of the music'. Their thunderous pizzicato is a sound that resonates from the guts of the orchestra.

Not everything is perfect. The leader makes a mistake near the start of the second part of *The Rite*. 'It's funny: I'm counting so hard, remembering bars of 3/4, 2/4, 4/4, and that's one bit I never thought would go wrong.' Over a beer – his first alcohol in a week – the orchestra's chief conductor finally relaxes into the easy society of his players. His piccolo player tells him, 'I feel I'm getting *La Mer* for the first time.' He tells her, 'I thought we played the opening of the second part of *The Rite* differently after what I said to you all. There were more lines.' Nott spoke to the audience before the concert, explaining that *La Mer* is far more elemental than impressionistic, and that the Stravinsky can sing as well as shout. That was the revelation of this concert: making moments like the end of the final movement of *La Mer* sound as violent as anything in the Stravinsky, an aesthetic more expressionist than impressionist. This was a nature infused with the turmoil of human emotion, a unique expressive consequence of the warm, deep colours of the Bamberg orchestra – and Nott's vision of the piece. And *The Rite of Spring* danced, convulsed, and sang its way to the annihilation of the individual dancer at the very end of the piece. Yet the music had a lyrical momentum as well as a rhythmic one, a side to this work I have never heard expressed so convincingly.

This concert is an upbeat for their tour to America. 'It's stupid saying to you that I don't get nervous before performances' – one of the first things Nott said to me when I arrived in Bamberg. 'Of course I do. It's just a question of how you channel it.' Through telepathy, commitment, and simple hard work, Nott and the Bambergers have channelled an energy that transforms this quiet, picture-postcard town into a place of seething emotions and shuddering expressive violence, a sonic intensity that leaves its echo even as the students beerily, cheerily dissipate into the streets and cobbles of Bamberg at night.

4

Simon Rattle
Berlin Philharmonic Orchestra

Even the words 'the Berlin Philharmonic Orchestra' are enough to induce a state of feverish excitement in the minds, hearts, and bellies of most music-lovers. The 'Berlin Phil' – or Berliner Philharmoniker, the forbidding Teutonicism the orchestra's management would rather we all employed – has become an institution and group of musicians endowed with almost mythical stature. When you first arrive at the Philharmonie, the orchestra's home – a modernist masterpiece that opened in 1963 within spitting distance of the Berlin Wall, an architectural life-form designed by Hans Scharoun that still manages to look new-minted next to the postmodern concoctions of today's Potsdamer Platz – you're hit with a queasy jolt of excitement and adrenalin, as a long-dreamed-of moment in your musical life comes true.

At least, that's how I felt in September 2002, when I first encountered the Berlin Philharmonic in the flesh. The occasion was Simon Rattle's inaugural concert as the orchestra's chief conductor, with a programme that both consolidated his previous relationship with the players, which began in 1987, and symbolised his intention to change the orchestra's repertoire and future priorities. The first work Rattle played was Thomas Adès's *Asyla*, an award-winning piece he had commissioned for his previous orchestra, the City of Birmingham Symphony Orchestra, in 1997. This was a bold choice: a piece that was still shimmeringly, dazzlingly new, by a composer the majority of the orchestra had never heard of, let alone played, and a work of uncompromising imagination with which to confront and surprise the public in the Philharmonie and vast international broadcast audience.

Rattle wanted to show that he was unafraid of upsetting the orchestra's naturally conservative – at least in the public perception – musical tastes. The Berlin Philharmonic is virtually synonymous with the great Austro-German tradition from Mozart to Mahler, from Beethoven to Bruckner and Brahms. The reason is not difficult to find: under the directorship of Herbert von Karajan, their conductor from 1955 until his death in 1989, the Berlin Phil became the most recorded, most famous, and most powerful orchestra on earth. Never before in history, and never afterwards either, had a conductor and orchestra been able to command such complete dominance of recorded musical media. The sound Karajan and his Berliners produced together was a deep, lustrous sensuousness that is still unparalleled and which became, for many music-lovers from the 1960s to the 1980s, the ideal to which all orchestral playing ought to aspire.

That's always been the theory, anyway. In practice, Karajan's tenure at the Berlin Phil was a story much more complex than one man's conjuring a musical ideal through benign, or not so benign, musical dictatorship. The truth about their repertoire, too, is much more nuanced than the impression you sometimes receive, that all Karajan and his musicians did was play Brahms and Beethoven cycles in an endless loop of ever more grandiloquent and perfection-obsessed interpretations. The current critical canard is that Karajan's compulsive search for a seamless sound-world rubbed the edges off the music he was conducting, so that his Beethoven was neutered by a veneer of aural artifice, his Brahms was a victory of superficial sheen over genuine structural integrity, and he was pretty well redundant in any music written after 1920, in which he supposedly had no interest. It's another critical commonplace that Karajan's eyes-closed conducting conveyed not a deep immersion in the spiritual world of the music he was conducting, but a self-regarding solipsism that turned music-making into the ultimate aggrandisement of ego: Karajan, the magus-like figure, communicating telepathically with his musicians, controlling their every note with his superhuman and invisible powers of persuasion, a musical sixth sense not available to mere mortal conductors who have to control their musicians using the mundane media of their eyes . . .

All of these are myths for which Karajan and his record companies are partly responsible. None of them is wholly true, but the one myth that stands up to scrutiny – even if only because frequent repetition has made it into a quasi-fact – is that the Berlin Philharmonic carries the soul of Austro-German music in its performance practice and in the collective will and energy of its musicians. Their repertoire really is centred on the orchestral music of Mozart, Beethoven, Brahms, Bruckner, Mahler, Strauss, and Wagner.

That remained true even during Claudio Abbado's years as Herbert von Karajan's successor (Abbado had the job from 1990 to 2002). As well as introducing far more genuinely contemporary music than Karajan ever played – the high modernism of Luigi Nono and Karlheinz Stockhausen was heard in the hallowed halls of the Philharmonie in the mid-1990s – much of the orchestra's personnel also changed under Abbado's leadership. This meant that the ensemble in front of Simon Rattle that September evening in 2002 was a much younger, more international group than the one Abbado inherited when he took over the job in 1990.

Yet this was still the Berlin Philharmonic. The vast majority of the tapes and CDs I bought as a music-obsessed teenager in Glasgow were of the Berlin Philharmonic, and nothing was more familiar to me than the sound the orchestra made. But even before hearing them play a note live, just being in the Philharmonie was an unexpectedly confronting experience. The auditorium has a unique architectural and acoustic structure. Instead of the musicians being raised in front of the audience at one end of the building, Scharoun's genius, working to Karajan's request, was to place the orchestra almost in the centre of the hall. At the true centre is the conductor's podium, a place visible from every seat in the house. To stand there is to command space as well as time: Karajan made himself the focus of the orchestra's and the audience's attention, a trans-dimensional conjuror seemingly capable of manipulating the architectural volume around you as well as the sounds you're hearing.

The hall's physiognomy has another feature that you feel as a physical phenomenon when you're sitting there. The spaces are arranged around the platform as a crazy geometry of interleaving terraces instead of conventionally demarcated areas like stalls, circle, and gallery. The effect is miraculously immersive, since it's not just that you can see all the performers from your seat, wherever you are in the hall, but you're aware of the rest of the audience around you as well. In no other hall that I know is the simple act of taking your seat such a dramatically democratic event.

In the Philharmonie the architecture makes you part of the performance, not simply a passive spectator. The performance begins before the orchestra and conductor have come on stage, before a note has reverberated through the auditorium. The air fizzes with a special energy and atmosphere, which is both inclusive – it's an electricity made by the collective expectation of the 2,440 people in the space (the Philharmonie is always full for Berlin Philharmonic concerts) – and forbidding: you have no choice once you're in your seat but to be propelled wherever the musicians want to take you. It's like being on a gigantic roller-coaster.

Thomas Adès told me after the concert that he had been worried in the rehearsals leading up to the performance of *Asyla*. The piece is a four-movement surrealist symphony, a vertiginous, virtuosic thrill-ride through music history from late romanticism to contemporary club music, and one of the most brilliantly achieved pieces of orchestral architecture in the contemporary repertoire. But by comparison with the quickfire precision of the City of Birmingham Symphony Orchestra, the Berlin Philharmonic players, unused to *Asyla*'s irrational rhythms and its sense of familiar patterns and ideas being put through a distorting kaleidoscope, were slower learners. The reason was that each player didn't want simply to perform the notes on their part accurately but to understand how that individual part fitted into the bigger picture, the whole score. The goal was to give not just a regular performance of the piece, but a Berlin Philharmonic interpretation. The period of ingestion was longer than for repertoire the orchestra has in its bloodstream. But *Asyla* had to become as much a part of the orchestra's muscle memory as a Brahms symphony. The culture of this new music had to meld with the culture of the orchestra, a complex process that involved the individual practice of each musician and the collective consciousness of the whole orchestral organism. A particular problem was *Asyla*'s third movement, 'Ecstasio', a late-twentieth-century scherzo that transplants the dance movements of historical symphonies – courtly minuets or Beethovenian rhythmic workouts – to contemporary clubs (the title is a typically Adèsian pun on the clubber's narcotic *du choix* in the 1990s and noughties). There's a passage in 'Ecstasio' where the conductor has to keep time for one section of the orchestra while the rest of the musicians continue in a different division of time, and hope that both sections reach the same point a minute or so later. That's a big ask for any orchestra but for one so uncompromisingly physical as the Berlin Philharmonic, it was a special challenge.

The effect, when the musicians locked into the music's hyper-complex groove, was viscerally powerful. The Berlin Phil's *primus inter pares*, its double-bass section, rocked out to Adès's thumping rhythms with a sheer abandon and power that made the wooden floor of the Philharmonie shake, while the woodwinds and violins hammered out an obsessive, shrieking melody. The music wasn't just recreated that night in the Philharmonie, it was reborn. *Asyla*'s finale, a dream of late romanticism that submerges shards of the textures and tonalities of music from the late nineteenth and early twentieth centuries in a context of floating, shimmering beauty, had new depths revealed in it. One reason was Rattle's developing interpretation of this music, since his first performances and recording of the work in Birmingham, another was the depth and richness of the Berlin Philharmonic's sound. The brilliance of Adès's writing for the upper-register instruments, the woodwinds and the violins, glowed with a greater radiance than in any previous performance of this piece, while the abyssal depth of the sounds Adès imagines in his bass lines throughout the four movements excavated previously unknown regions of orchestral resonance. Whatever I thought I knew of *Asyla*, the Berlin Philharmonic's performance was richer, stranger, and more moving than I imagined possible.

Rattle followed up his iconoclastic first half with something much more familiar to Berlin audiences: a Mahler symphony. Claudio Abbado chose the First for his inaugural concerts in 1990, but Rattle's choice was the Fifth. It was a revealing piece of programming because Sir Simon gave himself a deliberately difficult ride with this piece. As he confessed in an interview broadcast before the performance, the Fifth is a piece he has struggled with in the past, as he tried to get to grips with the work's effulgent mix of 'love and counterpoint', as he put it. The symphony is a characteristically Mahlerian fusion of vast reservoirs of personal feeling – in the love song of the Adagietto, that much misunderstood slow movement, famously used at state funerals in America and in the soundtrack to Visconti's film *Death in Venice* – with an over-abundance of strict counterpoint, especially in the fugues of the final movement, an unstoppable flow of hard-core fugal exactitude whose expression exceeds the bounds of its academic strictures and becomes a song to the sheer delight of existence. The difficulty is in giving free rein to the gigantic emotional trajectory of the music, from the funeral march of the first movement to the unfettered joy of the final movement, at the same time holding on to the structural integrity of Mahler's composition.

It was a fine balance that Rattle and the Berlin musicians achieved magnificently, thanks to the intensity of their performance and concentration, and the bonds of communication that joined them together. This performance was propelled by something else too, an energy that transcended the notes of Mahler's music. There was not a single musician on stage who did not give themselves completely to the performance, musically, intellectually, and physically. Rattle was the same. His body language on the podium has always been highly wrought and explosive, but that night, every grimace of his face, every gnarled fist in his left hand – a Rattle-ism that implores his orchestra to give him still more sound and more excitement, as if he was trying to squeeze the last drops out of a physically existing ball of energy – was intensified. This was an orchestra and conductor proving that they were capable of pushing each other to previously unknown heights. There were moments of imprecision, fleeting milliseconds where the correlation between the orchestra's gigantic musical will and Rattle's gestures did not coincide. This was, after all, the very start of their relationship together as orchestra and chief conductor, and they had yet to develop that orchestral sixth sense of knowing exactly how each other worked in the crucible of performance.

But those supposed imperfections had their roots in a much grander musical objective: a complete commitment to the moment of performance that went to the essence of Mahler's music, and made the finale an explosion of volcanic, elemental power. It was a quality of music-making that was alchemised by the tension of the situation, the sense of occasion, and the pressure that everyone on stage was under to prove to the world that the orchestra had made the right choice of chief conductor, and that Rattle was up to dealing with the history, status, and continuous exposure of the job. Even bus-stops and lamp-posts in Berlin were festooned with posters proclaiming 'Welcome, Sir Simon!' No one in Berlin can have been unaware of what was happening at the Philharmonie that night. However it happened, on that evening both Rattle and the orchestra were raised to superhuman levels of musical achievement. Later, Rattle will talk about the 'dangerous power' of the Berlin Philharmonic sound, and some of his players will allude to the 'fact' that 'the orchestra is greater than any of its conductors': two clues to the power struggles that lie beneath the surface of the dynamics between this orchestra and all of its maestros. But for those moments in September 2002, being the chief conductor or a member of the Berlin Philharmonic must have seemed like the best job in the world, and being in the Philharmonie as part of the audience – part of the performance, indeed – one of the best experiences you could ever hope to have as a listener.

It's May 2010. Rattle has immersed himself in the job for eight seasons. And in his 2009/2010 concerts he is continuing the ambitious expansion of the Berlin Philharmonic's repertoire that has been a defining feature of his tenure. Earlier years have seen him programme the complete works of Anton Webern, music that is more than sixty years old but which still has barely a finger-hold in the repertory, boldly programmed alongside Beethoven symphonies. Rattle has been building up a production of Wagner's *Ring* cycle at the Aix-en-Provence Festival, the Berlin Phil's first theatrical traversal of Wagner's epic tetralogy since

Karajan's in the late 1960s. He has invited new conductors with specialisms at extremes of the repertoire to work with the orchestra: Oliver Knussen and George Benjamin to conduct twentieth- and twenty-first-century music, including their own, and William Christie, Ton Koopman and Emmanuelle Haïm for baroque and classical works. He has also overseen the Zukunft@BPhil project, the orchestra's first-ever education programme, one of the conditions of his arrival to the job in 2002 and now a cornerstone of the orchestra's identity and sense of community. The programme works with children from Berlin's disadvantaged areas, giving musicians the chance to explore how their virtuosity can affect audiences who don't have the opportunity or the money to get a ticket for the Philharmonie.

In the 2009/2010 season, there's a typically Rattle-ish conjunction of Brahms symphonies and Schoenberg, a project that makes Fergus McWilliam, a horn player who has been with the orchestra for a quarter of a century, celebrate the new dimensions Rattle has revealed in music he thought he knew – the four Brahms symphonies, that is.

It's no longer just that people see Schoenberg pointing back at Brahms, and realise he was working that tradition in his own way. We all see now that Brahms is so forward-looking, that he was really the composer who opened the door to Schoenberg. That's typical of Simon's programming. He's a modernist as a musician, and they've not only benefited as composers by the juxtaposition, we as listeners and as an orchestra have benefited too. It's taken both composers out of the mossy museum and made them relevant to today.

Early 2010 also sees the recorded release of Rattle's Brahms symphony cycle with the Berlin Philharmonic, discs of these Berlin Phil warhorses that McWilliam rates as highly as any other he has played or heard.

Those four symphonies are the litmus test for us. Simon must have been under so much pressure. You know, I doff my cap to Vienna [the Vienna Philharmonic] when it comes to Mozart and Schubert – Mahler we can hold our own with them in – but when it comes to Brahms, we think as an orchestra, this is really our stuff. And Simon's cycle is really good. I actually prefer it to Karajan's. It's fantastic.

But there's another strand of concerts this season, music the orchestra doesn't know so well, which the play-ers could never claim was 'theirs'. In their 128-year history to that point, since their founding as a proudly independ-ent group of musicians in 1882, the Berlin Philharmonic musicians had never played one of the symphonic master-pieces of the early twentieth century – Jean Sibelius's Third. Rattle's biggest idea for the season was to give the Berlin Philharmonic's first-ever cycle of all seven symphonies by Finland's national musical hero. Earlier programmes juxtaposed Sibelius with Beethoven and Ligeti, but the series climaxed in May with a programme of unadulterated Finnishness: Sibelius's last three symphonies, the Fifth, Sixth and Seventh. These were the concerts I heard Rattle rehearse and perform.

There's a rich story behind what Rattle is trying to do with this cycle of symphonies. It touches on German ideas about Sibelius's worth as a composer, how his music is per-ceived to fit – or not fit – with the Berlin Philharmonic's core musical values, as well as on Rattle's own personal his-tory with these pieces, and his developing relationship with the Berlin musicians.

Rattle has a lot to prove to his musicians about the essential worth of Sibelius's music. Just how much is revealed to me by Olaf Maninger, one of the orchestra's principal cellists (or, in German, a *Solo-Cellist*), who sits within about fifty centimetres of the end of Rattle's baton, right in the middle of the orchestra (in common with many Central European ensembles, the Berlin Philharmonic have the violas to the conductor's right, the cellos next to them, and the first and second violins on the left of the podium). Olaf is also chairman of one of this self-governing orchestra's most important managerial bodies, the *Medien-Vorstand* ('Media Committee'), which looks after the orchestra's recording projects and payments. Together with Rattle, Olaf's committee spearheaded the development of the Philharmonic's Digital Concert Hall, the most successful web-based portal for any orchestra in the world, which has been available since 2008, and the orchestra has now even branched out into 3D. He may be one of the most important members and voices in the orchestra, but Olaf isn't a Sibelius fan.

Simon grew up with this music, but it's really not our tradition. We hardly ever play it, and it's different to so much of the music we're used to performing. It's very – Finnish, I have to say! It's a very strange harmonic language, and has such reduced themes. It's heavy and depressive, so what we're doing together is an adventure, and a struggle.

Olaf is right to say that the orchestra only plays the music infrequently. In the *Rattle-zeit* – literally, 'Rattle-time' – only Simon and the Finnish conductor Paavo Berglund have played any of the symphonies, and before the 2009/2010 season, only the more famous Second, Fifth, and Seventh. But if you rewind to the 1960s and 1970s in the Berlin

Philharmonic's history, or look in any of those thick tomes of recommended recordings of classical music, you'll see that Herbert von Karajan and the Berlin Philharmonic recorded all of the symphonies apart from the Third, interpretations that still count among the most powerful but polarising ever set down of these elemental pieces.

Karajan was already a Sibelius convert by the time he was officially appointed the Berlin Phil's conductor for life in 1955, having previously made recordings of the late symphonies with the Philharmonia. Ten years later, Karajan and his Berlin players were invited to give a concert in Helsinki to mark the Sibelius centenary. In 1965, Karajan saw himself doing exactly what Rattle says he wants to achieve with his cycle fifty-five years later. As Karajan's biographer Richard Osborne reports, Karajan gave a speech in Finland in which he emphasised the '*rejection* of Sibelius's music in the 1930s and 1940s – Sibelius the great Outsider – and his own determination to help right the wrong'. Karajan's advocacy came from the heart. Osborne says that Sibelius's brutal and unflinchingly bleak Fourth Symphony was one of only a handful of works that left Karajan 'emotionally exhausted for days afterwards'.

Today, Karajan is still a controversial Sibelian. The criticism that has been levelled at his Sibelius records reflects the general trend to hear in his music-making a triumph of sonic beauty over structural integrity and expressive intensity. Just after playing the piece in Helsinki in 1965, Karajan said. 'It can't be played more beautifully than that!' – a comment that seems to prove his critics' point. Sibelius's biographer Robert Layton explained to the BBC that he first heard Karajan's recording of this piece as 'like the Finnish landscape perceived through the windows of a limousine; there was a feeling of being insulated from experience'. But he later changed his mind. 'When I went back to the performance in later years, I didn't feel that. What I recognised later was great depth of feeling. That sense of something coming *between* the music and the listener had completely disappeared.'

But Layton's initial perception of Karajan's Sibelius persists in today's Berlin Philharmonic, among the few players who do know and love the music. Jonathan Kelly is one of the orchestra's principal oboists, who worked with Rattle in Birmingham for six years and who began his two-year probation period with the Berliners in 2002, the same year Rattle started. He argues:

The reason that so many British orchestras play Sibelius so well is that the style the music requires fits their way of playing better. British orchestras play with a finer, thinner, and cleaner sound than our natural way of doing things here, this fat, heavy, calorific sound that the Berlin Philharmonic makes. It's a bit like the Karajan recordings. You think, it's great, but is it Sibelius? It's fantastic, but it's just very different. But maybe it is, and we Brits are just used to a different style. It's like when you meet Finnish people and they have that reserve, and I think that reserved quality is in the music too. Maybe we understand the landscape more. Whatever the reason, I just think somehow that Sibelius speaks to the British soul more than to the German soul.

It's not just thanks to perceived national characteristics that Sibelius doesn't have a bigger place in the hearts, minds, and repertoires of the Berlin Philharmonic, or any other German or Austrian orchestra. As Rattle says to me during the days of rehearsals leading up to the three concerts of the last three symphonies, 'Adorno has a lot to answer for.' Rattle means the German philosopher and sometime composer Theodor W. Adorno, who was part of the Frankfurt School, and whose writing on sociology, culture, and music has been extraordinarily influential, particularly in German-speaking countries since his death in 1969. To give a thumbnail caricature of Adorno's philosophical position when it came to twentieth-century music: the progressive atonality of Schoenberg was the epoch's best answer to the question of finding a music that was new, in terms of the language it created; it was critical, in the sense of resisting the worst aspects of what Adorno called the 'culture industry'; and historically mediated, in the sense that Schoenberg's compositional discoveries were both a rejection of the exhausted models of tonality that had preceded him in the works of Wagner or Mahler, and their apotheosis. Schoenberg's oppositional pole, in Adorno's terms, was Stravinsky, whose re-imaginings of the past and use of pre-existing musics, whether folk tunes or jazz rhythms, were empty, decadent, and doomed only to regurgitate the worst aspects of the contemporary world back to a grateful audience, instead of progressing the future of music, and therefore, of society. (Schoenberg himself, however, had no time for Adorno, complaining of his 'pomposity' and 'oily pathos', despite the philosophic-aesthetic victory Adorno 'won' on his behalf.)

But if Stravinsky gets it in the neck from Theodor Adorno, that's nothing compared to what he thought of poor old Sibelius. The great Finn's music was worthy only of Adorno's utter contempt. This sort of thing, from 1966, the year after Karajan's trip to Helsinki, is typical:

I would like at least to suggest why attempts to go on speaking the traditional language of music are stricken with impotence. I refer you to Jean Sibelius. He wanted something of this kind.

Nowhere did he go beyond the limits of the existing, traditional tonal means. In spite of which – this much must be conceded – he found something like an individual style.

Thanks, Theodor ... but he goes on.

But individual style, by itself, is not yet a blessing or an achievement; one must look to see what is realized in it ... [And] in a demonstrable technical sense – one, at any rate, that can be demonstrated among musicians – all of Sibelius's works turned out so brittle, so inadequate that his attempt should be regarded as precisely what people are otherwise all too eager to criticize in modern music – as an experiment with a negative outcome.

No wonder Rattle thinks Adorno has a case to answer. However, there's another strand of ideology under Adorno's criticism, one that may prove to be more stubborn than the philosopher's frankly idiotic assertion that Sibelius's technical incompetence can be demonstrated 'among musicians'. (Karajan? Rattle? Are they not musicians? To say nothing of other great Sibelius interpreters that Adorno would have heard in his lifetime: Thomas Beecham, Serge Koussevitzky, Robert Kajanus.) There's an implicit association throughout Adorno's work between the 'impotent' attempt to continue to use tonality, Sibelius's so-called aesthetic conservatism, and political conservatism. That's because post-war musical aesthetics saw a connection between the overblown romanticism of tonality and the ways that fascist, communist, and oppressive regimes used that musical idiom as the soundtrack to their pernicious nationalisms and ideologies while suppressing more 'advanced' styles like those of Schoenberg. In Adorno's terms, to be a tonal composer was to cast yourself beyond the political as well as musical pale.

And it has to be admitted that Sibelius did not help himself or his posthumous reputation when it came to his politics: in 1942, he accepted a commendation from the Nazis. It's going too far, however, to suggest that Sibelius was a Nazi sympathiser, especially in the context in which the seventy-seven-year-old composer found himself in the 1940s. By then, Sibelius was the national figurehead of Finland, a country thrust into a complex wartime relationship between its old enemy Russia on one side, and the Nazis on the other. But that implicit connection between his music and some kind of conservative ideology didn't help his post-war reception in Germany, Austria, or France. The nadir – or high point, depending on your point of view – of anti-Sibelius invective comes from the French theorist and conductor René Leibowitz, who entitled a book *Sibelius, le plus mauvais compositeur du monde* ('the worst composer in the world').

Karajan was not well placed to engage in a debate about any composer's putative political conservatism, given his own relationship with the Nazi regime as a Party member. And the Berlin Philharmonic itself has a severely compromised relationship with the Third Reich: between 1933 and 1945, the ensemble was *Das Reichsorchester*. The orchestra was saved from bankruptcy by the Nazis, and for the first time in its history had to give up its financial and institutional independence in order to survive. Supported by Goebbels and the regime, the orchestra's musicians were protected from having to serve in the army, in return for the terrible price of having to play at the Nazi Party's behest, providing the official music of the Nuremberg rallies in the late 1930s and playing concerts for Hitler's birthday and German workers whenever the regime required them, in addition to their subscription series. It was in the

Nazis' interests that the Philharmonic should be a badge
of German cultural superiority throughout the world, and
it was during these years that the orchestra's international
reputation was cemented, in conjunction with their conductor, Wilhelm Furtwängler. Once, that is, the ensemble
had rid itself of its small but prominent percentage of
Jewish players, including its leader, Szymon Goldberg.
Some of the bureaucratic facts of the orchestra's tortuous
but complicitous relationship with the regime are told in
Misha Aster's *The Reich's Orchestra*. There are chilling
conclusions to be drawn from Aster's book; above all, the
disturbing coincidence that precisely the same repertoire
that Furtwängler performed as a badge of universal values
of humanity was used by the Nazis as a symbol of nation-
alistic, anti-Semitic chauvinism. There are some brilliant
and terrifying recordings of the orchestra during this time.
Two concerts from 1942 reveal both sides. There is the
demonic intensity and terror of Furtwängler's conducting
of Beethoven's Ninth Symphony at a concert for Hitler's
birthday in April. The end of the symphony sounds more
like an 'Ode to Hate' than an 'Ode to Joy', an expressive
horror that you would have hardly thought possible in this
of all pieces – until you hear this performance. Film foot-
age of the occasion shows the conductor warily shaking
Joseph Goebbels' hand – and then wiping his right hand
in apparent revulsion. But there is also a visionary, radiant
performance of Bruckner's Fifth Symphony from October
1942. No artefacts from the history of recorded sound pose
the same grave questions of musical value as the Berlin
Philharmonic's recordings from this period. The blazing
brilliance of that Bruckner performance is unassailable,
but to hear it in those terms, are we as listeners, sixty years

later, turning a complex cultural-historical happening into a narrowly aesthetic experience? Or is doing so to honour Furtwängler's, and Bruckner's, intentions, to pay tribute to musicians who remained fully committed to their musical ideals even if at the same time many of them were forced to traduce their political and moral beliefs? The questions will resonate, unanswered and possibly unanswerable, for just as long as the recordings.

To return to *Der Fall Karajan und Sibelius*, the case of Karajan and Sibelius: in terms of his recordings and the concerts he gave of the symphonies with the Berlin Philharmonic, Karajan was one of the most persuasive champions of Sibelius's music. But in turning the tide of Sibelius's reputation in Germany more generally, he manifestly failed, and in retrospect, even the musicians of his orchestra never took the Finnish 'great Outsider' to their hearts.

Back to 2010. Rattle remembers his previous performances of Sibelius with the Berlin Philharmonic over the last eight years. 'We did the Seventh in my first year and the Fifth three seasons ago, but with a very different orchestra.' Rattle means 'different' in terms of personnel; there has been another wave of new musicians joining the orchestra in recent years. 'And since we've been working on the symphonies since February, there hasn't been this slightly *hochnäsig* thing.' *Hochnäsig* literally means 'high-nosed' – in other words, 'snobbish'. The snobbism comes from Adorno, but also from generations of German musicians who have thought of Sibelius, disparagingly, as 'film music'.

But even if the players bring fewer preconceptions to the music than they might have done in the past, the simple fact is that the vast majority of the Berlin Philharmonic musicians just do not know these pieces. And neither do their audiences. Rattle tells me that he has heard during the week of rehearsals for the Fifth, Sixth and Seventh symphonies from Heiner Goebbels, one of the most celebrated contemporary composers in Germany. Goebbels told him, 'I'm such a German, I have never listened to these pieces, and people have been telling me it's great music, so I have to come to these concerts.' That's not a situation in which the virtuoso musicians of this orchestra often find themselves, where they don't know and can't relate to the music on the stands in front of them. 'It's a journey of discovery,' Rattle says.

So his first job is to convince the musicians that this whole Sibelius-cycle project is a good idea for the orchestra. And in 2010, he's in a better place to make that argument than he was in 2002. He tells me that when he first suggested the idea of a complete Sibelius cycle to one of the orchestra's committees, the reaction was laughter: 'You'll never get it past the players,' was the feeling. As Fergus McWilliam says:

Even a year ago, or eighteen months ago, the idea of playing three Sibelius symphonies in one night, especially the Fifth, Sixth, and Seventh, and especially as a horn player, would have been crazy. We'd have been asking Simon, 'Are you out of your mind?' But now, of course, we're all applauding him, and we're just wondering what he's going to come up with next.

The fact that Rattle's relationship with the orchestra has improved from then is a matter of public record. In 2008, the orchestra voted to give Rattle a new ten-year contract, taking him until 2018, six years after his initial contract was due to expire. This was not just a legal nicety, but a formal cementing of a relationship that many in the outside world had questioned. Rattle faced more direct criticism in his early years in Berlin than he has at any other time of his career, and the reasons for that aren't hard to explain. His tenure in Berlin has continued just as radically and iconoclastically as his choice of music for his first concert suggested. Rattle's whole project, endorsed by the players when they voted for him as Claudio Abbado's successor instead of the other most likely candidate, Daniel Barenboim, has been to make the Berlin Philharmonic as virtuosically versatile an ensemble as possible. That has meant exploring kinds of repertoire that some players actively dislike – Olaf Maninger refers to some of the contemporary music the orchestra plays as 'gruesome, really awful', but says that it's 'the orchestra's duty to play it, and be the most passionate advocates of it when we're on stage' – but for some observers, notably a handful of German critics, the effect on the Philharmonic's relationship with their core repertoire was potentially damaging. The notion was that the Berlin Philharmonic players were 'losing their sound', thanks to the extension of their repertoire into relatively uncharted waters and Rattle's unconventional attitude to the classics.

Fergus McWilliam rebuts these criticisms. 'That red herring about us "losing our sound" that was going around a few years ago would have been hilarious if it hadn't been so destructive. The people who were writing the articles had only heard Karajan on record' – the Karajan era is still held up as the blue-riband period for the establishment of what is thought of as the 'Philharmonic sound' – 'but no recording ever got close to capturing what we really sound like as an orchestra. It's taken until now, and our own Digital Concert Hall, to find the best sound I have ever heard electronically for this orchestra.' McWilliam questions the motives of critics like Axel Brüggemann, who were 'just trying to create a story', but the musicians' answer to the question of why Rattle has not fundamentally altered the sound of the Berlin Philharmonic is simple: it isn't his to change. The players are the ones who feel themselves responsible for the sound of the orchestra, not their conductors. As McWilliam says:

It sounds a wee bit arrogant, but it has to be true that the orchestra is bigger than any of its maestros. We as players have to accept that responsibility, and every conductor has to accept that reality. The Berlin Philharmonic is 128 years old. Conductors come and go, players stay a little longer, maybe thirty or thirty-five years – I've got seven years to go until I retire – and that collective identity is the most important thing. The player's first responsibility is to maintain the institution, hence the importance of continuing to find the best players, and to care for the institution in the way that we manage it. And after that comes the pollination of our relationships with our conductors. It's like the bee who visits the flower: we need the conductors to advance us, to keep the artistic direction of the orchestra going. But they do not define the orchestra any more than the bee is the flower, or the apple is the apple tree. It's an awesome feeling to be a member of this orchestra. You know, you walk round the building here and think, good grief, this is my orchestra – and I'm responsible for it. Every single one of us, from the wind soloists to every last player in the fiddles, is accountable for every performance. It's a huge responsibility.

There are inbuilt frictions in the Berlin Philharmonic's identity. They are a group of players who value themselves enormously as individual musicians, but who together create an instantly identifiable single sonic body in their performances, a 'tradition' that the present generation regards itself as inheriting and maintaining. Yet the conservation of that sound, that performance practice, is the opposite of 'conservative', Rattle and the players all tell me, since it is formed only through a complete and sometimes reckless commitment to the moment of performance. There's another tension too, in that for all their individual brilliance, and for all the democracy of the way they run the orchestra, these musicians nonetheless need and want to be led by a single person on the podium to whom they ultimately cede authority. The creative and sometimes combustible mix of all of these seemingly irresolvable contradictions is the paradoxical secret of their success. And they are tensions that are clearly exposed in the experience of putting together these Sibelius performances.

McWilliam admits how important and significant Rattle's particular brand of 'pollination' has been to the orchestra's sense of development in the few months leading up to these concerts. The month before I arrived, Rattle conducted Bach's *St Matthew Passion* with the orchestra. Programmed after Easter – that in itself was virtually a heresy for the Berlin orchestra and its audiences, because of the piece's sacred subject-matter – Rattle set out to make this a *St Matthew Passion* that no one in the orchestra or the Philharmonie would forget. McWilliam says, 'Look, I'm a horn player, and I wasn't even playing in it, but I'm sufficiently Germanised to feel the sacrilege of what Simon was proposing, playing the piece after Easter and having it directed and staged by Peter Sellars, for God's sake!' Sellars has always been a controversial stage animal; Rattle has a close association with him, having worked on Mozart with him at Glyndebourne. But Sellars, as even his staunchest apologist would admit, has done 'some, er, less than tremendous stuff', as McWilliam puts it. Added to which are the further heresies of the *St Matthew Passion* not being an opera or even a stage work, and the Philharmonie not being a theatre or opera house. The risks were huge: depending on what interpretation Sellars decided to visit on the Bach, there was massive potential for the whole project to misfire spectacularly as a staged event. Musically, there were dangers, too. Rattle's long involvement with period-instrument ensembles – he's a principal artist of the Orchestra of the Age of Enlightenment in the UK – might have scared some players that he was going to try and instil a pared-down, historically informed style among musicians whose instincts are often diametrically opposed, technically and philosophically, to the ideals of the early-music movement. It could all have been risible rather than reverential.

'Well, who's laughing now?' McWilliam says. 'This was one of the most important musical experiences of our lives, everyone in the orchestra is saying. And I wasn't even in the damn thing.' Rattle himself concurs.

I think this is the single most important thing we ever did here. After the performance, Emmanuel Pahud [one of the orchestra's solo flutes] said to me: 'Everything we've done seems almost secondary after that.' The achievement of Peter Sellars, and the effect he had on the whole house – it makes me well up just to think about it.

Sellars' brilliance was in making the Philharmonie a place in which the musical ritual was shared by everyone in the auditorium. Without any staging gimmickry but with sensitive lighting, subtle direction of the solo singers in their arias and recitatives (the cast was led by tenor Mark Padmore's Evangelist, with Rattle's wife, mezzo-soprano Magdalena Kožená, another of the soloists), and the placement of some of the choirs and singers among the audience, Sellars consecrated the space of the Philharmonie. He brilliantly but gently dramatised the heartbreaking universality of Bach's music and the Passion drama. Rattle's conducting and the Philharmonic's performance was the perfect musical analogue for the dramatic conception. Rattle allowed the musicians to play their solos without any conductorial diktats. This was not a performance of homogeneous stylistic integrity, but of democratic sharing: a group of individual players and singers each bearing witness. The players and vocal soloists brought their own authentic interpretative response to Bach's music to this performance. Rattle guided the performance's architecture in terms of tempo and the articulation and balance of the massed forces of players, choirs, and continuo groups. But he too was a musician giving witness to the Passion. A sense of generosity and inclusion radiated throughout the Philharmonie (and even over the ether to viewers of the Digital Concert Hall), and the energy of the whole performance was somehow transformed into an absolutely direct and moving spiritual experience.

It's no surprise that McWilliam says that Rattle 'has a lot of traction with us right now', a strength of connection he will need to call on in his journey with the orchestra through Sibelius's last three symphonies. But Rattle has the upper hand in this repertoire. He has been conducting Sibelius's symphonies since the 1970s, he already has a complete recorded cycle and hundreds of performances of this music with the City of Birmingham Symphony Orchestra to his credit, and he has the imprimatur in this music of Finland's *éminence grise* of conducting, Paavo Berglund (who died in early 2012). Before the first concert in the Philharmonie, Rattle is awarded the Sibelius Medal by the Finnish ambassador in Berlin for his decades-long contribution to the cause of Finnish music. The players will rely on Rattle's Sibelian pollination over the next few days. 'For me,' Rattle tells a Finnish interviewer, playing Sibelius is 'coming home. In Britain we all always feel that Sibelius is one of our greatest composers. Well, it's north, and not so far [from us]. But here it's a very different thing, because it's a very foreign land for German orchestras.' An alien territory Rattle and his players will have to navigate in their week of immersion in Sibelius's dark, cool waters.

In rehearsal in the Philharmonie (the Berlin Philharmonic, in common with so many of the world's great orchestras, rehearses in the same venue in which it performs), all these currents of personal relationships and collective histories, of musical reputation and individual responsibility, are flowing just beneath the surface of the music-making. Rattle is taking the orchestra through the Fifth Symphony, but sometimes it sounds like the other way round, as the gigantic accelerando that Sibelius writes in the second part of the first movement threatens to spiral out of control. It's one of the hardest things in the symphony to bring off, a speeding-up that happens over a huge span of time, about five minutes or so. It's a paradoxical phenomenon: the increase of tempo should be imperceptible, since it happens continuously rather than in stages, but the accelerative effect needs to be physical. The end of the movement should seem like a gigantic whirligig, a vision of the planets dancing in their orbits. Yet these huge musical forces need to be controlled and precise. Rattle is right to say that this kind of motion is a first in music history, and enormously influential on later composers:

The Fifth Symphony [composed between 1915 and 1919] is one of the great explorations of the idea of accelerando, this very, very gradual motion. As it comes to numbers Six and Seven [from 1923 and 1924], the tempos start weaving in and out of one another: one is suddenly in a slow movement without knowing it and just as suddenly in a fast movement. And this is one of Sibelius's great revolutionary discoveries, and of course a composer like Elliott Carter would be nowhere without them.

That's fine in musicological terms, but it's not the language in which he communicates with the orchestra. Instead, he has a story to tell the players about how he discovered the secret to creating this kind of motion, a poetic short cut to making the gradual accelerando in the Fifth Symphony work. Rattle speaks in English for this little musical parable, which is unusual in this rehearsal. His German has improved to a fluent but usable pidgin version of the language, enough to get him through most of the musical instructions he needs to issue to his players, but for the more whimsical or witty things he wants to communicate, he reverts to English. This story is about a ten-year-old Balinese girl. Rattle stayed in Bali for a few weeks learning the native gamelan music, and was amazed that the whole ensemble of percussionists and dancers could control vast, gradual speedings-up and slowings-down without a conductor, and without any obvious leadership or physical cues. When he asked this little girl about how it happened, she said, 'You've been here two weeks and you still haven't noticed that it's the dancers who control it? When they lift up their left hand, we play faster, and so on. That's how it works.' Rattle wants his players to think about this kind of Sibelian motion in a different way to the music they're more used to, for them to play it as unconsciously as the Balinese musicians. 'It's good if we can do it continuously, this accelerando.'

Rattle's combination of the poetic and the prosaic works. After running through the whole first movement, he says with a smile to his players, 'So, *guten Morgen*' – an ironic understatement, after the enormous musical powers he and the orchestra have just unleashed in the Philharmonie. This first part of the Fifth Symphony is Sibelius's unique fusion of a conventional first movement and a scherzo. In the original version of the symphony, these were two discrete sections. The masterstroke of Sibelius's later revision was realising a new kind of musical motion in symphonic form, creating a single line of ever-increasing speed and tension that connects the structures of both kinds of music. That's the academic theory of this piece anyway, but in thrilling practice in the Philharmonie, I've never heard this piece played with such overwhelming sonic force. And this is only a rehearsal, with a general rehearsal of the whole programme to come the next day, and the three concerts on consecutive evenings after that.

Rattle, too, is shocked.

I always have to kick myself – you know, this is just a rehearsal! It's amazing to have people playing at that level of intensity. Sometimes I forget that they don't really know this music, because a whole lot of it is more beautiful than I could ever imagine, and it goes so well. But then sometimes there are really obvious things that people don't seem to get.

* * *

But this sheer power of the orchestra is a double-edged sword, both in terms of the force of the individual personalities in the orchestra, and in their no-holds-barred approach to music-making. Rattle has to harness that power, not simply release it.

It's a completely different challenge and relationship from the one he created with the City of Birmingham Symphony Orchestra. In the West Midlands of England, Rattle's sheer enthusiasm and drive took the orchestra from provincial significance to world-class celebrity, and his energy was the dynamo behind the whole project. He changed the orchestra's repertoire, dragging it kicking and screaming into the late twentieth century (literally, in the case of Mark-Anthony Turnage's Francis Bacon-inspired work, *Three Screaming Popes*, which was commissioned for Rattle), and also charmed his audiences into coming with them – as well as convincing the city fathers to build a new concert hall for Birmingham, Symphony Hall, which opened in 1992 and is still the best acoustic for orchestral music in Britain.

Rattle's style of conducting in Birmingham, his continual imploring of his players to give greater intensity and commitment – embodied by those famous photographs of him, open-mouthed, left hand clenched, baton raised above his head and seemingly about to strike a physical as well as symbolic blow to the music and his musicians – has been modified in his years of working with the Berlin Philharmonic.

The danger with these people is that if you ask more and more, they will give more and more and more. Here, if you ask them, they'll drive off the cliff – with pleasure! I've watched a really wonderful conductor who I respect enormously start the Bartók *Divertimento* [for string orchestra] with the biggest upbeat I've ever seen, and they gave him this huge sound. But then he carried on with those gestures for the rest of the piece, and of course they just continued to give him that huge sound. You've never heard the Bartók *Divertimento* sound so deafening.

It was exactly that sort of conductorial dynamism that was necessary with the Birmingham orchestra, to force the players to come with him.

But here, I've had to learn something different. I've taken a lot of the edge off. The minute you have an edge, it stops them from being able to listen. American orchestras say to me, 'For God's sake, Simon, give us some clarity,' but there's a certain type of technique that works in America that doesn't work in Central Europe. It doesn't work here, and it wouldn't work in Austria, or with, say, the Israel Philharmonic either. And I've also had to learn it as I go.

What Rattle means by the 'edge' is the kind of absolute clarity of a technically perfect conducting style. This technique gives players their cues with an infallible click of the baton, carving out time in a geometrically consistent three-dimensional space, and ensuring togetherness and precision at all costs. It's a style epitomised by the extraordinary prowess of the American Lorin Maazel, a conductor who prides himself on the musical wizardry of his gestures. Such is the control over his musicians that Maazel exerts through his hands, you feel he can alter the loudness and softness of his players with all the exactitude of a digital mixing desk.

And that's the opposite of what Rattle wants to achieve in Berlin. That accelerando in the Fifth Symphony is a case in point. 'Eventually, it will run by itself, and I won't have to lead it. That's the wonderful thing here. The more I can withdraw myself from the process of how they actually listen to one another, the better it normally sounds.' Rattle identifies the same paradox as Mariss Jansons and Jonathan Nott, the counterintuitive notion that to best realise your musical intentions as a conductor, you have to set the frame of how the players work together – and then get out of the way. 'That's the hard thing,' Rattle says, 'that you have to learn to allow them to listen, and that means being less rather than more precise in your gestures.' Just as the players infused themselves with Thomas Adès's music, this is a process that comes from the ground up, from the roots of the music they're playing, rather than being imposed on them by a stick-wielding technocrat. It's a process that explains why the Berlin Philharmonic does not have a reputation as the most precise orchestra in the world. Rattle admits:

Just sometimes I have to say them: now we really have to do it all together. That's why pizzicato is famously so hard here, or those moments when the music requires the orchestra to play absolutely together with the piano or the percussion, the kind of thing [composer-conductor] Oliver Knussen does to perfection everywhere. Those moments are often more difficult to achieve here. As a special effect, they can do it, but normally the sound is better when they can breathe, when they have found the way to move together in a piece. It's like a wave motion that they need to create with whatever they're playing.

Oboist Jonathan Kelly, the only member of the orchestra to have experienced Rattle in both Berlin and Birmingham contexts, has a slightly different opinion about Sir Simon's relative precision.

We woodwind players always disagree with him, because he thinks that if his beat is clear and large, then we will play loudly. Sometimes I say to him, 'Simon, we just need a clear downbeat there. I'll do you a deal, if you give us a big downbeat there, I promise you we'll play quietly.' But he doesn't believe that we ever will. He thinks he should use a small, subtle beat, but sometimes it just makes it hard. Yet this has always been his theory, in Birmingham and in Berlin.

Kelly also suggests that Rattle is doing more in these Sibelius rehearsals than simply allowing the players to listen to each other.

What he does with us in Berlin that's very good is that he takes the music apart in such a way that even if you're not really concentrating, I mean if he's rehearsing the violas or a different section from yours, you subconsciously take in what's going on. You're made aware of what the whole orchestra is doing in the symphony, not just your part, and then the music falls together somehow. Like those tremolando sections that Sibelius writes so much of in the Fifth Symphony. You have the feeling that there's some edifice that's just waving around, but actually, it manages to stay together. That's because of the way he's rehearsed the music.

There are moments, though, when I can hear these two elemental beings – Sibelius's music and the Berlin Philharmonic's culture of playing – not quite coalescing, like two planets orbiting one another, each slightly out of phase with the other. A few minutes into the Fifth Symphony, there's a passage where the oboes and clarinets swap between them a skirling, repetitive phrase over a chiaroscuro of string tremolando, one of Kelly's wavering sonic edifices. The woodwind players play this music with a bold sense of character, individuality, and rhythmic swing.

Instead of a bland, cold rendition of Sibelius's music, they make this music sound improvised, even jazz-like. Rattle's response is, 'I love this so much – but it doesn't work. This big improvised thing doesn't work.' The problem is that it's hard enough for the strings to keep in time in the midst of a ever-changing shimmer of sound, but with the woodwind players giving their improvisational best to the melodic lines above them, the orchestra has no chance of staying together as an ensemble.

There's no question that Rattle is right, both for the orchestra's sake and for Sibelius's. There's a limit to how much expressive freedom this tightly wrought music can take before the relationship between its note-by-note structures and the overall sweep of the whole symphony falls apart. But the point proves one of the most important characteristics of this orchestra as opposed to any other. Jonathan Kelly explains the difference between the Berlin Philharmonic and the British orchestral culture he knew from the City of Birmingham Symphony Orchestra:

When I first came to the Berlin orchestra, I did some guest playing. And I remember going back to my colleagues in Birmingham and telling them that it's like a big free-for-all here, it's just such a mess. And it often was in the rehearsal, it just seemed like anarchy, really it did. It was a style of playing in which all the musicians – including all the string players – were performing as if they were the first solo or the leader, and I was thinking, you just can't do that. It was a very, very different way of being from the culture in Birmingham, and I needed a long time to get used to it.

Kelly's appointment to the Berlin Phil job was the fulfilment of a lifelong dream.

I always wanted to be in this orchestra. The reason was that my dad and grandmother had tons of recordings of the Berlin Phil and I would listen to them and play along with them, and try and imitate the sound. There were two principal oboes, Lothar Koch was the more famous, but there was Karl Steins as well, and I just loved the outrageousness of the way they played, the way the whole orchestra played. And on a lot of those Karajan-era recordings there are a lot of mistakes, which I grew to love as well, the things that were not completely together, because everything was done with such panache. The job that my colleague Albrecht Mayer [Kelly's fellow *Solo-Oboist*] got came up in this orchestra just after the time I got the position in Birmingham, and somehow I didn't think I was ready for it then.

When another principal oboe job in the orchestra came up a few years later – as with all of the principal woodwind and brass positions, there are two players who share the job – Kelly did audition. The audition process at the Berlin Philharmonic is notoriously nerve-racking. The whole orchestra votes on each position, so the candidates play on stage at the Philharmonie to their prospective colleagues, each of whom has a say in who gets through to the final round. For Jonathan's job, there were three finalists, who had to play the solos from the slow movement of Brahms's Violin Concerto, Strauss's *Don Juan*, and Rossini's *La Gazza Ladra* overture. All the finalists were on stage, playing the excerpts on their own, one after the other. 'It was like a penalty shoot-out,' Kelly said. 'And you're thinking, if you have to play last, Oh, I liked what he did with that bit of rubato, so what am I going to do? But finally, all you can do is stand up and just play it as yourself.' Half an hour later in the orchestra's canteen, which is just offstage at the Philharmonie, Kelly was milling around with the other candidates when they announced over the tannoy who was the successful applicant. 'I couldn't speak German, so I didn't even understand that I'd got it. Then there was this queue of people shaking my hand, so I thought, well, I must have got the job.'

That is already a brutal enough process, but Kelly's trial was really just beginning. As with every new member of the orchestra, there is a two-year-long probation period that the musicians have to go through, after which the orchestra votes again on whether to keep the player on and whether to offer them a permanent contract.

The hard thing was not to be intimidated by the whole experience. Having dreamt of all this for ever, it was hard not to think, oh my God, I'm on stage with the Berlin Philharmonic, and I'm sitting just where Lothar Koch used to sit. That was tough. And there were times I wouldn't have voted for myself, the way I was playing. When you're under that pressure, it can be difficult to perform. But at the end of the probation period I was getting exasperated: why does it take you lot so long to make your mind up? But now I understand why. Everyone needs that long, not just for the orchestra to decide, but for each player to adapt to the Berlin sound. No matter where you come from, you have to change to become a member of this orchestra in a musical sense. What you notice is that after the orchestra has voted a player in, you see and hear a blossoming in everything they do. It was the same with me, people would come up to me after a concert and say, 'Jonathan, your playing is just blooming.' And I wanted to say to them, 'Look, I'm just getting back to the level I was at before I joined this bloody orchestra.'

Aline Champion is a Geneva-born first violinist with the orchestra. For her, the graduation from probationary period to permanent contract was a complicated psychological moment.

The trial time was very hard for me. To be honest, it wasn't so much my colleagues making my own life difficult, it was much more myself. A few really good violinists hadn't made the vote after their probation just before I came, and knowing that put me under real pressure. The most difficult thing was actually to be able to be myself as much as I could and not to pretend or try to be better than I actually was. It sounds really easy to do, but when you feel watched all the time, it becomes really hard to be genuine. Also, I had to accept the fact that I couldn't please everybody, especially in a big group like the first violin group, with such strong and varied personalities.

So getting the job must have been a huge relief, the culmination of two years of work? 'Actually, it was more complicated than that! It was a really unexpected challenge after getting the job,' Aline tells me. She had already been an orchestral leader, with the South-West Radio Orchestra in Cologne, at a prodigiously young age, but the Berlin Philharmonic job, as for so many musicians, was a dream that would not go away.

Surprisingly, it took me a few weeks to get used to actually having the position. It was a strange feeling not to be under pressure any longer, not to have this continuous feeling of having to prove to everybody that you really deserve to be sitting there. Of course, I was very happy and having the vote was very liberating, but ironically, at the same time, I still felt I should prove to the colleagues who voted for me that they were right to have done so.

Until today, I am still trying to give my best at each concert. But I do it for me, for my responsibility to the audience and to the music. Honestly, this asks an enormous amount of energy, inner motivation and continuous self-discipline. But if I didn't do it, I would have a very bad conscience and would lose respect for myself.

That fusion of individual and collective responsibility is built in to the way the orchestra functions as a business, the way it hires musicians, and even the way it sits on stage. Uniquely among the orchestras in this book, the Berlin Philharmonic string players do not know where they are going to sit in their section before the first rehearsal of the week. Apart from the leaders of each group, from first violins to double basses, the rest of the placement is a free-for-all. Players decide on the spur of the moment to sit next to a player they haven't performed with for a while, to learn from each other's different technical and musical approaches. It's one of the small but significant features of the way the orchestra organises itself that ensures that when you watch the Berlin Philharmonic, whether you're focused on the leader of the first violins or the back desk of the violas, there is no sense of a hierarchical engagement with the music. Every player is leading their own performance in the concert, every musician is playing for themselves as if their musical life depended on it.

In whatever configuration you see it, the Berlin Philharmonic is made up of scores of these individual stories of how a musician comes to terms with this essential paradox: they are trying to be themselves as completely as they can be, in order to give themselves without compromise to the collective experience of being in the orchestra. Jonathan Kelly says that in British or American orchestras, the most important thing is to blend, to create a corporate sound.

Whereas for us in Berlin, the opposite is true. Our corporate sound, if we have one, only comes from everyone sticking out, from everyone throwing themselves into the experience. If you don't give a hundred per cent here, if you're just sitting there and playing *ganz bleich/bland* [blandly, passively], that's actually when you would stick out. That meant for me that I had to rediscover the slightly obnoxious teenager that I had been. I'd trained myself out of that kind of individualism. The hall has a part to play in all this too. In the Philharmonie, it's like being in a theatre in the round, that's why everyone is declaiming the whole time.

Aline Champion agrees. 'Everybody is taking risks all the time in this orchestra, in the tutti strings as well. In my eyes, this is the philosophy of the orchestra, and also what makes this orchestra so special. Of course when you risk something, you can lose, but no colleague is going to be annoyed with you if you risk something and it doesn't work. It would be worse not to have tried it!'

It's no surprise that Rattle has to rein in his ensemble of declamatory musicians from time to time. But his way of doing so is always courteous, often self-deprecating, and sometimes very funny. He talks of 'the time I could read music – before I got here'; he says that a moment in the second movement of the Fifth Symphony 'needs to be a bit more country and western – well, more country, anyway'; another few bars will work 'if we're not too gypsy', a few bars near the symphony's gigantic climax should be '*nicht zu Puccini*' (not too Puccini-like). To achieve the luminous quiescence of a place in the finale that Sibelius marks with four p's – pianissississimo, i.e. very quietly indeed – he tells his musicians, 'Do whatever you have to do: use raincoats, dusters,' to dampen the sound of their instruments. The effect of the way the orchestra finally plays that place is magical, and it symbolises Rattle's conception of this music, that the development of its sonic surfaces should go hand in hand with the unfolding of its structure, its musical geology. The whole of Sibelius's finale in the Fifth Symphony is a simultaneous slowing of speed and enlarging of scale, so the momentum of the whole piece is finally distilled into the spaces between the six gigantic chords that end the movement. Rattle's ultra-pianissimo shrinks the perspective of the orchestral players and his audience so that we all have to focus our whole attention on a sound that is just a shade above silence. The music almost seems to stop in that quietness, but from that musical inter-zone, suspended in the region between sound and silence, the final part of the symphony builds its enormous power.

In the general rehearsal, Sibelius's ending fools the groups of schoolchildren who have come to see the Berlin Philharmonic at work (another innovation of the *Rattle-zeit*, and a previously unprecedented opening of the Philharmonie's working environment to the general public). Rattle is masterly at welcoming the schoolkids to the hall – '*Wilkommen unseren Schulfreunden!*' – but even he can't make the children clap in the right place. After the first of the six chords, the children applaud. Rattle and the orchestra are unperturbed, but when it happens again after the second one, he stops. He is not cross with the kids. Just the opposite. He takes the children's instinctive reaction to heart, telling the orchestra about the first couple of chords that '*es ist sehr wichtig, dass es nicht wie eine Ende klingt*' (it's very important that it doesn't sound like an ending). Which means he has to find another way of making the orchestra play these chords, so that the audience in the

concerts don't think the same as the schoolkids, and imagine the symphony has ended before Sibelius's score says it
has. The secret is to make the musicians play through the
gaps between the chords. These are not individual mono-
liths of sound, but six interconnected menhirs that together
create a bigger form, a Stonehenge of sound. Asking the
players to think about a line connecting one chord to the
next solves the problem of how they play the music. Rattle
hasn't given them a specific technical solution but instead
offered them a new way of thinking about the music. When
they play it again, the six chords have a mysterious per-
ceptual doubleness: they are granite-hewn and static,
but they also have a definite internal motion. It's pure
Sibelian chemistry at its most distilled – and the children
don't clap in the wrong place this time.

Rattle achieves his musical goals with charm, inviting
his players to join him in hearing the music differently
rather than barking orders at them. As a general hint on
how to phrase this music, he says 'it's never Sibeli-US' but
'SI-belius', meaning that, just as in the Finnish language,
the accent, the stress, is often on the first part of the phrase,
not the final notes. After the orchestra have played the
Sixth and Seventh symphonies together, without a break
between them (an innovation Rattle is trying for the first
time in these concerts), he tells them, *Wir haben drei
Minuten Zahnarzt zu machen, tut mir leid*' (we have three
minutes' dentistry to do, I'm afraid). He then works the
strings of the Berlin Philharmonic through a passage of
the Sixth Symphony at half the speed it will be played in
the performance, to make sure their tuning is right. They
get the notes, but not the expressive character Rattle wants.
'It's a bit too clear; it should be more *nebelig* [foggy], more

Ligeti' – another of those Rattle-isms that has an immediate aural effect. This orchestra doesn't know much contemporary music like the back of its hand, but it does know its Ligeti, having recorded the complete orchestral works a few years previously with Jonathan Nott. Rattle's is an insightful comparison between Sibelius's textural fogginess and Ligeti's dense forests of micropolyphony.

But his strategy doesn't always work. 'Make it look like it's longer and it sounds much longer,' he tells the strings. They try altering their bowing, but tell him that it makes no difference to the sound. Rattle slaps his face in mock indignation and moves on. I wonder if his humour, which is full of typically English wordplay and punning, carries from the podium to the players. Jonathan Kelly confirms my suspicions. 'Sometimes he tries his humour in German, and it doesn't translate. And he'll say things in English which you don't quite get as well. There are a few people in the orchestra who don't understand English quite as well as he thinks they do.' What all the players agree on, though, is the positive atmosphere that Rattle creates in his rehearsals. Aline Champion says:

Simon always talks about us as a big family. I really appreciate how much he cares about creating and keeping a good and positive working atmosphere. He is extraordinarily friendly and open-minded. Even in some difficult situations, I have never seen him lose his temper. He is always exemplarily prepared for each rehearsal and also has a very clear idea of what he wants to hear. And if he makes everyone "crazy" until he gets what he wants, it is always with a smile.

That's true in the rehearsals I see. The closest Rattle gets to a direct criticism or frustration with the players is during the Seventh Symphony when, after some of Sibelius's tricky faster music has not worked as well as it should have done, he says to the orchestra, 'Just play what's there, and I will be so happy and surprised'; when the horns make a wrong entry he says, 'If you play one bar earlier, it will be even more beautiful.' Underneath the unthreatening rhetoric, though, I sense steel in Rattle's words. He means it, both when he says he will be happy if this orchestra of a hundred gigantic musical personalities were simply to play the notes in front of them, and he means it, too, that he would be surprised if it actually happened. And it's not quite true to say that Rattle has never lost his temper with the Berlin Philharmonic. Jonathan Kelly remembers an incident that shocked him.

Simon is very sensitive to mood, and if the mood is negative in rehearsal, it obviously affects him. During the time when we were making a decision about renewing his contract, there was naturally a lot of discussion. And although that discussion was mostly very positive, it still made everything electric, and the atmosphere was not so relaxed. In all my time working with Simon, I had never seen him lose it. I had seen most other conductors lose it, but Simon, never. But about a year ago in a rehearsal of a Haydn symphony, at one point, he just slammed his hands down on his stand, and said – something. I was shaking, thinking, oh my God, Simon's angry! I was stunned. But the rest of the orchestra thought nothing of it. They were saying, 'Yeah, it's good he got cross.' But normally even though he might be frustrated with things, he never actually shows it in the way he behaves.

That isolated incident reveals far more about the orchestra's expectation of how their conductor should behave than about Rattle's relationship with the orchestra. In all the interactions I see between him and his players, Rattle is a vision of a new model conductor as fraternal democrat rather than authoritarian father figure. The issue is that the Berlin Philharmonic is more accustomed to a different kind of authority. Fergus McWilliam remembers what the atmosphere was like during his first years with the orchestra, when Herbert von Karajan was still alive.

Karajan played up to the authoritarian image in public, which is actually at odds with who he was as a man. He was actually a softie, a warm-hearted, grandfatherly figure. But in rehearsal he would act up to the martinet image. And the orchestra liked being frightened a bit. I was new and an iconoclast: at that time, I was one of only twelve non-Germans in the orchestra, and now nearly half the orchestra don't come from Germany. I watched all this game-playing and was thinking, none of you actually believes in this, do you? It looked to me like the orchestra was pretending to be cowed by this guy, and he seemed to be pretending to be the despot. On stage during the concerts, they could allow him his artistic dominance, artistically. But backstage, when rehearsals were over, there were some serious battles. He and the orchestra fought all the time.

Aline Champion, one of the new non-German generation of players, confirms that the Berlin Phil can deal with conductors asserting their authority once in a while.

I personally can accept it if a conductor is getting impatient under pressure but only if what he is doing is serving the music. Democracy is a great thing, but that unfortunately doesn't always work in a big orchestra. With more than 120 people - and many of them are strong personalities with strong ideas - you do need someone to decide and set the main direction. A bit like a captain of a boat when he says: let's go this way!

(There's an assumption in Aline's words that 'the conductor' is a 'he' – the Berlin Philharmonic has been conducted by fifteen women in its entire history.) Claudio Abbado, Rattle's predecessor, was far less of a martinet than Karajan, 'but he was still a star, there was still this aura around him, that you couldn't really approach him. I absolutely loved him, and I was lucky he liked me. But he was still this big star. Simon is completely different.'

Rattle's main competition for the Berlin job before he was appointed was Daniel Barenboim, whose biggest job (in Germany at least) is across town at the Berliner Staatsoper. Barenboim is a different kind of personality too, fierier, more impatient, and more like the maestros of an older generation. They swapped orchestras in the first week in May, as Barenboim conducted the Berlin Phil's annual Europa-Konzert, the May Day concert for which the orchestra chooses the conductor and the city for a televised relay broadcast all over Europe. Rattle, meanwhile, conducted Chabrier's gently sardonic love-story *L'Étoile* in a new production of the opera at the Staatsoper, with performances before, during, and after his Sibelius rehearsals and concerts. Going from Chabrier to Sibelius is one of the biggest stylistic and psychological jumps that you can imagine. It's difficult to conceive of the energy you need to be on stage with two of the biggest cultural institutions in Berlin's musical life in such grotesquely varied repertoire, but Rattle tells me the musical difference between Sibelian seriousness and Chabrier-esque champagne refreshes him. He has watched the Europa-Konzert, from the Sheldonian Theatre in Oxford, in which Barenboim and the orchestra conjured a searing performance of Brahms's First Symphony. 'I thought it was one of the most extraordinary things I have ever heard from them. I was so touched and proud listening to it. And Daniel was in such good shape: he said to me afterwards, "I was in a good mood all week."'

The implication is that Barenboim isn't always of so sunny a disposition, but the players tell me that when he gets cross with them, they don't get angry back. Aline Champion says, 'It is true that he can sometimes be quite impatient and direct during rehearsals. In my opinion, it is always to serve the music first, and never for his own ego. The thing is that he simply cannot deal with mediocrity. I have an immense respect for Daniel Barenboim – he is one of the most amazing musicians I know – so his impatience doesn't matter to me, and in the end, we play better.'

This is another seeming contradiction at the heart of this orchestra of all orchestras. The players value above all their own reputations as musicians, individually and collectively. Fergus McWilliam speaks of each player as a 'stakeholder in the orchestra, not just artistically, but economically, too – our livelihood depends on us being at the top'; Olaf Maninger tells me 'the orchestra is greater than its conductors, that's a simple fact' – yet these players can give of their best only when they are alchemised, or 'pollinated' by a conductor, even if the person on the podium is shouting at them.

Yet this doesn't mean that the orchestra gives up all control to its conductors. Aline Champion describes how the process works for her:

Even if I don't agree with the conductor's idea, I always try to understand why he wants what he wants. I don't have to agree with his idea, but I generally find it much easier to accept something if I know where someone is coming from. Of course, that means I sometimes have to make some musical compromises, but that is part of my job. But I am not passive. The point is, I still feel a great responsibility towards the final result of the concert and that is why I would always try to make it sound as good as possible.

The way authority works in the Berlin Philharmonic is never a simple top-down flow of orders and their execution. The players are not willing merely to accept a diktat from on high and carry out the demands of any conductor without interrogating them, without asking the question – why? Fergus McWilliam compares the Berlin Philharmonic to a gigantic string quartet:

It's chamber music. Every single member of our orchestra partakes of the musical event that is happening. And that means that there are spontaneous decisions and improvisations that will suddenly happen in a performance. Someone will come up with an idea, suggest something in their playing, and the others have to work out what to do with it, to understand it, be convinced by it, and interpret it. So there's an awful lot of work that has to go on.

Especially in these Sibelius symphonies:

To get to the point where the music is digested into the metabolism of the whole body of our orchestra, so that we can improvise with it, it's not enough just to get through your own part. Everyone wants to know exactly what every instrument is doing. Which means that it doesn't matter if you've played these pieces before or not: this is new territory for all of us in this moment. Rattle has opened up Sibelius in a completely new way.

Olaf Maninger compares Rattle to an American-style 'manager', whose philosophy is to try and keep as many people happy as he can; solo bassoon Stefan Schweigert says he is 'the most democratic but also the most precise [*bestimmt*] conductor' the orchestra has ever had. It's a more vulnerable position for Rattle to put himself in than to adopt the posture of the Barenboim-style martinet, because it means that he has to earn the respect of the players not through the exercise of his will at all costs, but rather through the strength of his native personality and musicianship.

And seeing him at work in the Sixth and Seventh symphonies, he has finally got there. 'We're all so much closer now. We have been through a lot of different things together,' Rattle says.

It's much easier to take them further now, because we under-stand each other. Each side knows what we need to do more, and they're willing to go very, very far to achieve it. I loved the fact that today we went five minutes over time in the rehearsal and nobody made a peep. They're not so strict anyway because it's a completely non-unionised orchestra in that way. The fact is that they're working hard, and working with pleasure.

They are also working in a way that is changing funda-mentally how Rattle thinks of these symphonies, as close to his heart as any music.

The Sixth Symphony has been always been very difficult, even with wonderful orchestras, whenever I've played it. It's very elusive. And I said to the orchestra when we started three days ago: 'This piece is not hard to play, but it's hard to understand.' But in fact I was completely wrong, because from the moment this warm cantabile sound started [in the strings at the start of the symphony] I thought, this symphony is not as difficult as I thought. And they've eaten it up. The extraordinary energy of this orchestra means that the climaxes build themselves, instead of having to urge them on, really you just keep the big shape in mind, because, as I've said, if you give them too much, they will happily drive off the mountain.

Sibelius said of his 1923 Sixth Symphony that it 'reminds me of the scent of the first snow', and, reportedly, that 'while other composers were engaged in manufacturing cocktails [I] offered the public pure cold water'. Even if you look at the score of the symphony, you get an idea of what Sibelius means. Take the first page, an austere landscape of almost archaic polyphony and simple modality, a weave of voices in the string parts that is unadulterated by a single colour-giving accidental, whose long-breathed minims and semibreves, and the spaces on the paper that the shapes of the note-heads circumscribe, communicate the music's essential whiteness and stasis. The scent of the first snow: a frozen premonition that will coalesce into blizzards and blinding brilliance later in the four-movement symphony, but which at the start is a musical vision without any overt expressivity. This is music that is about a state of being rather than a way of feeling – it simply *is*. The music is marked mezzo-forte, the most non-committal of dynamic markings, as if Sibelius were saying to his performers: do not interpret this music, don't impose yourself on it, just let it be.

But this is the Berlin Philharmonic string section we're talking about: just 'letting it be' isn't what they do. And so the music is shot through with feverish intensity in the rehearsal, a quality of searching and unpredictability, as if we were travellers setting off into the snow, not simply watching it fall from behind a pane of glass. The whole symphony becomes a journey in a way that I have not experienced it before. The last page of the Sixth Symphony is another piece of Sibelian matter-of-factness: a straightforward chant of string sound that ascends and descends, an answering call in the woodwinds, an icy shimmer of timpani tremolo, and a plain pianissimo in the first and second violins that finishes the piece. It is music that has always sounded to me like a bleaching-out of human experience, as if nature were wiping out the traces of human intervention with another purifying, footprint-covering snowfall. Not in this rehearsal. The Berlin Philharmonic make the chant sing with the despair of a human soul lost in the wilderness, the woodwinds' response is a vain attempt at consolation, the very end of the piece a hollowed-out resignation to a higher power. It may not be a cocktail, but it sure isn't pure. After the rehearsal, and a similarly impassioned performance of the Seventh Symphony, I'm left with a flabbergasted sense of the new experience that Sibelius's music has become in the hands of Rattle and the Berlin Philharmonic, how different this is to any other approach to the composer I've heard before. And I'm stunned by the thought of how things may change and develop over the three concerts.

After all, the Berlin Philharmonic lives for its performances, for the arena in which they can drive as close as they dare to the edge of the mountain, and nobody apart from their conductor can stop them from going over the edge. Before the first concert, Rattle has a surprise for the audience. Completely by chance, he overheard a youth choir from Siberia rehearsing in the Philharmonie in the afternoon, and Rattle was so impressed that he asked them to sing at the start of the concert. In the evening, he tells the audience, in his English-accented German, 'Usually we have the encore at the end of the concert, but tonight we'll have it at the start.' It's an amazing act of generosity and curatorial inspiration on Rattle's part, and the hall is thrilled by the Russians' performances of Stravinsky and folk music. It's also a weirdly apposite upbeat to the start of the Fifth Symphony, the clear, powerful delivery of the Siberian singers opening up a northern vista of cold, open spaces.

The whole concert has some outstanding moments. Principal bassoonist Stefan Schweigert's solo halfway through the first movement is suspended above an undulating texture of string sound, like the outlines of a forest glimpsed through a thick morning mist, and the wedge shape of the Fifth Symphony's finale has a ferocious dynamism. Before the second half, Rattle again talks to the audience to tell us he will play the Sixth and Seventh symphonies *'ohne Pause'*, without a pause, to create a 'kind of gigantic five-movement symphony'. He is confident that the idea will work. It comes from his Sibelian mentor, Paavo Berglund, and makes sense in terms of texture and tonality. The D minor Sixth Symphony is driven by a never-resolved ambiguity created by a modal scale, starting on D, in which there are no accidentals – in other words, in which the pitches are the same as the scale of C major. These two poles of pitch, C and D, are centres of gravity around which the whole symphony spins. The Seventh Symphony is in C major, and begins with a quiet timpani stroke, an echo of what we have just heard at the end of the Sixth. There's another sense in which Sibelius himself might have given his imprimatur to Rattle's performance, as he composed both symphonies at the same time, and it's sometimes unclear from his letters which one he is talking about. They breathe the same air, even if the single-movement Seventh is a radically different structure from the Sixth.

The Seventh is a radically other emotional experience, too. The Berlin Philharmonic strings play a long section of grand, arcane, slow, and melodious counterpoint near the start of this twenty-minute symphonic journey with a vastness of scale and visceral emotional engagement that utterly reshapes this music. I had always heard this passage as an evocation of musical timelessness, another of those Sibelian moments in which human life is put in suspended animation in the face of the bigger forces of time and nature. Not here. Every note is embodied by the players, every phrase is infused with an intensity that transforms this music into a song of sadness for the fragility of human life, compared to the infinity of the cosmos. Somehow, the Berlin Philharmonic strings in the Philharmonie give you this feeling as direct physical experience. The hall is an arena of existential exploration, in which you as a listener are confronted with physical and sonic phenomena that are virtually beyond understanding, way past the limits of a conventional orchestral experience. During these few minutes in Sibelius's Seventh Symphony, there's a coming together of the music's essential power, revealed as if for the first time, and the expressive power of the playing.

And yet, and yet . . . by the end of the concert, I'm not sure that the whole experience has managed the complete vision of Sibelius that Rattle wanted to achieve, that sense of the 'big shapes' of the symphonies as well as their over-whelming details. Jonathan Kelly offers a clue as to why that might be after this first concert:

I thought the evening was really good, but Sibelius is still not this orchestra's music. For example, there's that moment in the first movement of the Fifth Symphony, when the sun comes out [the moment when the symphony's main theme is finally allowed to flourish, an unfurling of major-key optimism to which all of the mists and chills of the previous few minutes have been leading] and I was thinking, when we did this in Birmingham, every-body would be smiling at this point, smiling with the joy of the music. And I looked around at the same moment tonight, and we weren't smiling. This orchestra does not love this music! Personally, I think tomorrow and the next day will be much better. People were tired tonight. This music is so dense, and Simon worked us hard in the general rehearsal.

There are no rules about which of the three concerts the Berlin Philharmonic give of each programme in the Philharmonie is the most powerful. 'It's different every time,' Olaf Maninger tells me.

It can be that the first one is the best and the most exciting, and then the second one is more difficult. But then it's also good when you have had more time to get used to a piece or a repertoire, especially Sibelius. The third one is always the concert we broadcast live in our Digital Concert Hall, which makes it even more exciting. But look, I'm a professional musician, and the point is, when I'm out there in front of 2,400 people, I have to do my best all the time.

How does Maninger account for the differences between successive evenings, the fact that one performance can take off where another can still feel earthbound, despite the energy the players are giving to the music, the audience, and the conductor? 'There is the magic of the moment, of course, and then the public is important. I find the atmosphere with the audience unbelievably important.' Sitting where he does, in the front desk of the cellos, just to the right of the conductor, Olaf is in eye contact with a large percentage of the audience, and his charisma as a player makes him one of the most recognisable faces in the Berlin Philharmonic, someone through whom it's possible to read a whole performance if you were just to focus your attention on his playing.

We have three concerts, and three Berlin publics, but you can notice and experience a difference between them all. There are some evenings where you just enter the hall and know that every single member of the audience wants to experience something special in the next couple of hours. With that kind of expectation and atmosphere, there's no other possibility than that it will be an intense experience, that something special will happen. And everyone makes that happen – the audience as much as all of the orchestra.

On the Friday, the day of the second performance, the orchestra has the chance to relax during the day for the first time all week. And in the concert that night, there is a chemical reaction going on between Sibelius and the Berlin Philharmonic. The orchestra knows that last night was really the first time they had to experience this music fully, to know how the whole arc of the three symphonies felt in performance, to feel where the music is glacially slow, where it's gigantically quick, and to learn how to navigate between its musical and magnetic poles. There is no let-up of intensity, but the individual moments that were searingly impressive the night before seem now part of a grander design, the mysterious larger shapes of Sibelius's creative universe. The pauses between the chords at the end of the Fifth Symphony are not empty spaces but places that teem with the distilled essence of the previous half-hour's worth of music, somehow collapsed into the everything and nothing between these monuments of sound.

In the Sixth and Seventh Symphonies, the effect of this alignment between the energy of the Berlin Philharmonic's playing and the experience of Sibelius's music is still more overwhelming. This is a new Sibelius, a vision of the composer searched out with the laser-like intensity of the Berlin Philharmonic's playing, one in which 'cold, pure water' is replaced with rivers of lava and emotion. If you look at the end of the Seventh Symphony in the score, the music seems to clinch a resolution in C major, an affirmation of life and order in the face of the density and diversity of the rest of the symphony. But all is not as it seems. The journey on which Sibelius, Rattle, and the Berlin Philharmonic take us in the symphony encompasses as many moods and as much drama as a Mahler symphony, but compresses it all into a musical black hole that lasts just twenty minutes. Rattle describes the end of the piece as 'almost like a scream'.

It's the most depressed C major in all of musical literature. There's no other piece that ends in C major where you feel it's the end of the world. Look at how carefully he orchestrates it so that it doesn't sound like a victory, but as something you reach on the edge of death. You finally reach C major – and it's over. It should be a struggle for the strings to achieve this last note with their last bit of energy.

I never imagined that this was possible, but Rattle is right. The Berlin Philharmonic release an expressive violence in the final bars of the Seventh Symphony. The music is played by each musician wringing the last scintilla of sound from their instrument in the symphony's last two notes. Each player uses their own technique to achieve this ultimate instrumental intensity, so that the final tableau after the sound has died away, in the moment before the applause starts, is a crazy geometry of arms, elbows, hands, and violins, violas, and bows, instead of a neat uniformity. The very end of the piece tears at the limits of instrumental possibility as well as at the limits of Sibelius's symphonic structure. It is a congruence of two of the most concentrated phenomena in musical culture: the dangerous viscerality of the Berlin Philharmonic, and the white-hot compression of Sibelius's music.

And at the absolute centre of both, just as he is physically at the centre of the Philharmonie, is Simon Rattle. The combination of his command of the music's architecture with his technical and personal communicativeness as a conductor has given this performance its transcendence. Rattle lets the players build Sibelius's climaxes apparently without his intervention, but at the same time, he controls and moulds their journey through this music. Members of the orchestra may say that theirs is the greater responsibility for what happens in their concerts, but the truth is, this orchestra would never have chosen this music to play without Rattle's ambition and vision for these symphonies, without his insistence that the Sibelius symphonies should be at the core of what these players do, alongside Brahms, Beethoven, and Bruckner.

It's no wonder that when I see Rattle in the wood and green velvet-clad room that Herbert von Karajan designed for himself backstage at the Philharmonie, about twenty yards from the conductor's podium, he looks so drained. I catch him at the interval of the concert, blundering in on him alone with a large glass of *Apfelschorle*, that uniquely refreshing and uniquely Germanic fizzy-apple concoction, and was struck by how small and how lonely he looked. I blurt something to him about these two gigantic edifices of music and orchestra coming together, and how spectacular the performance of the Fifth Symphony was. His response is disarming in its modesty. 'Well, let's hope we can keep it going for the second half.'

That image of Rattle haunted me, vulnerable without his musicians around him, a figure alone and apart despite the huge forces that he unleashed in the Philharmonie that evening. It was a reminder of how fragile and complex are the factors that enable concerts of this life-altering quality: the story of Sibelius and Germany and the orchestra's previous relationship with the music, the times of difficulty that Rattle and the players have been through together, the sense of continual friction that is this orchestra and conductor's curse but which also produces the Berlin Phil's indelible place in musical culture, the hundreds of individual stories of personal achievement, crisis, and transcendence that lie just beneath the surface of the orchestra, and the paradoxical isolation of Rattle's position as somebody they simultaneously regard as essential and dispensable.

The third concert was the most technically polished of them all, but I had the sense that the orchestra thought that they could trump even the level of the previous evening by exaggerating the extremes of their music-making, and the performance felt forced in comparison to the Friday. Orchestra and composer were once again separate entities, for all Rattle's attempts to lash them together. But in the whole sweep of these concerts, Rattle completed what Karajan started in the 1960s. These performances were a vindication of Rattle's belief in the essentialness of Sibelius's music, a stunning proof that these symphonies could be part of the orchestra's DNA, and the most important effort in a generation to surmount the baseless prejudice against the composer in Germany. They were also a realisation of the potential, and the limits, of the relationship between Rattle and the orchestra. Rattle's advocacy of Sibelius will never be enough to convince every member of the Berlin

Philharmonic that they should love this 'depressive Finn'.
But as Stefan Schweigert says:

It was a fantastic chance to play all of these symphonies. But since
they are not in our usual repertoire, the conductor needs to have
unbelievable power to make the music live. And Simon has this
way of creating a huge arc in his performances, connecting the
beginning of the piece with the end. Last night, it felt so good
with these pieces. The music was a living organism that was
changing all the time. It had an unbelievable energy.

Rattle's victory in these concerts was really Sibelius's. His
final gesture in the Philharmonie was to hold up the score
of the Seventh Symphony to the audience – to an extra-
loud cheer from 2,440 people who were already on their
feet. 'The worst composer in the world'? Not any longer
in Berlin.

5

Iván Fischer
Budapest Festival Orchestra

It starts with something I have never experienced outside youth orchestras I have played in and seen at work. In the upstairs room of an old cinema on the Pest side of the Danube, the Budapest Festival Orchestra is beginning its rehearsal. There are over a hundred players crammed into the room, filling the space completely; their conductor, the fifty-eight-year-old Hungarian Iván Fischer, takes a single step through the door and he's up on his podium. What happens next is remarkable for its simplicity, its concentration, and its apparent naivety. Fischer asks the string players of his orchestra to play their open strings together. He tells them which to play and how loudly or quietly, and engineers a spare harmonic tapestry by combining the five notes available to him from the string section: C, G, D, A, and E. When orchestras tune, it's usually up to the players themselves to take responsibility for tuning after the oboist plays an A, and the players calibrate their intonation with the finest microtonal adjustments of their individual strings. But here in Budapest, the players are led through their tuning by their conductor. The ritual is startling because it's both an invitation for the musicians to listen to one another, to hear how their instrument resonates with those of their desk partner and section, and also a conducted exercise in which their choice of how to tune, how to balance with one another, is taken by the conductor rather than by the players themselves. As Fischer explains to his musicians – intermittently translating from Hungarian into English for the benefit of the handful of non-native players – this exercise is for 'the fine tuning, the narrowing of the fifths', the interval between each of the strings of the violins, violas, and cellos.

Players in other professional orchestras might think instead that this was unnecessarily didactic spoon-feeding. In the context of a youth orchestra or even a semi-professional ensemble, there would be nothing extraordinary about it: eccentric, maybe, but not unexpected. But when the players have known each other for up to a quarter of a century, and when the orchestra is internationally famous as Hungary's most celebrated classical-music export, it's a surprise. The atmosphere seems more like that of a schoolroom than a place of professional music-making. Yet the effect of this exploratory intonation-improvisation is weirdly musical, as Fischer asks the violas and cellos to sustain their low C while the violins harmonise above them with their G and E strings, slowly creating a sonorous C major chord, a moment which Fischer asks his musicians to sustain and meditate upon. It's as if Arvo Pärt were improvising with a live orchestra.

And the apparent didacticism continues. It's not just the strings that are put through their paces. Fischer says: 'Bach', and the orchestra turns to blue-covered folders on their music stands. 'Let's explore the piano range of the instruments,' he says to the wind and brass players. And after the principal oboist plays a cursory A, the musicians of the Budapest Festival Orchestra softly play a Bach chorale, one among hundreds of four-part versions of Lutheran hymn tunes that Bach made throughout his life. It's music that has been used since the mid-eighteenth century as a testing ground for music students learning the theory of harmony. The chorales are touchstones of how one chord should flow into the next, how the internal voices of a harmony need to be satisfying, logical, and expressive lines in their own right. In Budapest, these tiny, exemplary harmony lessons are used for the woodwind and brass players for the most prosaic reason of staying in tune with one another. And Fischer also wants them to understand how the individual players' timbres and styles of playing should blend together. 'Don't give too much now, we are finding each other in each group. I am exploring how we will sound together.' The strings join in for the final cadence of each little performance, thickening the harmony when Fischer tells them in which key the chorale finishes. They play three different chorales with different articulations, exploring how Bach's micro-masterpieces highlight sometimes the middle voices, played by the clarinets and the horns; sometimes the bass instruments, the trombones, tuba, and bass clarinet; as well as the highest voice, the chorale melody in the flutes and oboes.

In the eighteenth century, entire musical forms, the prelude and the toccata, were derived from the way musicians would explore their instruments, especially the unreliable, variously tuned keyboard instruments of the time, to sound out the range and expressive possibilities of what they had at their disposal. It was a way of tuning themselves into a performance before the serious business of the fugue, the sonata, or the improvisation, got under way. That's what Iván Fischer is doing with the Budapest Festival Orchestra at the start of every day's rehearsal, testing out his instrument before he plays it. And then, after ten minutes of

orchestral chorale practice, he says, 'OK – Mahler now.'
And the orchestra begins the epic, thunderous first movement of Mahler's Sixth Symphony.

Bach's warm-up chorales won't feature in the concert
programmes the orchestra will play in a week's time, in
Budapest's new concert hall, MUPA, as part of their annual
Mahler Festival. The Sixth Symphony is the main work,
along with a new cello concerto by Sicilian composer and
cellist Giovanni Sollima; there are also staged performances
of Hans Krása's children's opera *Brundibár*, with a cast of
Hungarian schoolkids. These are the blue-riband performances of the orchestra's season in Hungary, the opening of
their musical year, and the latest manifestation of Fischer
and the orchestra's long-term association with Mahler's
music. But it's their association with each other that is the
defining feature of their music-making. This is, above all,
Fischer's orchestra. The story of its foundation is enmeshed
with the recent history of Hungary, and watching the
orchestra in the autumn of 2009, during celebrations for
the twentieth anniversary of the fall of the Iron Curtain,
reinforces how strongly the orchestra's life is bound up
with the way Budapest and the whole country has changed
and developed in the last couple of decades.

The orchestra's very existence in its early years seems
almost unbelievable in the context of Hungary's authoritarian regime and the bureaucratic strictness with which
the musical life of the communist state was run. The orchestra was founded in 1983 by Fischer and pianist-conductor
Zoltán Kocsis – who would subsequently have a creative
falling-out, making the Budapest Festival Orchestra the
sole dominion of Fischer – with a combination of musical

and institutional idealism. The clue is in 'Festival'. The idea was to create an independent ensemble that would not rely on the machinery of the communist musical institutions, bureaucratic behemoths like the National Cultural Fund (which still survives today, coordinating Budapest's musical life, albeit without the all-embracing power over artistic policy it had before independence). Coming together for a handful of concert series each year, Fischer and Kocsis were able to create an ensemble of Hungary's finest instrumentalists, who were paid entirely through private money, but also had none of the usual rights accorded to orchestral musicians. Since this was, effectively, a luxury pick-up band of players who convened for these concerts, there was no need for the committees, unions, or players' representative councils that are commonplace in any full-time orchestra elsewhere in the world.

The problem was that the Budapest Festival Orchestra was too successful for its own good, because of the quality of its concerts and what it symbolised for Hungarians. Fischer says:

It created a sensation in the 1980s, because everybody in the city was behind us. I remember taxi drivers, shopkeepers, and hairdressers asking me: are you going to survive? What's going to happen to the Budapest Festival Orchestra? We were a model of individual initiative, so the question was, could we survive as competition to the state orchestras, and would the state tolerate us?

Whatever the regime's feelings about Fischer and Kocsis's private musical enterprise, the orchestra survived until the fall of the Berlin Wall. 'In which we played a funny part, actually,' Fischer says. In August 1989, East German refugees had taken asylum in the West German embassies of Central European cities, including Prague and Budapest, having tried to escape over the border from humanitarian camps. The four hundred who were in Budapest were invited to an all-Beethoven programme Fischer was giving with the orchestra at the Congress Centre, the largest hall in town. 'It was a bold gesture to invite them,' Fischer remembers, 'but it came out of a mistake.'

We forgot to sell one of the balconies for this concert, so I said we should invite the refugees. After all, this was a concert of music by their composer, Beethoven, and they had nothing better to do. A West German diplomatic delegation came to my dressing room to say what a good gesture this was, because they could inform the refugees about what was going to happen the next day. After the concert, the East Germans agreed that they would go to this picnic on the Austro-Hungarian border, right beside the fence. That was the historical occasion when the Hungarian government opened the fence and let six hundred people go into Austria, including the four hundred who had come to our concert. And that was the start of the whole process, the beginning of the end of the Iron Curtain. I remember exactly when it was: our concert was on 18 August, the picnic, the 19th. But funnily enough, it was not our intention to bring this political cascade of events – just to ask them to come to a concert!

The Budapest Festival Orchestra's symbolic role as an independent institution, a herald of a wider political freedom, meant that the orchestra was an important part of Hungary's cultural life after 1992, and the establishment of the country's full independence.

In the new, democratic leadership, it was natural for the new mayor of Budapest to think, here is this very popular non-communist orchestra, let's make this the main orchestra of the city of Budapest. We were fortunate with this first generation of leadership, since they really wanted to do something cultural which wasn't just taking over the communist institutions. But that was only the first wave of enthusiasm – which faded.

Yet there was a major problem. The Budapest Festival Orchestra was not full-time. To turn this pick-up band into a permanent organisation and the city's main orchestra would require an injection of state money. Even more importantly, it would mean changing the culture of the ensemble: instead of the best players from the rest of Hungary's orchestras and elsewhere coming together to focus on individual projects, with all the excitement of doing something out of the ordinary, the orchestra would have to become a regular, everyday, concert-giving orchestra, and the players would have to leave their other jobs to focus on their music-making with Fischer (Kocsis officially left the orchestra in 1997).

'I was partly forced into this change,' Fischer says.

By 1992 there were anyway more and more demands on the orchestra. Since it was becoming more and more successful with international tours and recordings, it was getting to the stage where I couldn't always guarantee the quality of the players. Since they all had jobs all over the place, I was dependent on other orchestras releasing people to play for me. We had signed a recording contract with Phillips, which made for even more of a headache in terms of finding who would play. So when the offer came from the City of Budapest to subsidise us – at a very modest level, but enough to make it work – it was a relief, since I could then book people on a long-term basis. But the decision wasn't an easy one. Because I was very aware of the threat that it would become a normal orchestra, an idea I absolutely wanted to resist. That was, and is, my greatest fear: that this would become a normal, everyday orchestra.

Fischer's concern was to maintain the enthusiasm and commitment of a project-based festival orchestra in the context of an ensemble that would now meet every week.

In the early days, we had a very high spirit, but we also had the insecurity that comes from not knowing, say, which of your flute players are going to be free for a planned concert or recording. So when we turned to this second phase, it was a wonderful mental challenge, how to keep the festival orchestra spirit with the set-up of a permanent structure.

What Fischer did was create strategies for keeping the motivation of the individual musicians as high as possible.

There are a large number of subtle things that help avoid a sense of routine. That's our biggest fear, that routine which becomes apathy and jadedness, which I think somehow is a virus that affects most orchestras in the world. People say that the biggest problem in orchestral culture today is that everything has become globalised, that there are no national schools of different sound any more. But my observation is that the main problem is apathy, a lack of emotional involvement in the playing. So these strategies are designed to avoid that.

Fischer limits the full orchestra to working for just over half of the year, and he ensures friendly rivalry within the ranks with an annual concerto competition, in which members of the orchestra compete for a handful of slots to play as a soloist with their colleagues. In addition, musicians are asked to lead chamber orchestra projects, and the string players regularly rotate seats in the orchestra. The format of the orchestra's concerts varies greatly too, from standard concerts at the Liszt Academy or Budapest's new hall, to children's concerts and 'surprise concerts', in which no programme is announced and the audience wait with bated breath to see what Fischer and the orchestra will play, and still other occasions when the listeners in their seats have the chance to vote on which piece they want to hear next in a programme. These are all ways to avoid 'the collective feeling of the orchestra being mentally tired', Fischer says.

However they achieve it administratively, the strategy works when it comes to their performances. The concerts that Fischer and the Budapest Festival Orchestra have given on tour over the last couple of decades have been among the most memorable and distinctive of any conductor-orchestra partnership anywhere. There is a sense of adventure about every programme I have seen them play, like a Mozart Requiem that re-imagined the sound-world of Mozart's posthumous masterpiece by placing the three trombones all around the rest of the orchestra to communicate better with the chorus, and the basset clarinets and bassoons right in front of the conductor's podium, creating a tenebrous continuo section for Mozart's most progressive but simultaneously most baroque work. The same spirit of not taking any interpretive decisions for granted coursed through Dvořák's Cello Concerto and Bruckner's little-played Symphony no. 0. (The strange designation of the latter results from Bruckner's disappointment with the piece: he deemed it unworthy of a number or a place within his symphonic canon, and it was not premiered until after his death.)

Fischer's long arms seem to embrace his musicians when he invites them to play at the start of each piece, and with his aristocratically long baton – a curiosity among today's conductors, much more common in maestros of past generations, like Toscanini or Adrian Boult – he has a huge wing-span that seems to take in the whole stage, the whole concert hall. He told me that his job as a conductor is 'to search for the truth – like an eagle after its prey', and he does a good impression of a musical raptor on the podium, especially in works that are at the heart of his repertoire with the orchestra, like Bartók's unstoppable *Music for Strings, Percussion, and Celesta*. But the essential vitality of what he and his orchestra create is not only the Dionysian dimension of earthy, irresistible rhythm – although they were responsible for one of the most thrilling, danceable, and lyrical performances of Stravinsky's *Rite of Spring* I've ever heard. There is also a sense of naturalness of flow, and of song, that made *Das Lied von der Erde* a draining but life-affirming experience when Fischer performed Mahler's song-symphony on yet another of the orchestra's tours.

But if there's an edge-of-the-seat feeling to the Budapest Festival Orchestra's performances, there's a mundane as well as musical reason for it. This is an orchestra without any job security. Each player is on a two-year contract which is renewed at Fischer's discretion. 'We have basically created a pre-war situation here,' he says.

'There are no committees and no unions. This decision was taken by the founding musicians by a democratic vote. They wanted quality, competitiveness with no secured jobs. This first generation of enthusiastic young musicians had experienced the usual system of committees and trade unions with other orchestras and they wanted a change. They wanted an orchestra in which only music and quality matter. Their vote is still binding today, after twenty-five years, and nobody regrets it.'

There is advice from the players: whether on the artistic side, or the question of who plays in the orchestra, but the final decision is mine. But what I find is that instead of an American-style 'tenure' system [meaning jobs for life, with the pensions, health insurance, and other perks that go with being a musician in one of the big orchestras in the States] is that there is no necessity to fire people with our system. It practically never happens that I have to kick somebody out. But what does happen with us is that people maybe play better in the later part of their musical lives than they do when they have total job security, because they have to keep up their own standard of playing to stay in the orchestra. However, it's absolutely not necessary to come in with an axe and threaten people, because they somehow motivate themselves.

There's a direct connection between the atmosphere of taking nothing for granted when Fischer and the orchestra are on stage, and the way the orchestra is set up as an institution, since the players can't be complacent about their futures. And neither can they be complacent about the musical direction of the orchestra. It's not just that they don't decide programmes: even when a concert has started, they don't always know what's going to happen. In Mahler's Sixth Symphony, one of the biggest decisions a conductor has to make is in which order to play the two central movements. Mahler himself originally intended the scherzo to be played before the Andante, but during rehearsals for the first performance in Essen in 1906, he changed his mind, placing the slow movement second and the scherzo third, before the gigantic, half-hour finale, one of the most imposing and complex single spans of music in the orchestral repertoire. Mahler's intentions during his lifetime seem to have been clear, since he requested that a second edition be published with the movements in this new order, and that an erratum slip notifying readers of the change should be inserted into any unsold copies of the first edition. He only ever conducted the symphony with the slow movement second. And yet, Erwin Ratz's critical edition of the Sixth Symphony reverts to Mahler's original idea, saying (without apparent evidence) that the composer changed his mind a second time, putting the scherzo first. This may or may not have been based on a telegram that Alma, then the composer's widow, sent the conductor Willem Mengelberg in 1919, telling him to play the symphony in that sequence. Whatever its provenance, and however much it seems to go against Mahler's express intentions, the idea has stuck, and many conductors continue to play the scherzo second and then the andante.

Most conductors feel the need to favour one order or the other, and stick with their choice through their careers. But not Fischer. In the three performances of the symphony in Budapest, he experimented with both of these different musical and psychological paths through the piece. You would have thought he would have told the orchestra before each concert which order would be adopted for that performance. In fact, after the first movement finishes, Fischer mouths to the orchestra 'scherzo' or 'andante', giving the players just a heartbeat to turn to the right page in their scores. It's a split-second musical judgement, the single most important choice any conductor or orchestra has to make in this symphony – and Fischer leaves it to chance, as if improvising with the gigantic building blocks of Mahler's music. It's testament to the strength of his relationship with his players that they tolerate this aleatoric approach to interpretation – and relish the quality of live-in-the-moment excitement that Fischer wants to create.

But Fischer's complete control of his orchestra is not, he says, at the expense of the individual members of the ensemble, or their well-being. In no other rehearsal room of a symphony orchestra that I have seen in Europe does each member have their own framed photograph on the wall, a hall of fame past which the musicians walk a few times a day, on the way to buy coffee and cakes in the rehearsal breaks. In the middle of the wall, Fischer's face is just one among many, valued with the same space as any of his musicians.

I look after them almost as a rabbi would look after a Hasidic community. My main concern is that they are looked after well so they can concentrate on the music. To make music one needs to be joyous and have an environment of mutual trust. We have an atmosphere of a happy family here. If I notice any sign of apathy or unhappiness, I tak to them, try to help and if possible ease the disturbing circumstances. And there are things that are easier for a leader to do than for a colleague. Say, for example, if somebody doesn't play the trumpet very well. There are many ways of trying to bring that person back to good-quality playing. You can talk, you can rehearse, you can release them from certain difficult parts. I do all that. But at a certain point, if it comes to the place where you have to say, sorry, you really damage the quality of this orchestra, maybe you should not be first trumpet with us; maybe only third trumpet in certain works – or maybe not play at all – that is easier to say, and to do, for a leader than a colleague. Imagine saying that to someone you've spent thirty years with, who you sit on the bus with, who you socialise with. This is tough. A leader has to take responsibility for doing these things. An orchestra should be led, in a conscientious and responsible way. Now, of course people talk to me about certain issues – a musician comes to me and says we should rehearse this piece a little bit more, another says, why don't we play more Schumann? I usually follow their advice. It's like in a family. But they need to be led by a music director.

This conductor–orchestra relationship has lasted for twenty-five years. So they know me. And I know them. And somehow this takes the orchestra to a new level. I notice this when they work with guest conductors [who are, naturally, picked by Fischer himself] and when I go and guest-conduct other orchestras. In both cases, it seems like suddenly I or they go back to a 'getting acquainted' level, a complicated web of politeness and misunderstandings. But when you are working with a good friend who has been in your life for a quarter of a century and who you know completely inside out, you don't have to say the unnecessary things. You can read the mind of the other person. It's just an entirely other level of communication that we have here.

*   *   *

In the cramped rehearsal room, a percussionist who looks like a body-builder and whose biceps are bulging out of his T-shirt is preparing his instrumentarium for the finale of Mahler's Sixth Symphony. It's appropriate that this Hungarian man-mountain has at his disposal the biggest and most brutal instrument on stage: a hollow wooden coffer, about six feet long and two feet wide. It's the least sophisticated musical instrument in the room, a huge sounding board that he will twice hit with a hammer in Mahler's last movement. This is extreme percussion-playing: he will need to swing a sledgehammer over his head, and bring it down exactly in time with the more than hundred other players in the orchestra. In any performance of Mahler Six, these are moments of huge theatrical as well as musical tension. Will the percussionist get the hammer-blow in time? Will this huge Hungarian break the wooden box? (That isn't what Mahler wants: he is after a hollow, resonant boom rather than a sharp, life-endangering splintering.)

It's Fischer's job to lead these huge forces in the less-than-ideal acoustics of the rehearsal room.

He says that the ideal for his orchestra is that 'we start work where others finish': what he means is that his musicians should be technically prepared enough so that the only considerations of the rehearsal period are to do with the musical, expressive, and emotional world of the music. That means that much of what he says to his players is concerned with colour, spirit, and metaphor. On the page, the opening of Mahler's slow movement could hardly be simpler: a serene, melancholic song in the first violins, accompanied by the gentlest of harmonic supports in the second violins and violas, a lullaby-like rocking in the cellos, and soft, pizzicato heartbeats in the double basses. Mahler's expressive instruction, *zart, aber ausdrucksvoll* ('tenderly, but full of expression'), suggests to the first violins that this melody is about something more than its notes. Outwardly, the movement is full of a tender love music, but the theme is shot through with minor-key inflections, dark shadows of doubt that disturb the music's radiance. Somehow, the first violins' playing has to suggest all of this in just a few seconds. But that's easier said than done, and Fischer starts and restarts his orchestra a handful of times before he finds the right expressive register. After the first time, he throws a mock clowning fit of physical theatrics, stopping the orchestra by launching his baton in the air, pirouetting a full 360 degrees, and catching it again. His frustration is to do with the chaos that's created when there's a complete disconnect between how he knows the music should go and the sound his players actually produce. The second time he says the music needs to be 'quieter, quieter'; the third, 'for me, it is too *con moto* [with movement], it needs to flow, but be less clear'; after the fourth, he claps out the music's tempo 'because if it becomes completely mechanical inside you, then we can trust each other enough to move'. The fifth time, he says, 'whisper, whisper, whisper! It should be like a dream, a beautiful dream . . . yes: that is the pianissimo, it's beautiful now.' Later in the movement, Fischer demands a different colour, a transformation of the main tune that he says should sound like Bach: 'It's like baroque music here, a different style, like polyphony.' But there are technical remarks, too, like the place where Mahler's colouristic imagination gives an important melody to the contrabassoon, with a low, rumbling minor-key transfiguration of the opening theme. It's a moment that reveals the psychological genius of Mahler's orchestration: the tune has descended from the serenity of the first few bars in the first violins to the gloomy ruminations of the lowest instruments of the orchestra. Fischer has to remind the rest of the orchestra to respect the contrabassoon's moment in the spotlight: 'The high notes have to be so precise because the most soloistic instrument is the double-bassoon.' There's a bit of baton-biting, too, another of Fischer's physicalisations of his frustration: during the slow movement's climactic, cowbell-festooned peroration, the violas and cellos get out of sync with their colleagues, prompting Fischer to stare at them, baton in mouth, in exasperation.

The grotesque cavalcade of characters of the scherzo movement gives Fischer more chance to set his imagination free. When the players spiral out of control on the first run-through after just a couple of pages of the movement, he mimes a drowning man flailing for his survival as Mahler's symphony melts into a musical maelstrom. The trombones are asked to play a particular passage of slippy chromaticism 'not too much like a snake'; another moment in the low brass where Mahler virtually quotes the sliding semitones of Fafner – the giant who is transformed into a dragon in Wagner's *Ring* cycle – gives Fischer the opportunity to do his impression of a mythical fire-breathing creature on the podium for a few bars. When Mahler's music clambers out of this cauldron of dissonance into sunnier, major-key climes in the strings, Fischer says the moment should be 'like plucking eyebrows'. It's a description that's both a metaphorical suggestion of how the violins should think about the character of the music, and a brilliant physical characterisation of the technique they should use to play it: 'the notes have to be as short as possible.' There's a cast of thousands of musical characters in this thirteen-minute movement, which includes the scatological as well as the seraphic: Fischer looks over at the horns and mimes a bout of explosive nausea; it's not a comment on their performance so far, but a violently expressive indication of how he wants their next entry to sound. Underneath some grunting clarinets, the horns duly oblige with some seasick-making semitones, complete with dynamics swaying woozily from loud to soft and back again.

Another bite of the baton signifies a break in the rehearsal. Fischer and the orchestra played and recorded Mahler's Sixth only a few years ago. I ask him whether he is consciously trying to change his interpretation this time around.

I don't even like the word interpretation. What we try to do is the piece – just that, itself! Of course interpretation comes into it because I take a certain tempo and not another one, but that could be because our new young principal horn player takes a little more time over a particular phrase, or a clarinet player rushes a little somewhere else. There's flexibility in the way I feel the music. In no way do I come with a complete idea and simply try to realise it with the orchestra. The whole thing grows throughout the rehearsal, because of what the orchestra is doing. The main idea of the rehearsal is not that the musicians should just deliver on my instructions. It is about developing together. And because of all of those factors, maybe it will sound a little bit different than last time. I'm not aware of that, though. We may have played it those years ago, but we have to start all over again for these performances.

There are contradictions in what Fischer says. Whether he likes it or not, no conductor can escape the paradox that however much they focus on 'the piece itself', what results has to be a one-off performance that amounts to a provisional realisation of the possibilities of the piece at that time and place – a definition perilously close to an 'interpretation'. In any case, Fischer wants each perform-ance to be a consecration of the moment of its creation, a unique musical happening that is dependent on the coming together of the infinite variables of performance, from how well the orchestra is playing to how he is feeling, from the atmosphere in the hall to the attentiveness of the audience. Unlike Mariss Jansons, however, he does not come to his rehearsals in search of a translation of his ideas about the piece into sound. Fischer wants there to be a two-way pro-cess of communication between him and his players:

It's not just that a conductor must inspire orchestras: I think orchestras should also inspire conductors! That's why most of the time I try to say things in rehearsal that are not as clear as instructions; they are more like suggestions or metaphors. I'm trying to open up possibilities, so it's about saying I want more colour or character in a certain place rather than 'more crescendo here, more accent there'. I want to involve their creativity in the process.

Despite the top-down autocracy of Fischer's administrative and artistic leadership, he wants his rehearsals to be collaborations between him and his players. He expects his players to give their complete engagement to every second of the journey from rehearsal to performance. There is the narrowest gap of any orchestra in this book between the Budapest Festival Orchestra's attitude and energy in rehearsal and what happens in the concerts. 'If there is a certain switched-off attitude from the players, then you feel like you're fighting against a wall, and you can very easily lose your motivation. The spirit of our rehearsals comes from the emotional involvement of everybody involved. And of course that means I get a lot from the players.' That's borne out in the rehearsal room, even down to the smallest details: at a place in the first movement where Mahler's expressive markings suggest how the music should move 'always peacefully, without hurrying', Fischer says to his musicians, 'this place is a collective rubato; if everyone feels those changes of tempo, I will follow you.'

Fischer's ideal of what rehearsal should be is different from that of Valery Gergiev, Mariss Jansons, or Simon Rattle.

I think this idea which a lot of orchestras and conductors who work together for a long time have developed, that the rehearsal is where you save your energy, and then, as the Viennese say, *es wird schon gehen* – it'll be all right on the night – is completely wrong. For me it's not even arguable. It's pure laziness. I'll try to explain in rational terms: it reminds me very strongly of how an actor works. If an actor did the same thing, taking the

rehearsal period easily and then on the night, putting on a special energy, then he or she would come up with gimmicks and
superficial clichés rather than a real artistic development of the
character. What I recognise as artistic development is precisely
described in the Stanislawski method of acting. You should try to
understand the role, and then understand the difference between
the character you're playing and who you really are. And then
you constantly try and narrow the gap between yourself, your
situation, and the role. You have to make a journey into the
part.

What we have to do in rehearsal is experiment with the character of the music. It's a question of, say, how much salt, how
much pepper, how much sugar to add, how much adrenalin! But
finding the balance of all of these things wouldn't work if we just
saved all that for what happens on the night. If you were to do
that, you would only get musical gimmicks and clichés, because
you haven't really gone through a proper musical journey. I
really disagree with that way of working.

There's a combination of discipline and imagination that
defines the Budapest Festival Orchestra's rehearsals. In one
three-hour rehearsal for the winds and brass alone, a piccolo player has nothing to play for the entire time, because
Fischer only rehearses the first three movements of the
symphony, in which she has nothing to play. But there is
no hint of frustration from her, or any of the musicians.
With the full orchestra, Fischer has occasionally to shush
his musicians up, but even when the brass or percussion
players have to count dozens of bars' rest before their
next entry, or when Fischer rehearses the string section
alone, there is no crackle of restlessness in the room. Gabi
Karácsony, Fischer's personal assistant says: 'You are not
allowed to read or do anything else in this orchestra during the rehearsal.' That sounds like an orchestral rule or

stricture, but in practice, it seems like collective will and concentration.

And Fischer's zaniness on the podium helps too: the orchestra is energised by the imagery he uses to get an idea across and his exaggerated physicality. One of the percussionists, who has been working with him for the past four years, says he is attracted to musicians like him who are a little bit 'crazy'. There's a reason no one wants to read newspapers in Fischer's rehearsals. 'It's never boring here. It's like a philosophical position: if you are bored, don't do it. It's a mistake in life to be bored. I like very much Iván's way of playing music here, his style, his whole approach. And the fact that he likes to take crazy guys like me and my colleagues in the orchestra.' Fischer's music-making does not admit the possibility of a laissez-faire attitude to rehearsal or performance. 'Music is an emotional art, whether you like it or not. It's highly charged. And it doesn't work if you perform it in a detached way.'

If that's true of any piece of music, it's axiomatic in the last movement of Mahler's Sixth, the longest, most complex, most dramatic finale in any of his symphonies. It is a gigantic journey through a doomed musical universe, which sounds as if the rest of the symphony were being filtered through a disturbing, distorting prism. The melodies and the characters from previous movements are here heightened and transfigured, and the huge climaxes in the thirty-five-minute movement symbolise the apotheosis of Mahler's musical hero. Mahler exposes whoever or whatever this unfortunate protagonist is – himself? the ideal of romantic love? the struggle of humanity against forces outside our control? – to a tortuous musical tornado from which there is no escape. At the very end of the symphony, the music creates for one last time the swirling, enveloping dreamscape that started the finale, but the hero finds only oblivion with the repetition of the fatalistic rhythm that has permeated the whole symphony, hammered out by two timpani players, and a defeated pizzicato in the strings.

It's music that is hard enough to listen to, let alone perform, but after nearly an hour of some of Mahler's densest music in the three movements before the finale even starts, there are real issues of stamina for all of the musicians, especially the wind and brass players (and even more so since the players will have to get through a forty-minute cello concerto in the first half before beginning the Mahler). During rehearsals, Fischer has taken himself and his players to extremes. The building on Selmeci Street in Budapest shakes to its foundations at the climactic moments of the final movement; I worry that the bicep-clad percussionist may have the power to demolish the whole place when he first brings his hammer down, perfectly in sync with Fischer's downbeat. Even Fischer seems surprised by what he has unleashed, collapsing into his score after this climax with feigned terror and aural assault.

There's a strange feeling at the end of the last rehearsal. As soon as the final note of the Sixth Symphony has disappeared into silence, after its dry, pizzicato death-knell, there's the usual fiddling about that all orchestral players indulge in – the bass clarinettist noodles around his instrument, the strings make that strange improvised chaos that comes from fifty musicians simultaneously trying out different passages of their parts. But there's something else. It's impossible to go through the finale of Mahler's Sixth without any emotional response. As a listener in that confined space in Selmeci, the experience was overwhelming, sonically as well as expressively. This was already a no-holds-barred performance of the piece. It just happened to be called a rehearsal. The players needed to diffuse the enormous tension in the music, and to remind themselves that Mahler's emotional abyss is something they have created, whose terrors they have to confront, but from whose brink they can finally step back – at least in the rehearsal. Having played the whole movement without a single stop for criticism or fine-tuning, Fischer gives his musicians a pep talk, at first in Hungarian, which he then translates for the non-Hungarophones in the orchestra – not least the guest leader, Philippe Aïche from the Orchestre de Paris.

This movement is so long, and sometimes I notice that some people become a little bit dizzy with it. It's such a wonderful long composition, probably the most amazing and *full* that has ever been written for a symphony orchestra. And if it ever crosses your mind that it is tiring, then the best way to play this movement is in a complete state of ecstasy. Play it from beginning to end as if you're in a trance. Then you can forget about the fact that it's tiring, and then at the end, you will feel like you can start the whole thing again, without a problem.

Fischer wants to induce in his players, and his audience, a collective hypnosis in the course of Mahler's huge symphony. And the way he leaves his musicians with this state of being in their imaginations before the performance reminds me of something else he tells me about his role. He compares conducting to being a basketball coach:

You must have seen these smaller people, next to the players, who run around the side of the game, and write strategy on a board?

I think they are great conductors! Because they are absolutely fully involved for the best result of their team, and it's not about being nice and satisfying all the players, they want the result. They want what is going to make their team win, not what is going to make everyone happy. And that is what a conductor has to do, too.

Fischer's pep talk before the performance of Mahler Six is both a coach's final exhortation to his team before they get on the field of play, to help keep their stamina going over the whole ninety minutes, and an acute psychological observation that gives them a clue to thesurreally powerful vision he wants to communicate in the performances.

*   *   *

For all the focus of their preparation, neither Fischer nor the players can guarantee that their performance will generate the expressive power they need to realise the full range of Mahler's musical universe. The postmodernist barn of the MUPA's auditorium is bedecked with a gigantic portrait of Mahler, directly above Fischer's podium. From my seat at the back of the hall, the portrait is slightly skew-whiff, and in the first concert, that's true of the performance, too. Fischer plays the symphony in the published order, saying 'scherzo!' to his musicians after the first movement. Maybe it's the sheer effort of all that A minor tempestuousness, or the after-effects of having had a morning rehearsal on the day of the concert, or a delayed reaction to the long and turgid cello concerto in the first half, but the performance does not have the same intensity as the music had in that cramped rehearsal room.

That's a necessary danger of Fischer's philosophy. If you give all you have, all the time, the question is, what's left

for the concerts? The answer comes in the second performance. Fischer changes the order of movements from the
night before, playing the slow movement second, but that's
only the biggest difference from the first performance.
From the opening bar, the music is energised by a collective
will from the orchestra to make all the characters, colours,
and contrasts that Fischer had developed in the week of
rehearsals as vivid as possible. From the vice-like grip of
the implacable repeated notes at the start of the first movement, the symphony creates an energy that is impossible to
resist. It's a performance of gigantic structural momentum,
a vindication of Mahler's self-conscious classical preten-
sions in this piece. More than any other of his symphonies,
this piece takes the forms of the conventional nineteenth-
century symphony and stretches them to breaking point.
But it's also a thrilling existential drama, in which symphonic form is transmuted into psychological experience.
The immediacy of the relationship between Fischer and
his players releases something I have never heard in this
music before. For those ninety minutes in MUPA, there
is no distance between us, the composer, the performers,
and the piece: the Sixth Symphony is a journey we go on
together, which Fischer and the players unflinchingly take
to ecstatic, tragic extremes. By the end of the finale, the
performance has created a trance that I find difficult to
escape. The terrifying reality of the music makes the world
of applause, of people, of social interaction after the concert
seem a hollow illusion. It takes hours before the trance – or
the truth – of Mahler's music recedes.

It's dangerous, all-consuming music-making. And it's
unrepeatable, at least in the short term: the third performance is a good impression of the gestures of the night before,

with all the surface intensity but without the transfiguring internal dynamism of the previous concert. After the concert, I ask Fischer why he had chosen a different order of movements for the second concert.

This goes back to the question of why Mahler changed the order in the first place. I have tried to imagine. Was it because the orchestra in the first performance couldn't characterise the scherzo well enough? The thing is, musicologically, structurally, the published order [Allegro–scherzo–Andante–finale] makes sense, in terms of the relationship between the movements, the way the scherzo uses the music of the opening movement, how the scherzo ends softly, which elides with the start of the slow movement, which then flows into the start of the finale. It all makes sense. But practically and musically, I feel that Mahler's performance order [Allegro–Andante–scherzo–finale] is more digestible for an audience and for the players too. The contrasts between the movements make the whole symphony less tiring. I cannot say that one solution is right and the other one is wrong. On one night I choose for the perfect structure, another night for digestibility because it feels necessary.

Fischer agrees that the second performance 'was for me the best. It has to do with a lot of things: how fresh I am, how tired I am, little things, personal differences'. Fischer's musical philosophy of a hundred per cent – or a hundred and ten per cent, to use the sports coach's cliché – commitment means that the finest physical or psychological factors make the difference between a concert that reaches that rare but immediately recognisable place where there is no choice but to surrender to the musical experience, and the more mundane realm of the 'good performance'.

The crazy risk-taking on the concert platform and in the rehearsal room can only happen in a situation in which all of Fischer's players know him, trust him, respect him, and want to follow him on his journeys inside these pieces of music. But that quality of unquestioning respect for a conductor is rare among today's orchestras. For Fischer, it's a throwback to the era of the great autocratic figures of the earlier twentieth century:

It's crystal-clear to me when you look at the old films of the pre-war conductors, when you look at the faces of the musicians who play, that there is respect for, say, Arturo Toscanini, for Fritz Reiner, for Thomas Beecham, for Wilhelm Furtwängler, for Georg Szell. And when you look at them in rehearsal, you see that everyone stops and pays attention immediately. The conductor says something, and the musicians do it, without reservation. I think it's that authority and respect that created the magic of those recordings of the pre-war period.

Things are different now, Fischer says.

The present-day orchestra–conductor relationships in 'everyday' orchestras are a complicated mixture of resentment and respect. The respect might come from thinking, well, he's good at composer x's music, and not good at composer y. But sometimes there is open questioning from the players, who say, 'Why are we doing it in this way?' That sort of dissent is one of the major reasons why orchestral performances in general are losing their personality. What you end up with in that dissenting situation is a half-hearted performance: the conductor does one thing, and the orchestra follows, but only in a grudging way. What you end up with is a sort of neutral music-making. What we have today is a generation of conductors who are capable of beating very clearly, who always say the right thing, who never insult anybody, who take the right tempos – and that's about all they do. This is the type of conductor who is encouraged by the current system of so-called democracy in most conventional orchestras.

Fischer comes back to the issue of respect.

Think again about the pre-war generation: these conductors were the respected musicians of their communities. They could be nice guys, or tyrants – we hear that Hans Richter was a pleasure to work for, but that Gustav Mahler was a neurotic wreck – but they were the respected musicians of their music societies, and their countries. Of course it's a disaster if you have to work for somebody as difficult as Fritz Reiner, and you lose your job or have to take tranquilisers to get through it. One can understand why unions have been created to defend musicians – but there are strong side effects. The old conductors made no compromises about music. They were real musical leaders and orchestras followed them without reservations. In contrast, this modern type of conductor, this polished, nice guy who is nice to the players and is entertaining to the audience, is less respected musically and more respected because of his good manners. That's the difference between then and now.

So one of the dreams of the Budapest Festival Orchestra is to recreate a pre-war relationship between the players and their maestro. 'If you don't have that respect for the conductor, you can't play with complete commitment as a musician. Respect is the number one thing. If that's not there, you can only have an average performance of any piece of music.' I tell Fischer about the players of the Berlin Philharmonic, an orchestra he regularly guest conducts, and their collective view that they are bigger and better than any of their conductors.

I don't even understand what that means. The roles are so different, for one thing. But I think this is pure nonsense. An orchestra can have great qualities, technical qualities, and sensitive musicianship. But there are a hundred musicians with obvious differences! Because this particular art-form, the symphony orchestra, is a conducted art-form, there is one person whose job is to absorb the composition and to radiate the composition. His task is to make sure that there is a single, unified expression of the orchestra. Everyone must follow this one way of playing. The proof is that you cannot have a great performance from the combination of a great orchestra and a mediocre conductor. That's like having a Rolls-Royce with a mediocre driver. If that were the case, there could be no such thing as good concerts. For me, the only combination that makes sense is a very good orchestra which has complete, unreserved respect for a very good conductor. That is the only thing which leads to success. Nothing else.

Fischer has created a non-democratic throwback to his idealised version of the conductor–orchestra relationship, in which he calls the shots artistically and administratively, and the players go along with every decision he takes. The respect he commands from his players is based on a mix of mutual trust of each other's abilities and mutual distrust of reaching a plateau of routine or stability. In every concert, the musicians are playing for their right to continue to be members of the orchestra, and Fischer is doing all he can to ensure that the musical journeys they go on are always developing, always new. The Budapest Festival Orchestra is a thoroughly contemporary anachronism. Ironically, it's a model of the sort of unquestioned, top-down leadership from which the Hungarians fought so hard to be free in the late 1980s and early 1990s. Fischer argues:

The question of democracy in orchestras is: what would its purpose be? If you compare orchestral democracy with democracy in a society: the purpose of political democracy is that people should live well, peacefully, and reasonably happily, and that their voices should be heard. Life itself is the purpose. But in the case of an orchestra, great art, exceptional quality, and engaging listeners through that intensity and quality, are the ultimate purposes. And orchestral democracy can easily be influenced by the welfare interests of the musicians, and then you've lost the focus on highest possible quality. I don't think democracy is the best tool to achieve these artistic goals.

Formed in the last years of the Soviet regime as a symbol of what might be possible away from the yoke of the state in a privatised free market, the Budapest Festival Orchestra, in an independent and democratic Hungary, is an aberration: a partly state-sponsored example of artistic and organisational dictatorship, in which Fischer wields unquestioned authority over his players. And paradoxically, it is because of the unadulterated respect the musicians give to Fischer that they play with such freedom, such lack of restraint, such intensity, and such quality.

Fischer identifies one last, definitive problem in the culture of orchestral music-making:

It's the notion that music, musical performance, and the reality of having a full-time job don't really mesh. If you see music as your job, which sustains your family and gives you your livelihood, it inevitably leads to the apathy of the modern type of symphony orchestra. As a musician, you don't want to work for a Fritz Reiner-style tyrant, you want employment rights, things that defend your situation. But somehow music – musical quality – works best when the culture is more vulnerable – as vulnerable as the relationship between the coach and the football player, or the director and the actor in the freelance world, where everyone gives their utmost to make the best impression and do the best for the result. But I do agree that if you have spent your whole life learning the horn or the violin you should have a certain security, you should be able to have a normal life.

I do have an idea how this paradox could possibly be solved, but it would require far-reaching reforms. One would need to divert subsidy and donations from orchestras offering tenures to concert promoters who would engage the best orchestras. Musicians wouldn't earn less but there would be some competition in a flourishing freelance environment. Meanwhile our experiment here is an alternative to the usual system. It is up to the players. If they prefer tenure, they can go to join other orchestras. If they like our ambitious rules they can stay here. In fact we have lost two or three musicians in the past twenty-five years who left for safe jobs elsewhere, but the large majority stayed. There is a long list of musicians who would love to play here and they all say that there is a reputation of this orchestra being happier than other orchestras. Well, our musicians certainly smile more. We attract players who prefer the more risk-taking, entrepreneurial world of a freelance existence. What we are doing here is our little personal solution, where music matters more than welfare, but it is also an utterly human and caring organisation. It works for us: but I'm not saying it solves the problem for everyone.

Maybe not. But it's not just good for Fischer and his players: as those concerts showed, it's good for Mahler, too.

6

Claudio Abbado
Lucerne Festival Orchestra

There is such a thing as a loud silence, a silence that fills your being with a presence more tangible than the biggest orchestral tutti, more visceral than the grandest peroration. At the end of Mahler's Ninth Symphony at the KKL Concert Hall in Lucerne in 2010, the audience and musicians were held in a suspended animation that lasted fully three minutes after the final notes had finished, and those aching, etiolated appoggiaturas in the violas had melted into silence. But this was not a temporal space to be counted merely in the marking of clock time. The players of the Lucerne Festival Orchestra and their conductor, Claudio Abbado, had turned this symphony into a meditation on mortality that was both a riotous, violent celebration of life, in the vitality and dynamism of the climaxes of the opening movement, and a terrifying apostrophe on death, in the overwhelming song of the final movement.

That finale is Mahler's slowest piece, and his most extreme emotional journey. If you see the final page of the score, the music looks as it sounds, as filaments of the melodies you have been listening to for half an hour in the last movement become gossamer threads, then spider-web traces, and at last, quantum distillations of musical material, marked to be played ever quieter and ever slower. This is a piece that has been heard and performed by conductors from Bruno Walter to Leonard Bernstein as an image of

Mahler's holding on to life as tightly as possible, a refusal to relinquish music to silence until the last possible moment. The very last bar of all is marked *ersterbend*, 'dying', as if the performers needed any more clue to what the piece is about.

This is dangerous music to listen to and to perform. If the concentration of any single listener in the audience is anything less than total, these fine etchings of sound and memory are all too delicate: a single cough, a single shuffle of feet, let alone a stray mobile phone, ruin the power of the moment. For the performers, it's even more confronting. The physicality of their movements on their instruments is put under an unflinching microscope, where each tremor in the bow-arm of a violinist, viola player, or cellist is translated into sound. Anything above the quietest of strokes of bow-hair on the string would be a scar on silence, any unwanted slip of hand or arm, or even an audible intake of breath, would spoil the atmosphere of this passage of musical time.

And all that is just to achieve what Mahler asks of his performers in this part of the symphony – but to truly realise the fragile phenomenology of this unique moment in musical history there's even more the performers need to do. The preceding eighty minutes of the performance need to have been similarly concentrated and characterised, because if the previous three and three-quarter movements of the symphony have not been played at the required pitch of Mahlerian intensity, this last page of the last symphony he lived to complete sounds simply like a slow and quiet conclusion, instead of what it should be: a searching for the boundaries of musical and human possibility.

In Lucerne, that's exactly what happened. This was a performance that was not only a vivid representation of the dots on the page that comprise Mahler's Ninth Symphony. It was an orchestral performance that offered a special kind of knowledge and experience, which transcended the limits that even Mahler might have imagined for his symphony. Bruno Walter premiered the Ninth in 1912, the year after Mahler's death; and although that final bar is an aural image of 'dying', in Lucerne, something extraordinary happened after the symphony had ended.

Which is that it *didn't* end. Instead, in the leave-taking of the final notes of the music – the end of the sound, but not the substance, of Mahler's Ninth Symphony – the collective silence the audience and the musicians created afterwards was a journey into another dimension. It's a place not marked in the score, a place whose geometries and physicalities are almost impossible to describe, but which is tangibly *there* when you experience it. There must have been a moment when it happened, when the soundwaves of the final chord – already some of the gentlest you could imagine, as if the string section of the Lucerne Festival Orchestra had caressed the air rather than done anything as physical as play their instruments – lost their energy to the surrounding space of the concert hall. But in a phenomenon that would take quantum physics to define, that dissipating sound opened up another universe exactly at the moment it disappeared from our ears and from our sensory consciousness. The sound was a passage to another world, and in those minutes at the end of the performance – not 'after the performance', since this experience defined this account of Mahler's symphony, and was irreducibly part of the fabric of the piece – we in the hall followed it there. All of us who were in the audience that night know what that place is, should we ever encounter it again in our lives.

That was the power of the experience the KKL in Lucerne hosted that evening in the summer of 2010, and at its still centre was a small, elegant, but elderly man, with his back to the audience, his large hands and long arms hanging loosely in front of his body. There wasn't a fibre of tension in his being, but he held the hall in the silence for as long as the collective consciousness of the audience and the performers wanted it, a witness to the journey of the whole symphony but also the catalyst through which everything that evening had happened. Seventy-eight-year-old Claudio Abbado allowed this experience to take place, and as the audience began to edge back from the sublimity of Mahler's symphony into the physical world of the concert hall, of shifting in seats and thinking about how they had forgotten, so far, to clap – a journey of zero distance in metres or miles, but a huge existential voyage from one way of being to another – Abbado subtly shifted his shoulders, and the world of applause and acclaim, relief and release flooded violently in. The noise was deserved, but the suspended animation was the real prize of this performance.

Or, indeed, any performance. That evening in Lucerne was a revelation of how the alchemies in the relationships between a conductor, an ensemble of the world's finest musicians, and an audience enraptured by the brilliance of what they're hearing, can create something emotionally, expressively, and physically transformational, a kind of experience you're lucky to have, ever, in your life. The concert marks one of the high points in the history of the performance of symphonic music, and yet the story of how it happened can be told, through a constellation of circumstances of place, time, personality, career, and chance – all of which have been combining since 2003, when Abbado first conducted his Lucerne Festival Orchestra.

It should never have worked. The laws that underlie stories of great orchestral playing, like the ones in this book, are all broken by the Lucerne Festival Orchestra. This is an orchestra with no history, no playing tradition, no heritage: an ad hoc ensemble of (admittedly brilliant) musicians who come together for a few weeks in the summer as opposed to a seasoned, decades- or centuries-old orchestra. The players have no rights in the orchestra, there are no committees, no unions, no rules about how much or how little the orchestra should rehearse, and there is, naturally, no job security. And yet this weird and unique experiment, this glorified pick-up band, made from musicians who all choose to give up their summers to spend precious weeks away from the rest of their musical lives working on the shores of Lake Lucerne, is the fulfilment of a lifelong ambition of Abbado's. 'It is a dream come true,' he told me at his home on Sardinia, as a seraphic smile crossed his lined face, and his eyes twinkled with the scarcely suppressed joy of a child in a sweet store, as if hardly able to believe his luck in bringing a long-cherished idea to fruition.

That idea is a simple one: to translate the sheer love of making music that individual musicians feel when they play solo repertoire or chamber music on to the largest symphonic scale. Abbado wanted to found an orchestra that could perform Mahler, Bruckner, or Berlioz with the same focus, attention, engagement, and joy that players find in their own music-making. And to do that, he needed to create something that would not exist within the boundaries of a conventional, everyday orchestra. To make it happen, he needed the right place, the right partner, the right money – and the right players.

The place is special. Lucerne is a town that has resounded with musical inspiration for hundreds of years. It nestles at the western end of the gigantic Vierwaldstätter-see, Switzerland's most geographically improbable and beautiful lake, and the jaw-dropping backdrop to the city, with the grandeur of its two great mountains, the near-perfect pyramid of Pilatus and the voluptuous curve of the Rigi, has inspired composers from Mendelssohn to Wagner, from Brahms to Rachmaninov. In the weeks that were left to Felix Mendelssohn between his beloved sister, Fanny, dying and his own death, he took a grief-stricken sojourn through the Swiss mountains in 1847, staying in Lucerne and drawing some ethereal, haunted water-colours of the city- and mountainscape. His view of the Sankt-Leodagar Kirche is as limpid and diaphanous as his emotions must have been churning and desperate, an expressive intensity he would turn into music in his great String Quartet in F minor. The horn-call that catalyses the final movement of Brahms's First Symphony was also a Lucerne discovery, a transcription of an alphorn call that Brahms heard in one of the valleys and pastures above the town, an instrument that appealed to the horn-playing composer.

Rachmaninov composed his *Rhapsody on a Theme of Paganini* on the shores of the lake. Sergei's house is just a little further up the water from Lucerne's most famous contribution to nineteenth-century music history, the villa at Tribschen where Richard Wagner lived from 1866 to 1872, a period during which he was bankrolled by his unfortunate, obsessive, and all-too-credulous sponsor, the mad King Ludwig of Bavaria. This was the house where Wagner cuckolded his friend and champion, the pianist and conductor Hans von Bülow, with his wife Cosima, who was also Liszt's daughter; where he completed *Die Meistersinger von Nürnberg*, continued work on the *Ring* cycle, and where, having finally married Cosima himself in 1870 in Lucerne, he composed *Siegfried Idyll* for her birthday. That piece was first performed on Christmas morning 1870 in the stairwell of Tribschen, as his young wife woke up to the strains of the most charming and intimate music Wagner ever wrote. And yet Tribschen also hosted Wagner's redrafting of some of his prose works, including the notorious and poisonous essay *Jewishness in Music*. As with any shrine to Wagnerian inspiration, it's a place of musical genius and personal and political darkness. Today, the house is a weird and wonderful museum of Wagneriana, with a bizarre collection of artefacts among the manuscripts and scores: an ornate, gilt-framed case that houses Wagner's dog-whip, with which he would bring his beloved German shepherds to heel, and an incongruous display of instruments from all over the world on the top floor (not collected by Wagner, whose racial theories would certainly not permit a relativistic celebration of the diversity of world musical culture). There's also an out-of-tune piano in an upstairs corridor that could possibly have belonged to Wagner. That's the instrument on which British composer George Benjamin played the opening bars of the overture to *Die Meistersinger* when I visited Tribschen with him, creating a hilarious honky-tonk cacophony from the hallowed themes of the Mastersingers.

But Tribschen was also the site of a remarkable musical happening in the twentieth century. In 1938, Italian conductor Arturo Toscanini, in self-imposed exile from Wagner's theatre at Bayreuth in protest at how the Nazis were treating Jews and Jewish musicians, incarnated the Lucerne Festival with a performance in the grounds of the villa. He convened a so-called 'Elite Orchestra' of the greatest players in the world, including Jewish musicians, and on the little meadow in front of the villa, just above the pontoon where the boats still stop today with their freightloads of tourists and Wagnerites, Toscanini conducted the *Siegfried Idyll* in a performance that reclaimed the piece as the world's property, not just Germany's. That ensemble is the distant ancestor of the present-day Lucerne Festival Orchestra, similarly made from a hand-picked selection of the best soloists, chamber musicians, and players in the world's orchestras.

Abbado gives a snapshot of the constitution of his orchestra:

It's so wonderful. We are all friends, and they are the best players from each orchestra, from each nation, from each capital city. If you think there are seven or eight principal cellos in the cello section, there's Wolfram Christ, who used to lead the violas in the Berlin Philharmonic, and Alois Posch, who was principal double bass with the Vienna Philharmonic – amazing. And I don't know how many leaders there are in the first violins.

During rehearsals in 2008, I counted: there were nine. Toscanini's example is one thing, but the real pre-history of Abbado's orchestra is to be found in the story of his own musical career, his relationships with the great orchestras, ensembles, and opera houses where he was chief conductor, and the suite of other orchestras, usually for young people, he has set up over the last forty years.

Abbado grew up in a family of musicians in Milan, surrounded by an atmosphere of chamber music-making with his father, a violinist, his mother, brother and sister. Even during the war, and the tyranny of Italian fascism, it was Abbado's musical obsessions that were at the top of his mind: as a twelve-year-old, he daubed the motto 'Viva Bartók!' on the wall of a house in the city; the Gestapo came to his home and asked his parents, 'Where is the partisan Bartók?' Abbado studied as a pianist, composer, and conductor, and his decision to devote himself to music came through a Damascene moment in La Scala, Milan, when he was seven years old, as he told me. 'The three *Nocturnes* of Debussy' – music Abbado has conducted in Lucerne – 'was the first music I heard. Guarnieri was conducting. And I decided there and then to be a musician, to be a conductor. I wanted to realise again this magic thing. You know, that moment when you hear this harp and the trumpets . . .' Talking to him on the shores of Lake Lucerne, in another villa not far from Tribschen, the year he was rehearsing the *Nocturnes*, Abbado trailed off into a reverie as he recalled the defining memory of his musical life. And with his harp player and the solo trumpets of the Lucerne orchestra, he magicked those joyful faery sounds of Debussy's *Fêtes* ('Festivals') more shimmeringly than I have ever heard them.

But Abbado's progress as a conductor has not followed a conventional path. In his early twenties, he faced a crisis moment, having to decide to which of the three potential paths of composing, conducting, or piano-playing to devote himself. Talking to Leonard Bernstein in 1963, when he spent a year as his assistant in New York, he remembered the moment – in curious circumstances. At dinner after one of Abbado's concerts there, Bernstein suddenly asked him, 'Tell me, what is it I'm doing wrong? I'm not Karajan, you can tell me everything!' Abbado was shocked, and didn't know what to think or say to the composer of *West Side Story* and some of the most successful contemporary classical pieces of that era, the most uniquely communicative conductor of his generation, a brilliant pianist, music educationalist and proselytiser of genius. Abbado at last said, knowing he didn't play the piano or compose as well as Bernstein, that he himself had the choice to be a composer, conductor, or pianist after his studies in Milan and Vienna, and had realised that he couldn't do all of them at the same time, but would have to choose one and forsake the others in order to realise himself completely.

Even after that decision, Abbado's relationship with conducting was about trying to put his relationship, knowledge and understanding of music before his ego. In his mid-twenties, he won the conducting competition at the Tanglewood summer school, near Boston, but instead of taking up an appointment with an American orchestra, which was offered to him, he returned to Italy to teach chamber music in Parma for three years. 'Teaching was a great experience. I learnt a lot from these young musicians. We played everything – Stravinsky's *Soldier's Tale* without conductor, Bartók's Sonata for Two Pianos and Percussion – making chamber music with large groups.' Chamber music with large groups: that was the ideal to which Abbado's life in conducting would aspire, even when he was at the helm of the iconic institutions he ran from 1968 until

2002: the opera house at La Scala, Milan, the London Symphony Orchestra, the Vienna State Opera, and the Berlin Philharmonic, where he succeeded Herbert von Karajan in 1989.

Yet Abbado always felt a sense of frustration with these opera houses and orchestras, however glamorous. 'I knew that you could get better music in a better way: with a different way of listening. You know, in America, there are wonderful orchestras everywhere, but I never accepted a position over there.' America's orchestras are notoriously unionised, run by regulations that must be adhered to. 'In Vienna and Berlin it was better because there are many more musicians playing chamber music,' Abbado says.

But in American orchestras, they have maybe one string quartet, and it's the mentality. The terrible thing is that the players of orchestras like that, they finish the rehearsal not because the music is finished, but because the time is finished. But here in Lucerne, we can continue, shorter, longer, just as we like it. And you know, during the concert, even more than during the rehearsal, it's fantastic to hear not just how they play, but how they follow. It's like we breathe together.

And Abbado has consistently found other ways in life to foster this 'different way of listening', this desire to turn the orchestra into a vastly expanded chamber ensemble of intimate musical relationships and human interactions. He has harnessed the idealism – and lack of unions – among young musicians, setting up a series of major international youth orchestras and ensembles of young professionals. He began in 1978 with the European Community (now European Union) Youth Orchestra, followed in 1986 by the Gustav Mahler Youth Orchestra, which included play-ers from outside the European Union, especially Eastern Europe and Russia. Abbado was a guiding inspiration behind the Chamber Orchestra of Europe, and when the brilliant players of the Gustav Mahler orchestra ensemble wanted to extend their philosophy and their way of play-ing in their professional lives, Abbado set up the Mahler Chamber Orchestra. The Mahler Chamber players are at the core of the Lucerne orchestra, but Abbado has con-tinued to found other ensembles: Orchestra Mozart in Bologna, a laboratory for performance practice and new approaches to classical repertoire, and he has close ties with the Simón Bolívar Symphony Orchestra in Venezuela, the blue-riband ensemble of the most remarkable phenomenon in music education and social transformation of our time, El Sistema. Among other conductors, it has produced the brilliant young maestro Gustavo Dudamel, and the even younger Diego Matheuz, who was recently appointed to run La Fenice, Venice's opera house, and both have ben-efited from Abbado's advice and imprimatur.

This apparently public labour invested in orchestra-building is a realisation of Abbado's intensely private phi-losophy of listening. It was something inculcated in him by 'the most inspiring person in my life', Abbado says: his grandfather on his mother's side. The fullness of his life was one example:

He taught ancient languages at the university in Palermo in Sicily. And every five years, he learnt a new language. He was studying Aramaic, and he made a translation of the Bible that spoke about the brothers and sisters of Jesus. So he was excom-municated from the church in 1915. He was so open. You know, when he died, he was ninety-six, and to the last days, students still used to ask him, please can you tell us, what is the meaning of this hieroglyph?

But the most important lessons the grandfather taught the child were about silence, nature, and listening. Walking in the mountains of the Swiss–Italian border near Monte Cervino (the Italian name for the Matterhorn), immersed in a world of grand geology and microscopic alpine flowers – the extremes of the expressive universe charted by Mahler's symphonies – Abbado and his grandfather spent time together. 'He used just a few words. And I learnt such a lot from him. For me, listening is the most important thing: to listen to each other, to listen to what people say, to listen to music. And to listen to silence.' To make others listen to silence, too: Abbado is a man of famously few words in his rehearsals.

In Lucerne, Abbado has embarked on a cycle of the symphonies closest to his heart, which have run like a chain of Alpine mountains through his life: Mahler's nine completed symphonies and the Adagio of the Tenth. In 1965, Abbado was asked by Karajan to lead the Vienna Philharmonic in the Second Symphony, the 'Resurrection', a performance that marked his debut with an orchestra he would go on to lead in the 1980s, and which shot him to international fame and attention. It was the same work that Abbado conducted as the climax of his first series of concerts with the Lucerne Festival Orchestra in 2003. The choice was telling. Aside from what it has meant for his career, Mahler's Second has talismanic importance for Abbado. In its choral finale, a vision of spiritual rebirth, Abbado sees and hears a metaphor for the musical experience, too. Within Mahler's text for that movement are the following words:

What was created, must pass away
What passed away, must rise!
Cease to tremble!
Prepare yourself!
Prepare yourself to live!

Abbado sees this as meaning that music is both destroyed and redeemed by its temporality: it exists and is extinguished in a moment, but has the endless possibility of being created anew in time.

The same has been true of Abbado's career – and in recent years, his life, and his health, too. In 2000, in the last couple of years of his tenure at the Berlin Philharmonic, he was struck by serious, life-threatening illness. Abbado's sleek, well-groomed appearance in the 1990s was changed utterly by the severity of his illness and his treatment. But music kept him going, and still sustains him. Martin Baeza de Rubio, a trumpeter with the Berlin Philharmonic and the Lucerne Festival Orchestra, remembers a performance of *Tristan and Isolde* in Tokyo with the Berliners in 2000, for which Abbado seemed scarcely able to mount the podium, let alone conduct the four tortuous, transcendent hours of Wagner's score. Yet he did, gripped by a mania and utter commitment to the music that drained him completely and reduced the orchestra to tears. And just before his illness, Abbado met up with the Lucerne Festival's artistic director, Michael Haefliger, in Salzburg in 1999. He came to Haefliger with his dream for an orchestra without rules and without limits, which would be made up of musicians hand-picked by Abbado, including players like the chamber musicians of the Hagen Quartet, soloists like cellist Natalia Gutman, clarinettist Sabine Meyer and the brilliant members of her woodwind ensemble, principal players from the Berlin and Vienna Philharmonics, and energised by the youthful brilliance of the Mahler Chamber Orchestra.

There was scepticism even from the musicians who were initially asked. Wolfram Christ led the Berlin Philharmonic's violas from 1978 until 1999, working closely with Abbado for the decade of his tenure. Christ decided to leave the orchestra to turn to teaching, conducting, and a solo career, but Abbado asked him before he left whether he would be interested in playing with his dream orchestra.

I wasn't sure if it would really happen, but I told him I would play – if he managed to get the people he said he would, like trumpeter Reinhold Friedrich, Kolja Blacher [leader of the Berlin Philharmonic in Abbado's time], the Hagen Quartet, Natalia Gutman. If they all came, it would be a dream. And dreams usually do not get fulfilled. But in this case it did, and it was a long time in his mind before it happened. Amazing.

Soloist and chamber musician Kolja Blacher had never played in an orchestra before Abbado asked him to go for the job of leading the Berlin Philharmonic in 1993. And for six years, Blacher sat at Abbado's left hand in the Philharmonie in Berlin. But even after working with him for that length of time, Blacher was unsure about the Lucerne idea.

In the first year, it had an amazing hype, and I have to say I was completely unsure that it would work. I said, look, I will do it for a year, fine, to see what happens, and if it doesn't work, I'm just going to leave. He was talking about putting together a huge orchestra with people who had never played in an orchestra before, who had never played with each other before. So we needed very intense sectional rehearsals. And then – it worked. Better than anybody had expected.

Etienne Abelin, a Swiss freelance violinist who plays in Abbado's Orchestra Mozart, remembers that first year.

We were like, my God, this is actually taking place, we never thought it would happen! He thanked us after the very first concerts of Debussy, and everyone was in tears after that. He was thanking us really for a new life. And then there was Mahler Two, a musical resurrection. It was really thanks for being here – thanks for sharing this with me. You know, at the end of these concerts, you feel privileged, because he may never perform these pieces again.

The 'Resurrection' Symphony was a symbolic celebration of Abbado's life after illness, and with his orchestra in Lucerne, the fulfilment of a dream.

Kolja Blacher says that Abbado's illness only heightened the qualities that were always there in his music-making, the phenomenon that 'nobody gets people to play as well for them as Claudio'. But the physical changes in him, the way the musicians react to him, the fact that they all know him and love him, has sharpened the responses of the musicians in the orchestra. 'Of course after an illness you really know what you're living for, and the only thing he is living for is the music.' The resonances of the 'Resurrection' were as personal as they were musical for Abbado and his musicians in 2003, but as the summers have passed, the conductor has looked stronger and stronger, and while none of the players take it for granted that they will be playing in the Lucerne Festival Orchestra every year, it is now an ensemble with its own special history and a unique performance practice. For Italian flautist Chiara Tonelli, principal of the Mahler Chamber Orchestra and second flute of the Festival Orchestra ever since its inception, the LFO is 'the high point of my year'.

At the beginning of every summer, I think, is it really possible that this orchestra exists and that I'm sitting in it? It's only rarely that you sit in an orchestra and think, during a rehearsal, oh my God, that's so beautiful, what that string section sounded like, how that trumpet solo was played. This is the only orchestra I know where that happens, where there is a fundamental sense of wonder, every day we're together.

Tonelli talks of the 'the big "Yes!"' in the total commitment of the Lucerne orchestra.

Because we all want to work with Abbado, he can go higher with us than he can with other orchestras because he receives this absolute *'Ja!'* from us. He has this amazing ability not to do anything to the music. He leaves it, you have the feeling he is leaving the musicians alone to play. And this is the strange contradiction – but I have experienced that he does it, that it happens. You have the feeling in the orchestra that he is letting the music play, so you think he's just standing there and coordinating what's happening, not leading it. But that's naturally not the case! He has the whole thing completely in his head, in his body. And that's what makes you so lucky as a musician in this orchestra: it's not that somebody is telling you what to do, but you are doing it yourself. You play exactly as you want to play, he allows us to do that – but in spite of that, he is in charge of it, he has such a strong personality that he is leading what is happening.

Tonelli hits on the essential paradox, and miracle, of Abbado's way of making music, and the culture of listening he wants to create in the Lucerne orchestra. The musicians feel that they are totally realised as individuals, that they are interpreting the music the way they want to, and yet they are also part of a collective vision and experience.

Kolja Blacher puts it more bluntly.

Look, in a way, one has to talk sociologically about this: you have a creative group of people who are being led by a person who in a way has to be a dictator. It's completely contradictory. But it works. And what Abbado gets here is something that works for four weeks in the year, but it would not work for two years or four years, if the orchestra were to become a 'normal' orchestra. At this stage in his life, he has got what he really wanted ten years ago.

What he has is an orchestra of friends, the best and most brilliant musicians he has worked with throughout his life, and the complete freedom of their playing and listening because of each player's love for him. It's a situation that every other conductor on earth can only dream about. Blacher goes on. 'Being completely clear about it – this orchestra only works because it's in Switzerland, and there's a lot of money behind it. A lot of money.' Around two million Swiss francs, in fact, which Michael Haefliger finds in private cash (the whole Lucerne Festival is almost completely privately funded) to realise his and Abbado's dream each year.

Blacher gives his side of how the orchestra has developed over the years. 'Even in the second summer there was still this excitement about whether it will work or not, and then afterwards, things got in a way easier,' as many of the same players came back to renew their once-a-year relationships with one another.

But then there was the danger of the hype going and the thing becoming normal: 'Oh, it's you again ... here we go, then ...' But I think we managed that transition in the next couple of years and didn't lose the orchestra's sense of specialness. And you could see how good things were at the Proms [Abbado and the Orchestra came to the Royal Albert Hall in 2007 with Mahler's Third Symphony] and now I think it's a good balance of being exciting and new and having a little security: it worked before, it will work this time, too.

The first time I heard the orchestra live was in 2006, when Abbado led them in Mahler's Sixth Symphony, that dark and single-mindedly tragic composition. Its brilliance was in making the music both completely clear in its structure and devastating in its expressive impact. Because the orchestra were able to communicate clearly the narrative of Mahler's huge symphonic story, making every strand of the story audible even in the densest textures of the final movement or the opening Allegro, you heard the violence and tortuous contortions through which Mahler puts his themes. Whether the hero of the symphony was Mahler himself or a fictional, doomed protagonist, you followed every twist and turn of his demise, as the music's dreams of love, redemption, and escape were all crushed by the hollow thud of the end of the symphony. And yet despite, or perhaps because of the darkness, the cathartic power of the whole performance was weirdly life-affirming. Having looked the music's terror and fear and premonitions of death square in the face, it was possible to return to the world drained but renewed.

This was one of the first performances I heard after leaving hospital myself, after months of operations for cancer. If I identified with the symphony's emotional trajectory, and with what I knew had happened to the conductor, that was not only subjective or sentimental identification, but proof of the potentially healing experience of Mahler's music and the Lucerne Festival Orchestra's playing. The next year, the huge hymn to love of Mahler's Third Symphony in Switzerland and at the Proms was a more obvious reason to celebrate the virtuosity of listening in the Lucerne orchestra's way of making music, and it was one of the concerts that the Royal Albert Hall audience will never forget.

So in August 2008, I'm waiting outside the stage door of the Kultur- und Kongresszentrum Luzern as rehearsals are due to start for that year's Lucerne Festival Orchestra programmes. It's right by the lake, but the artists' entrance is a forbidding steel door that opens on to a faceless lobby area, in which a small Swiss army of fierce, be-bereted attendants are waiting to check the musicians' passes and, hopefully, allow me access to the inner sanctum of the 'Salle Blanche', the white auditorium of the main hall. The front of the building is a postmodernist riot of invention – a gigantic steel roof juts out fifty metres from the curvaceous wooden shell of the Salle Blanche, and the waters of the lake run all the way through one level of the building, a surreal incursion of the natural within the starkly industrial interior of black surfaces and metallic angles – but the hall itself is an updated version of the oldest and best architectural shape for housing a symphony orchestra and a large audience. It's a narrow shoebox, like the Musikverein in Vienna, or the Concertgebouw in Amsterdam, and it sounds just as good as they do. For a hall built in 1998, that's some achievement.

Making my way through a scrum of players who are milling around the cafe just beside the stage door into the hall, there's an unusual atmosphere for a rehearsal that includes music that will challenge even the best players, and in which the musicians, many giving up a sixth summer in a row, are again putting themselves on the line for the reputation of the Lucerne Festival Orchestra. There's laughter, warm embraces at the renewal of friendships old and new: the oldest player in the orchestra is seventy-eight-year-old violinist Hanns-Joachim Westphal, who sits next to the youngest, Raphael Christ, Wolfram's son, who leads the second violin section as well as Abbado's Orchestra Mozart. Stories are swapped over cups of coffee and quickly stubbed-out cigarettes, and some late arrivals sweep past me on scooters, a good way of getting round the couple of miles of lake-front from the musicians' hotel to the concert hall. On stage, as the players warm up, there's a sense of relaxed excitement before Abbado comes on to the platform, wearing trainers, his shirt sleeves rolled up, and a red sweater swung casually but elegantly around his shoulders.

He doesn't know it, but there's a twinge of disappointment among some of the players this year. The reason is that for the only time in the Lucerne Festival Orchestra's short history, there isn't a note of Mahler on either of the two programmes they will play. Instead, Abbado has chosen French and Russian music: one of the pieces he is most famous for, Stravinsky's *Firebird* suite, to partner Rachmaninov's Second Piano Concerto, and Tchaikovsky's rarely-heard tone-poem, *The Tempest*. In the first concert, meanwhile, there is Berlioz's *Symphonie fantastique*, Ravel's miniature orientalist song-cycle, *Shéhérazade*, and the pieces that converted Abbado to music and conducting all those decades ago, Debussy's *Nocturnes*. The Tchaikovsky causes controversy because some of the players tell me they don't think it's a good enough piece of music, but they're prepared to trust Abbado's judgement. It's the lack of Mahler that is the biggest surprise, however. Chiara Tonelli tells me:

It's good that it's different, it's a chance to be more flexible in French and Russian repertoire. And Abbado does these things amazingly. I'm looking forward to it. And it's wonderful that it's not just about Bruckner and Mahler. Yesterday, in the woodwind sectional [before the whole orchestra played together] there was such grace in the way he conducted the melodies in the first movement. I was so happy for him – he was finding the joy he is still looking for. But of course, we have the hope [in 2008] that Mahler's Ninth will still come. And it's good to have that hope!

With the huge weight of anticipation arising from the performances I've heard this orchestra give in previous years, with the quality of players I can see in front of me, those string sections stuffed full of leaders, great chamber musicians and soloists, and all the other close musical friends of Abbado's, it's possible I expect too much from the first time I hear Abbado work with the players in rehearsal. Because what happens in the second section of Debussy's *Nocturnes* – precisely the *Fêtes* movement that was Abbado's signal inspiration as a child – is bizarre and unexpected. It's music that's among the least technically challenging that the orchestra, or the conductor, will face in their few weeks together. The two violin sections play the same rhythm, a celebratory firework of triplets, played fortissimo, and *très marqué*, very marked and accented, and the upper woodwinds have a single open chord. In fact, there are just three notes that all these instruments play, two Cs an octave apart and an F at the top of the treble-clef stave. The music is even cast in that simplest of time signatures, 4/4. It's not something that should tax any half-decent group of amateurs, let alone an ensemble whose constitution places it among the finest in the world, led by a conductor whom Wolfram Christ describes as 'in a class of his own – there is no one as good as Claudio at the moment'.

And yet, what happens is a chaos of different interpretations of Abbado's upbeat, a lack of coordination between the two violin sections, even though they're sitting next to one another. That's at least partly explicable since they have different parts of the chord to play; what's less comprehensible is the disagreement from one desk to the next, one desk partner to another. Even the woodwinds, charged with their sustained blast of Cs and Fs, don't come in together. It's all even more puzzling when Abbado restarts the ensemble, using the same gesture to try and achieve the effect he wants – and it doesn't work, for a second time. A third time; but the violins play at a faster speed than Abbado wants, followed by a fourth, still unsuccessful attempt.

It's a revealing moment because of what it shows about the priorities of Abbado's conducting and the things on which he isn't prepared to compromise. He does not change his gestures or try to correct what the violins and the wood-winds were doing by being clearer or more direct in his beating. Watching his arms, baton, and body move in the split second before the orchestra started to play, what he was giving his musicians was not simply an upbeat in the technical sense that the conducting manuals describe, but an impulse of movement, drama, and character for his players to translate into sound. In *Fêtes*, he wants the opening to sound like the joyful crack of a firework, a scintillating explosion of sound and colour that provides the dynamic and expressive propulsion for the rest of the movement. That's more information than a humble upbeat could possibly provide. It would have been much easier for him to have simply made his beat sharper, to have drawn a clear 'three–four–one' in the air and then to have enjoyed the results of his orchestra playing perfectly in time. After all, the function of a conductor's upbeat, strictly speaking, is to convey the right speed for the music, and to make sure that information is succinctly displayed to all the members of the orchestra who will perform the first bar of the music. Instead, in the chaos of the first few attempts at this passage, the magic thread that usually connects him to these musicians in Lucerne is broken.

Abbado's solution is simply to keep going, trusting that the musicians will work out what to do – and refusing to change his own interpretation. That would be a dangerous tactic in a 'normal' orchestra of players who could easily say it was the conductor's fault, not theirs, that they weren't getting this moment right. They would have a point, too. But here, the players want to keep Claudio happy. That's why the musicians come to Lucerne in the summer, because they all trust Abbado to be able to provide those dramatic and emotional dimensions that they can't achieve on their own. And he, in turn, trusts them to be able to play as precisely as necessary. Which all means that Abbado does not have to compromise on the musical substance of what he's trying to achieve at every moment of the *Nocturnes*, or Berlioz's *Symphonie fantastique*. What he's doing goes to the heart of what the gestural language of a conductor means. For

Abbado and his musicians, the fact of playing accurately and together is assumed, so it's providing the extra, expressive factors that are the conductor's job.

What happened at the beginning of *Fêtes* would not happen in the Berlin Philharmonic, the Concertgebouw, or the Bamberg Symphony. Those regular ensembles take for granted a playing tradition built up over the years, decades, and centuries. And however good the players are in Lucerne, they don't have the same collective experience as a single body of musicians as those other orchestras. Coming from different playing traditions – from Caracas to Berlin, from Gran Canaria to Liverpool, from Hilversum to Bologna, from Munich to Madrid, from Florence to Moscow – the things that usually glue orchestral playing together in a conventional context have to be discovered in an instant. The Lucerne situation is more comparable to what groups like the Gustav Mahler or European Union youth orchestras have to do each summer, when groups of young players who have never met before get together to form an orchestra. Reinhold Friedrich, the Lucerne orchestra's solo trumpet since 2003, describes the atmosphere in the Festival Orchestra as being like 'a youth orchestra for professionals, with the same joy in playing together'.

Back in the rehearsal, Abbado's perplexity never becomes anger at his players. It's more as if he is mystified by things not going the way in which they were pre-ordained. His thought process is, 'I can do this, you can do this, it has to work!' rather than, 'We need to find a different way of doing things.' Abbado does not question whether he is right or not: this is simply the way the music goes. And when the players do find those finest of calibrations with each other and with Abbado's gestures, at the fifth time of asking, the result is stunning, even during this initial rehearsal of the movement. Driven by the relief of playing together and getting over this hurdle, there's a freedom to the music-making that is already a pre-echo of the level they will find together when they play this music in the concerts. Later, I ask him about this moment. 'It was strange that it didn't work immediately. But I was never cross with them.'

The double basses don't come in until later, and when they do – with the same rhythm that caused the violins such an issue, there's no problem. Their leader is Alois Posch, who led the basses of the Vienna Philharmonic for twenty-five years and was with the orchestra for three decades, having joined when he was eighteen. For him, there's a clear reason why the Lucerne orchestra will do whatever it can as a collective and as individuals to turn Abbado's gestures into sound.

The orchestra here in Lucerne is not a mature *Klangkörper* [sound-body]. There is no connecting culture of playing between us. Whereas in Vienna or Berlin, there are extremely strong traditions. In Vienna, we play together in the opera every night, and we have really developed together as musicians, so there's a huge understanding between every member of the orchestra. And there isn't that here in Lucerne. But that lack is compensated for by the idealism of the musicians here, and the *Spiel-freudigkeit* [joy of playing], so it's really not a problem. We can play well together here and find a beautiful sound. But here's what one really has to say: the Vienna Philharmonic or Berlin Phiharmonic have their own souls as orchestras. Here, the soul is Abbado, not the orchestra. That's the biggest difference. The conventional orchestras define their own culture, but the binding element here is Claudio. And what's so special about it is that everyone is here because they want to make music with Claudio. There is a fundamentally positive atmosphere here, which you encounter only very rarely. It's about the music and the hard work – and Abbado.

Posch says that even with the colossus-like names of previous generations, conductors did not have the same conditions that Abbado has managed to create for himself in Lucerne.

I remember working with Carlos Kleiber, with Leonard Bernstein, and with Karajan, names we now think of as so great: well, there were problems working with all of them! And there were always different opinions in the orchestra about each of them. But here there is none of that, only a unity of working on the music with Abbado.

The atmosphere of a youth orchestra made of the best professional musicians in the world, who can come with their family for a few weeks for the ultimate busman's holiday in one of the most sheerly beautiful places in Europe and luxuriate in music-making in an atmosphere of friendship and mutual admiration, makes the Lucerne experience close to ideal conditions for orchestral playing, Posch says.

You can't say that here is the highlight of orchestral life, because in Berlin, Cleveland, or Vienna, those big orchestras can manage a similar quality. But there is a difference. Here, the chance that something really special will happen in each concert is very high. Sometimes we play only very good concerts, not *Sternstunden* [literally, 'hours of the stars', concerts that go to the 'cosmic' level that Mariss Jansons talks about]. But it's more likely that we will create a *Sternstunde* here than anywhere else.

'Souls' and 'star-hours' are one thing, but to realise all that, Abbado has to be a physical presence. There must be a way that this soul, these stars, are physically communicated to the musicians. It turns on something that all of the players in this orchestra tell me, so much so that it becomes an article of faith. It's the idea that there is a direct relationship between Abbado's gestures and the sound the orchestra makes. And not just the movements of his hands or his baton, when he uses one, but his entire body, his eyes, his face, his torso. Abbado's body language is a sound-language in Lucerne. Wolfram Christ says:

The gestures of Abbado are unique. He has gestures that no other conductors have. Especially with his left hand. His left hand is an example of freedom, how to create freedom. The only other conductor who had the same freedom in his conduct-ing was Carlos Kleiber. Most other conductors try to beat, to beat time. And this is the last thing Claudio wants. He doesn't want to beat the music. He wants to be there, to be leading it with gestures that are sensitive to the atmosphere of the music of Debussy or Ravel. It's like watercolours, it's like he creates a thousand different shades of colours that melt into each other. And you cannot do that by only beating one, two, three, four! But that's also why when he was in Berlin with the Philhar-monic, there were sometimes people who said, we cannot see the beat, where is the one, the two of the bar? But for me he is very clear. He doesn't need to speak, I can see it in his face, that we're too loud, or whatever it is. He doesn't need to tell me. You can read everything from his hands. You must just let yourself go with that. And you must have the knowledge and technical security to be able to follow him, and all the players have that here in Lucerne. But you need to trust yourself, and you need to trust what he does. Especially in concerts. He's a magician in concerts.

Christ's position in the orchestra, immediately to Abba-do's right on the concert platform (Abbado has the Lucerne Festival Orchestra set up like the Berlin and Vienna Phil-harmonics, the two groups of violins on his left, the violas on the extreme right, with the cellos tucked in beside them) means he's in one of the best positions in the orchestra to be able to commune with the conductor's gestures. But trumpeter Reinhold Friedrich, sitting all the way behind the woodwinds, with only the percussionists further away from the podium, says the same is true up there, too.

Claudio is engaged with everything that's going on in the wind and the brass. And I want him to feel that there is a lot of interaction from us, that we are there to think with him musically. When we played the Fifth of Mahler here [which opens with a famous – and famously exposed – trumpet solo that Friedrich played in 2004], I said to him, 'I'm wax in your hands, I will do anything you want: you tell me, and I'll do it.' But he said to me, 'Don't change anything, everything is wonderful.' I had the feeling he trusted me a lot. Often there's an attitude from conductors that the brass are so far away, the trumpets play always the same, always loud, and it's all about dealing with the string players in the front desks. But with Claudio it's the whole orchestra.

Flautist Chiara Tonelli, who has played with Abbado since her teenage years in the Gustav Mahler Youth Orchestra and the Mahler Chamber Orchestra, says that 'such a long period of working with him creates a deep level of trust. The art of Abbado is unreachable by anyone else. Each concert is a one-off, unrepeatable experience. He really makes everything build towards the concert situation.'

It's the same everywhere I turn in the Lucerne Festival Orchestra, expressions of trust, love, even outright idolatry. That beautiful German word *musizieren*, 'to make music together', crops up a lot, as musicians from the percussion section to the second violins talk of what it's like to make music together with Abbado. What the musicians are mostly too modest to say is that this trust, this transparency between each of Abbado's minuscule facial tics and sweeping gestures of his left arm, is a two-way street. Abbado's gestures are not in themselves enough to communicate music – although they are beautiful in an aesthetic sense: the most graceful, flowing, balletic shapes conjured by any living conductor – and not just because of the obviousness of conducting being more than a mime act. Abbado needs his musicians to make music, to interpret his gestures, but more than that, in Lucerne, he needs their faith. Abbado's body language is only translatable into sound because the musicians in the Lucerne Festival Orchestra believe that's possible. It's a self-fulfilling prophecy in Lucerne, a virtuous circle in which the musicians' faith that Abbado's gestures communicate everything that they need to know about how to play Berlioz or Bruckner, Mahler or Mozart, means that is precisely what happens, in rehearsal and in performance. The fact that they know Abbado trusts them and has chosen them to be there means they can safely go further into the music and their musicality than they could otherwise, and Abbado himself is pushed to explore the extremes of what's possible because he knows there are no limitations imposed by institutional politics or personal conflicts. That's part of the secret of the musical miracle manufactured in Lucerne.

Chiara Tonelli and Kolja Blacher describe the mutual enrichment that is possible in this atmosphere of unquestioning respect that conductor and musicians feel for one another. Tonelli observes:

It's not maybe that he can learn from us, but he can go further in his art in this context, with an orchestra who all want to work with him, and want to go with him. That's different from a normal orchestra where you have some people who don't want to go with him completely. Even though he has done these pieces a hundred times, he can still make a progression.

For Blacher, 'the reason that people play so well for him is that he will even sometimes change his concept of a piece a little to allow them to really play what they want. That helps give you the illusion that you really can just play how you want in this orchestra. That's what he's trying to create here.'

And yet, even if there is partly a self-willed illusion in the players all giving themselves to Abbado's music-making, there is something inherent in his gestures that creates the sense of freedom and responsibility he wants from his orchestra. Wolfram Christ says that Abbado has an 'absolute fascination with legato playing, which is one of the difficult things for strings and woodwind players to do: to make a melody that is not limited by the length of the bow or breath. Don't limit the melody with your bow, but try to follow the melodic line of the whole piece of music. He is a legato fanatic.'

That sense of endless line is exactly what Abbado's gestures communicate: it's the musical idea his left hand is continually communicating, showing that there's a higher musical flow that exists above the individual lines the instruments have to play. Abbado wants the musicians to be part of a gigantic musical line that connects the beginning of a Mahler symphony, or the *Symphonie fantastique*, with its end. That's a flow of time bigger than any bow, longer than any breath. I asked him how he conceived this idea, and he told me he builds up his knowledge of any work he conducts by analysing how the lines of harmony function in the piece, from the lowest line in the double basses to the highest melodic part in the first violins, creating an image of the piece as a network of interrelated strata of musical material, rather than a sequence of moment-to-moment happenings. It's a tectonic, generative approach to music architecture, in which Abbado knows how each part relates to the other, how shifting weights and densities in one part of the musical texture will affect and shape the whole landscape of the symphony.

Abbado's way of thinking about music, his way of hearing, is relative and dynamic. His conducting is a kind of heightened consciousness. Being aware of every aspect of the *Symphonie fantastique*'s structure at every point in the rehearsal and the performance is not just a feat of knowledge and memory. It's also something that gives him the freedom to change details of tempo or balance, to react to what the players do, to shape each performance as a new experience. His philosophy of conducting is to give that freedom to his musicians as well, to invite them to hear the piece as he does, to think of it as he does.

Kolja Blacher admits it's not easy, because it demands that the players take almost as much responsibility for their performance as Abbado does.

Abbado was one of the first to try to push democracy into this very hierarchical job when we were working together in Berlin, and that was why it was new and difficult there. The thing is, as a group of people, you have to be able to deal with democracy and personal freedom. And it's much easier when somebody just tells you what to do, you know?

The freedom the players have is to interpret Abbado's gestures the way they want to, to give themselves to the moment of their music-making. But to do that in the context of orchestral performance, their responsibilities are greater. They need to know how their part fits in to the bigger tectonics of what's happening in the rest of the orchestra at the same time – whether they need to subdue themselves to allow the solo cor anglais to be heard, to accompany the melody in the cellos, to give support to the trombones, or to play out as fully as possible – and they need to know the piece as well as Abbado does to fully understand where each moment sits in the contours of the journey of the whole symphony, the whole piece of music.

Above all, they need to listen. Second violinist Etienne Abelin remembers a moment during a performance of Mahler's Third Symphony when Abbado didn't even start the music going, but waited for a collective act of will, of listening, from the orchestra to bring the piece into being.

It was the beginning of the finale of the symphony [a soft hymn for strings alone]. And he didn't give a beat! His hands were just sort of up there, and he just knew the sound would come in. And I knew when he didn't give that beat, that it would be perfect. You sensed that you just had to wait for something, together, and the sound would sneak in. It was only because he avoided giving any kind of entrance that the moment sounded so perfectly.

That's conducting as the opposite of leading; conducting as allowing-to-listen, allowing-to-happen.

In the Lucerne Festival Orchestra's rehearsals for the Berlioz, what I see happening is utterly mysterious, according to the normal practices of the rehearsal room. Abbado doesn't so much lead the music-making as set the orchestra off in the first movement – and then watch and listen to what happens. He is as seemingly passive as it's possible for a conductor to be, gently suggesting that the strings play less to allow a clarinet solo to be heard, showing the brass that they aren't the centre of attention by pointing to the cellos, as if saying, 'The melody's here, listen to them play,' or having an apparently private conversation with Blacher or Christ while the rest of the orchestra plays on. Presumably, he is issuing instructions to some of his most trusted players to pass on to their sections, but he doesn't do anything as vulgar as stop the orchestra to tell them what to do.

What is actually going on? As long chunks of the first movement are played, replayed, and played again, without Abbado saying why he wants to repeat the passage, or what he wants done differently each time, it's hard to work out the trajectory of this rehearsal. In my score of Berlioz's *Symphonie* with which I followed these sessions, I marked down every word that Abbado said over three days of work on the piece. And there isn't a lot there. He asked the strings to play 'more *tasto* [on the fingerboard], not so "real"' in their opening music; he tried out the woodwind's nightmarishly exposed music in the first two bars of the symphony a few times, without correcting tuning that was never perfect, only showing that he wanted the music quieter, quieter, quieter; he says he wants the music around the first entry of Berlioz's '*idée fixe*', his musical hero and alter ego, to be more 'agitato'; he wants more legato in a place that's usually too accented – and that's about it. Without much else to write down, I even had time to notice that Wolfram Christ and Claudio Abbado wear the same kind of leather slip-on shoes, according to one of my notations in the first movement.

There are no anecdotes, there is no choice use of metaphor, no obvious show of discipline or authority, democratic or dictatorial, and no psychological finesse to what Abbado is doing. There are, however, two constants: the word Abbado uses more than any other, and which peppers my score of the Berlioz, is 'listen . . .' 'Listen', he says to the rest of the orchestra, to the oboe's melody, to the violin's tune, to the tuba's interjection, to the double basses' fundamental note, giving glimpses of how he hears the music and how he wants the orchestra to communicate it to the audience. The other constant is that there is a smile on his face for almost the whole rehearsal.

This repeated 'listen' heightens the awareness of the musicians. Instead of commanding the brass players, say, to 'play quieter', Abbado shows them what they should be hearing, that their music is only an accompaniment for the oboe, the violins, the clarinets. It's an invitation rather than a command, an instruction that suggests participation rather than proscription. If the brass players listen to the oboist and accompany him, the music will work the way Abbado wants it to. He doesn't have to issue admonitory commands or use those crass limiting gestures, like putting a hand over the mouth of a screaming child, that conductors usually do when they want musicians to play more quietly. It's a culture of sharing and responsibility that Abbado wants to create, rather than an atmosphere of strictures and 'thou shalt nots'. Smiles and 'listens': if it were that simple, every conductor could do it. The reason it works in Lucerne is biographical, in the close personal and professional relationships that Abbado has with nearly every member of the orchestra, and, simply, that Abbado doesn't have to try to convince any of the musicians that his approach works. They are all here because they want it to.

It wasn't always this way in Abbado's career. Clive Gillinson was a cellist with the London Symphony Orchestra in Abbado's time, later becoming the LSO's general manager, and he now runs Carnegie Hall in New York. He remembers Abbado's rehearsal technique:

People actually got quite bored in his rehearsals, because he speaks so quietly and is so shy. I remember one terribly funny thing. He'd been with us for a long time at the LSO and he decided he was going to give a dinner for the entire orchestra, when we were on tour in Italy. The chairman of the orchestra gave a speech and said, 'Claudio, would you like to say anything?' – Claudio never made speeches – and he said, 'OK, I'll make a speech.' And he said, 'Thank you all very much.' And that was the longest speech he ever made! But the reason it worked with the LSO and in Berlin is that the performances were so great. The rehearsals may be frustrating – and if a conductor who didn't do great performances said so little in rehearsal it would be a catastrophe – but everybody knows the performances were amazing. Just as they are in Lucerne. Even if people in the LSO were thinking, God I wish I knew what he was saying, or I wish I could actually hear him, that never meant the orchestra didn't want to see him, didn't want to work with him. The thing is, I've never known anybody more compelling. He tells you everything you need to know through his conducting. He's the most natural conductor in the world. It's all about serving the music for him, and his humility in front of the music. He cares desperately about it. For Claudio, music is his entire life, it's what he thinks about all the time, so there's an urgency and importance about the performances. It's life or death for him. It's that Bill Shankly thing: is music a life or death thing? No – it's more important than that.

In Lucerne, as the rehearsals go on, something does begin to change. It's not as simple as saying the playing gets more together, or becomes more accurate, or more homogeneous. But it slowly transforms so that the difference from the first rehearsal to the last is a contrast between two kinds of orchestra. The difference is especially clear in the big tuttis of the first movement of the *Symphonie fantastique*, and in the last two sections, Berlioz's hallucinogenic vision of the destruction of the hero's ego first by grim execution and then through the still more ghoulish ritual of the 'Witches' Sabbath', the final bacchanal. Jörgen van Rijen, principal trombone of the Concertgebouw Orchestra, whom we met earlier in this book, first played in the Lucerne orchestra in 2007. Among the first notes he played with the orchestra were some of the most exposed and challenging in the trombonist's repertoire: the long, soulful solo in the first movement of Mahler's Third Symphony. He was replacing the previous first trombone in the Lucerne Festival Orchestra at the last minute, and had played neither this symphony nor with Abbado before. 'It was quite a scary situation,' he says with the Dutch dryness I remember from Amsterdam. 'In the solo, he was always showing what he wanted, whether he wanted something shorter or longer. He is always busy with you when you're playing a solo.' Talking about the difference between his orchestra, the Concertgebouw, and the Lucerne ensemble, he says:

What is great here is the power of this orchestra. If you look at the last desks of the violins, there are concertmasters in there. That's the power of sound that this orchestra is capable of, this high-testosterone sound. In the Concertgebouw, we will never play this powerfully, but there are all the subtle things that go with that orchestra's 120-year history that you haven't got in Lucerne.

At the start of the week's Berlioz rehearsals, what I heard was the power, what van Rijen calls 'testosterone', a wall of huge, rich sound, especially in the string section. It's a way of playing that suits the big Germanic repertoire the orchestra has been used to playing – above all, Mahler. But this was not the sound that would get the most from Berlioz's *Symphonie*, its world of diaphanous colours and quicksilver emotional ups and downs. The orchestra needed to recalibrate itself, to change from a Mahlerian powerhouse of an ensemble to a flightier, finer orchestra, a group that could explode with hellish ferocity but then immediately conjure a scene of pastoral contemplation, which could rouse itself to the heights of sensual abandon and then sink into suicidal despair. It needed to become a truly Berliozian orchestra, one that the great French composer and orchestral visionary would recognise.

And over four days of rehearsing, that's exactly what happens. It doesn't take a sermon from Abbado on the finer points of Berlioz's orchestration: he simply allows the players to find their way of playing together, to find a different way of listening to each other to create the right sound-world for Berlioz's symphony. That's what this rehearsal process has really been about. Abbado has surreptitiously led his musicians, with that palette of thousands of water-colour shades that Wolfram Christ describes, to hear the symphony as he does, to listen to Berlioz's music as he does. This is an idea of listening that is the opposite of passive: it's listening as a doing, an active verb. Abbado's apparently passive rehearsal technique, the way he lets the players themselves deal with the technical problems that occur in any orchestral run-through, the way he seems content to play the same passage, the same movement, over and over again, is part of the same process. He too is listening. He becomes gradually more animated over the four days – not in what he says, but what he does. Those flowing gestures of his left hand begin to soar as the week goes by, giving glimpses of the voluptuous melodiousness he wants the orchestra to find in their three performances of the *Symphonie*. And when he does so, there's a special electricity to the orchestra's playing. They are being allowed to give full flight to their ideas, their way of playing, their way of listening.

As Clive Gillinson says, Abbado's strategy of preparing his performances in this way works best if all of the players, as in Lucerne, go along with the project. In Berlin, Hanns-Joachim Westphal tells me, they used to say, 'For rehearsals, give us [Nikolaus] Harnoncourt' – whose inspirational and scholarly insights into all of the repertoire he plays are loved by every orchestra he conducts – 'and for the concerts, give us Abbado.' In Lucerne, they want him for both, but it's the performances where everything changes, and the promise of the orchestra's playing is fulfilled.

Not that the rehearsals are completely without their own kind of magic. In Stravinsky's *Firebird* suite, there's a place just before the final hymn where the music is reduced to a shimmer of tremolo chords in the strings, vibrations of the air that sink down and down through the music's fairy-tale harmonic sequences until they find a soft ground on to which a solo horn places the gentle melody that will sing out in grand peroration at the very end of the piece. Stravinsky marks his music piano-pianissimo, *ppp*, but even he cannot have imagined what happened the first time the Lucerne Festival Orchestra rehearsed this place. Abbado's gestures make it clear what he wants: less and less sound. From a gigantic string section of nearly a hundred musicians, you would have thought it impossible to make a small sound of any kind, let alone create a new kind of quiet. But that's what happens. The music is quiet, then it's on the edge of silence, and then it gets quieter still, so that for those of us listening in the hall our ears feel as if they have extended outwards to try and catch the sound. And it gets quieter yet again, and then there is still less, until the players must hardly be touching the strings with their bows. It's an experience that becomes more rather than less intense the quieter they play, opening up a realm of sound I have never heard before, the possibility of music at the edge of silence. It's a magical effect. Composer George Benjamin hears it too, as Stravinsky's notes become ethereal tremors of something just above nothing, and exclaims to me – quietly – after the solo horn has begun its melody: 'Amazing – they transformed harmony into texture.'

The three concerts of Debussy, Ravel, and Berlioz follow a pattern set by previous Lucerne Festival Orchestra programmes. Many of the musicians say that the performances in Lucerne grow towards the final concert they play, and that's true this time. Simply put, they get better, but all of them are different, and each has an individual character and excitement. Nothing is taken for granted in any of them. The first, performed to the stiffest audience in the whole Lucerne Festival calendar, the glitterati who attend the gala opening of the event, complete with speeches, politicians, and Swiss pomp and circumstance, is the least free, but it is still scintillating. The opening of *Nuages*, the first of Debussy's *Nocturnes*, is the sonic definition of floating clouds; Elina Garanča's singing in Ravel's *Shéhérazade* is in a different league from her rehearsals; and the Berlioz is a gleeful and grotesque cavalcade. It's impressive, but the second performance is finer still. Having proved to each other that they can play this music in the tensions of a concert, the second night is freer, more elastic, more expressive. It's the finest performance of the Debussy the orchestra will play, as Abbado dares them to become still more cloud-like in the opening movement, and still more evanescent in the final section, *Sirènes*, music in which the sixteen female singers of the Bavarian Radio Symphony Chorus become part of the orchestral texture as well. His gestures are traces on the air that have nothing whatever to do with the mechanics of beating Debussy's six in a bar or five in a bar, and everything instead to do with creating an atmosphere of infinite subtlety and flexibility. It's a dangerous game to play, taking the orchestra to the edge of what's possible in terms of what they need to be able to play the notes in front of them, and asking them to interpret the music on another level of meaning and expression. But in Lucerne, with these players and under these conditions, it works.

'They will go through fire for me,' Abbado says, and sometimes, they have to. Etienne Abelin, sitting in the second violins, says:

When he goes into the Debussy, you feel like he has never heard the piece before – in a positive way! He's just thinking, what do we do with this? How do we create it right now? It's very impulsive. He's asking himself questions all the time: how do we make the music sound even freer, how can we play around with this moment, how can we move everything around, without ever losing a sense of balance?

And *Fêtes*? The performance is a vindication of that difficult moment in rehearsal, music of pure explosive colour, which also includes the best and quietest trumpet playing from Reinhold Friedrich and his section that I have ever heard. Somehow, they manage to sound as if they start playing their music on a mountain top outside the concert hall and slowly, slowly, get closer and closer until their fanfare fills the hall. It's a moment that does justice to Abbado's early memory of this piece.

In its second performance, though, the Berlioz is more exciting but also less accurate than the first, as if the orchestra had decided they can play the piece and can just give themselves to Berlioz's flights of fantasy. It's the third performance where the *Symphonie fantastique* fully realises the potential of the musicians, the conductor, and the symbiotic relationship between them. The previous concerts have happened impressively in front of us, the audience, but the third one happens inside us as well. In the act of listening, we in the audience are also participating in this performance. We're not mere passive recipients of musical information that is projected into the auditorium, but an integral part of the experience. 'Listen': Abbado's main desire for his musicians extends to us as well. Abelin accounts for the impact the audience has on the performance. 'There's a different atmosphere in the space with different groups of listeners. As a musician, you sense that and feel it. Somehow what you are doing resonates with how people are hearing. It's one experience, one community.'

And that circle of listening, created through the complete attention of the two thousand pairs of eyes and ears in the audience and the hundreds on stage, creates the space for something remarkable to happen in Berlioz's

Symphonie. The fantastical imaginings of the music aren't mere metaphors for experience, for the 'Ball', the 'Scene in the Meadow', the 'March to the Scaffold' and the 'Witches' Sabbath', but experiences in their own right. That means we aren't just watching something happen to a fictional hero on a journey to the destruction of his body and soul, but going through it all ourselves. We all become Berlioz's doomed protagonist that night, wracked by obsessive love, experiencing moments of sensual joy and pastoral calm, and then going through the fires of hallucinogenic hell until the ultimate extinguishment of our collective ego in the final moments of the noisiest bacchanal in orchestral music. The freedom that Abbado gives his musicians, and the way they respond, means that the music is made in the real time of the performance. This isn't a performance of a pre-existing interpretation of Berlioz's *Symphonie fantastique*, but the creation, the incarnation of an experience that has never existed before.

Etienne Abelin describes what it was like to be in the middle of this tumult.

In the performance, you're at a higher level of thinking about the music. You're able to dig much deeper into what it's all about: what kind of euphoria the first movement ends in, what's the relationship of that to the second movement, where does the craziness of what happens at the end come from? As a musician, I want to ask those questions – and Abbado lets you. He's going in there too with a philosophical mindset to each performance, questioning the piece more and more each time. He's a catalyst for that process. He wants to go on that journey too, so if you're going there as well in your own way, he's always providing the space in which you can feel at ease. In the third performance, I was really thinking, this is an incredibly disturbing piece, and how does it do that, how does it make you feel so disturbed? I don't know any other conductor who allows you the space to ask these questions more than Abbado. So in the performance, it's like he inspires us, and we inspire him back. There's a lot of interplay going on. And the more we know a piece, the more we can give ourselves to it in the moment of performance. It's not a case of, 'We did that yesterday', it's more, 'What else can we discover tonight?' That's why the third performance was the best.

Abelin also suggests why the players feel so free to explore their playing in performances with Abbado. 'I think his is an art of anticipation. Every moment, every gesture, it's thought *for* you in some way. He's anticipated it already, somehow. So whatever you do – it's already done! It's so easy to play like that, because you're free to just go there, just to play the way you want.'

The performances in Lucerne are a kind of experiential knowledge. Because of the way Abbado's rehearsal process gathers momentum towards the concerts, it is only in the performances that he and the musicians really know what they can create together in Berlioz, Mahler, or Bruckner. It's only there that their vision – their way of listening – for a piece can reach its full potential. And in going on those journeys together with the necessary inspiration of an audience, they discover new dimensions to music they might have thought they knew, or that the listeners in the hall might have thought they understood. In committing themselves to a new creation every time they perform, everything is at stake in each of their concerts, each one an arc of coming to life and leaving it in the beginnings and ends of every piece they play. As Raymond Curfs, the Lucerne orchestra's timpanist since 2003, puts it, 'In these performances, it's like there's a beautiful line that just goes and goes, on and on, and maybe it ends up in heaven. And you cannot explain it. It's like the gods touch you. It's amazing. Amazing.' That's how much it matters to Abbado too. You can see it etched on his face during concerts, where there seems to be no gap between the expressive content of the music, the journey he is going through inside himself, and how that is communicated to the players, and the audience.

And then, a couple of years after those Berlioz concerts, there was that performance of Mahler's Ninth Symphony. The essence of that collective silence that Abbado, the orchestra, and the audience achieved together at the end of the symphony is both more mysterious and more explicable than it seems. That other realm, that different dimension that opened as the music crossed a border into silence and beyond, was the revelation of the dark matter behind all of the Lucerne Festival Orchestra's performances, without which none of them would exist: it was the sound of listening, the sound of all of us – audience, musicians, conductor – listening to Mahler, to music, to each other.

*

In January 2014, Claudio Abbado died. His last concerts with the Lucerne Festival Orchestra the summer before – the last music he conducted – contained two unfinished symphonies, Schubert's 8th and Bruckner's 9th. Abbado and his musicians made these symphonies ask questions about the beginnings and ends of pieces of music, about the borders of sound and silence, about the mirror-like membrane that separates life from death; questions that still ring, quietly but profoundly, in the imaginations of anyone who heard them.

Epilogue

Abbado's performance of Mahler's Ninth Symphony with his orchestra in Lucerne is a realisation of the transformative power of orchestral music. But so too are Gergiev's Rachmaninov in London, Jansons' Dvořák in Amsterdam, Rattle's Sibelius with his Berliners, Nott's Stravinsky in Bamberg, and Iván Fischer's Mahler Sixth in Hungary. They are the result of diverse approaches to the orchestra, to the cultural place of music, to the ethics and practice of music-making. Above all they are all concerts, experiences, and musical-chemical processes that are made through the culture in which musicians live and participate, the repertoire they play, and the dynamics of those living, breathing relationships between orchestral players and their conductors.

There are, of course, still other ways of doing it, just as many as there are orchestras and conductors in the world: from the octogenarian wisdom of Bernard Haitink or Colin Davis to the wildness and energy of an astonishingly talented younger breed of conductors like the Venezuelan Gustavo Dudamel at the Los Angeles Philharmonic, the Latvian Andris Nelsons at the City of Birmingham Symphony Orchestra, the Canadian Yannick Nézet-Séguin at the Philadelphia Orchestra, or the young British conductor Robin Ticciati at the Scottish Chamber Orchestra and Glyndebourne opera house, all of them in their late twenties or early thirties. These are all musicians who thrive on the easy internationalism of today's conducting careers, but whose charisma is capable of getting their own sound and their own vision of the music from all the orchestras they conduct. The Philharmonics of Vienna and Berlin have been astonished at the fire, passion, and intensity that Nelsons, Dudamel, and Nézet-Séguin have brought to their performances of the great classical and romantic repertoire. The effect and excitement that these young conductors have for audiences is another factor in their success. Despite their differences, all of them share a physical language of conducting that is unafraid of showing emotion, passion, and intensity. Audiences can read the emotional journey of any music that Nelsons or Dudamel conduct through their fearless, and fearlessly energetic, gestures, leaps, and grimaces on the podium. These young conductors have a desperate need to communicate the essence of the music they're performing, and they are breathing new life into music from Mahler to Shostakovich, Wagner to Bruckner, showing that this music still matters and still means as much as it ever did for today's youngest generation, giving the repertoires of orchestral music new sounds, new possibilities, and new audiences along the way.

There is also a dazzling generation above them, including the brilliant, insightful British conductor Daniel Harding, a protégé of both Abbado and Rattle, who conducts the Mahler Chamber Orchestra and the Stockholm Radio Philharmonic and regularly guests in Vienna and Berlin; the fiercely intense and analytical Vladimir Jurowski at the London Philharmonic; the inspirational Susanna Mälkki at the Ensemble Intercontemporain; and Alan Gilbert at the New York Philharmonic, whose adventurous programmes are revitalising what was in danger of becoming an irredeemably conservative institution. Then there are the older *éminences grises* of conducting like Seiji Ozawa, Charles Dutoit, James Levine, Riccardo Muti, Lorin Maazel and Zubin Mehta, as well as the revolutionary geniuses of the early-music movement who are now essential parts of orchestral culture in general, like Nicholas Harnoncourt, John Eliot Gardiner, Roger Norrington, Christopher Hogwood, and Trevor Pinnock. All of them have their own philosophies of music-making, and all of them are responsible for making classical musical culture as ceaselessly energetic as it has always been.

But there are ways of doing it without a conductor too. A remarkable recent phenomenon in orchestral culture is Spira Mirabilis, a collection of brilliant young orchestral musicians from all over Europe and the rest of the world, who get together a few times a year to work intensively on single symphonies: Mozart's 'Jupiter', Beethoven's 'Eroica', Schubert's Fourth. They have no conductor, and their aim, according to one of their four Italian founders, Lorenza Borrani, is to do the work that a conductor would normally do, but do it together, and be collectively responsible for every musical decision the group makes. This isn't the sort of conductorless ensemble that is led by the first violinist, which is so often what happens when a group decides to do without the person who wields a stick. Spira Mirabilis is the closest thing I have ever witnessed to genuine orchestral democracy. I saw them rehearse and perform Beethoven's Fourth Symphony at the Aldeburgh Festival in Suffolk. In rehearsal, the thirty-four players sat in a circle, and every single one of them had a copy of the full score of the symphony, in the latest Bärenreiter edition, as well as their own part. They all agreed on the most fundamental question of tempi and shared a broad sense of how the music should be articulated – with as much life, variety, and difference as possible – but beyond that, everything was up for grabs in the rehearsal room. And in the three hours I saw, most of the members of the group had their say at some point. A second violinist suggested a way of phrasing for the woodwinds; the winds tried it out but this new flexibility felt too extreme. But the rest of the orchestra liked the novelty of what they heard, so the woodwinds stuck with their experimental phraseology. Every bar of the music was dissected like this, every moment fought and argued for. As in all democracies, not everyone gets what they want, but everyone is allowed to share their views, and the result is an ear-opening vitality to the music-making. As in Lucerne, this music, this two-hundred-year-old symphony, is revealed as if for the first time, because every musician on stage knows each bar inside out, knows why they are playing the way they're playing, and feels connected to the creative process of the performance. In performance, everything feels like it's at stake, and each moment of each movement sounds as if it is being discovered anew.

It's no wonder Spira Mirabilis play just one piece on their programmes: the amount of work that each concert costs is in a different dimension to the preparation time an orchestra would usually allow for symphonies like Beethoven's Fourth, which are core parts of the repertoire. But it's worth it. As in Lucerne, I felt the intensity of participation, of listening, from the orchestra extend into the audience so that as a spectator, you were made part of the experience.

Spira Mirabilis proves that you don't need a conductor to get to those cosmic levels of orchestral music-making that the conductors in this book all spend their lives striving to reach. But the Spira Mirabilis example proves something else: that the essential work of the conductor has never really been about the exercise of authority. As the musicians of Spira say, they want to experience the kind of work that conductors routinely do, or should do, before they even get to the first rehearsal, to be responsible for those decisions themselves. And what conducting is really about is the creation of a culture of responsibility, of respect, of musical and social awareness, and of listening. It's possible to achieve some of those goals through fear and force, as previous generations of conductors did, and however democratic the ideals of today's maestros might be, they are all still involved in a top-down transmission of power of one sort or another. But it's the responsibilities of that power that are the real achievements of the conductors like the ones in this book. Through the extension of a virtuous circle of listening, which starts with the conductor working on the piece when they are preparing it, continues in the enlarged space of the rehearsal room, and finds the outermost of these concentric circles in the inclusion of the audience in the final performance, conducting is a metaphor not for absolute power but for shared experience, for collaboration, for listening.

There are social and political dimensions to all this. In Venezuela, El Sistema uses classical music as a driver of social change, and crucial to the success of this music–education 'system' is the way it employs the idea of the orchestra as a metaphor for society as a whole, for individual components all contributing to a greater whole. Around four hundred thousand children have benefitted from the scheme over the last three decades, which was set up by the economist, politician, and conductor José Antonio Abreu. For some (including Simon Rattle and Claudio Abbado, who both regularly work in Venezuela), El Sistema is the most remarkable phenomenon in classical music in the world today. The project has transformed children's lives from the barrios of Caracas and elsewhere in Venezuela, turning futures that could have been destined for drugs, poverty, and fear into lives of hope, opportunity, and meaning. What's truly remarkable, though, is that El Sistema reveals the shared, democratic, egalitarian values that classical orchestral music realises in its practice and performance. Along with the focus on technique and playing orchestral instruments to as high a standard as possible, it's the spirit of making music together in a large group on which El Sistema thrives. The joy for the children who play in El Sistema's hundreds of orchestras comes not from doing what the conductor says, but because they know that they are progressing on their instrument, becoming better as individual musicians and people. In El Sistema, the conductor is not the wielder of total control, but someone who inculcates a culture of shared passion and energy to serve a larger purpose. The explosive international success of El Sistema's top ensemble, the Simón Bolívar Symphony Orchestra, and its conductor Gustavo Dudamel proves the sheer musical potential of the idea, but it's the social message that comes from their music-making that is even more powerful.

Conducting and conductors increasingly matter in today's world as models of a way of transforming authority into creativity. As Colin Davis told me, 'In orchestras we find a way of making a large group of incredibly strong personalities work together, so why on earth aren't politicians interested in learning from us?' The alchemies of conducting are as much social and cultural as they are musical. Conducting matters because orchestras matter, and orchestral music matters because of its transformative power, and because it embodies a way of relating to the world that is based on an essential principle that keeps renewing itself and is the route to knowing ourselves and each other: listen, only listen.

Acknowledgements

This book is indebted to all of the conductors, musicians, and orchestras who so generously gave me their time, their testimony, their honesty, and above all, who allowed me into the crucibles of their musical creation in the rehearsals and concerts I observed over three years from 2008 to 2010. 'Observed'? That's too passive a word for what I felt happened. It may have been an illusion – at least, it might seem that way to the orchestras in Berlin, Lucerne, London, Budapest, Bamberg, and Amsterdam, for whom I was mostly a rapt onlooker sitting somewhere in the stalls, or sometimes behind and occasionally actually within the percussion section – but because of the insight I was given into the cultures of each orchestra, these were experiences in which I felt included, as if I too were taking part in them. Music-making needs witnesses, it needs audiences and listeners to become meaningful. This book is an attempt to define at least some of the meanings of the astonishing music-making I was able to witness, from first rehearsals to final concerts.

Above all, this is a book of things that happen, of music being made and performances catalysed and created. But in turn, it could not have been made without the collaboration of the orchestral administrations, managers, agents, press-relations agencies, and personal assistants who make up the courts of the six conductors in each of the chapters.

Acknowledgements

Without their help, it would have been impossible to go on the musical journeys this book describes. In particular, Judy Grahame, Elisabeth Hilsdorf, Gabi Karácsony and Dvora Lewis dealt miraculously with my patience-stretching requests. Equally, it could not have happened without Belinda Matthews at Faber, and her editorial perspicacity and gentle yet ruthless insistence on deadlines, without Mary Morris, also at Faber, whose insightful and practical advice was invaluable, and without the patience and tolerance of my friends and family, upon whom chapters-in-progress were thrust without warning. I am also indebted to the wise and continual counsel and inspiration of my agent, Kerry Glencorse at Susanna Lea Associates. Above all, this book could not have happened without my parents, Jo and MacIain, without whose unstinting support a life spent in the strange career of writing and communicating about the unfathomable power of the musical experience could never have happened. It is to them, with love, that the book is dedicated.

Index

Main entries are shown in **bold**. Concert venues are indexed under their location.

Index

Index

Index

Index